D1488254

SELECTED ~~~~~~ RADIO AND TELEVISION ~~~~~~ CRITICISM

edited by
Anthony Slide

The Scarecrow Press, Inc.
Metuchen, N.J., & London
1987

Also edited by Anthony Slide

Library of Congress Cataloging-in-Publication Data

Selected radio and television criticism.

   Includes indexes.
   1. Broadcasting--United States. 2. Broadcasters--
United States--Biography. 3. Radio programs--
United States--Reviews. 4. Television programs--
United States--Reviews. I. Slide, Anthony.
PN1990.6.U5S4 1987   791.44'75'0973   86-27891
ISBN 0-8108-1942-2

• CONTENTS •

iii

• INTRODUCTION •

This volume gathers together a group of articles on radio and television from the late twenties through the late fifties. Unlike the earlier multi-volume sets devoted to Selected Film Criticism and Selected Theatre Criticism, the material included here is not limited to reviews of individual shows or series, but also includes critical articles and commentary on various radio and television personalities. The articles are interfiled, in alphabetical order, with the reviews of the shows.

As Bob Landry notes in his article "Critics and Criticism in Radio," reprinted here, "Most publications do not provide the conditions indispensable to criticism.... There are no incentives to careful listening." Hence, there was little radio criticism from which to select suitable items. Similarly, television, during its so-called "golden era," was never particularly well served by criticism other than from the trade papers. (John Crosby, writing in the New York Herald Tribune, is, of course, an honorable exception.)

I have tried in my selection to include pieces that are either literate or entertaining (hopefully both). An attempt was made to include items on as many different shows and personalities as possible; certainly all of the major ones are represented here. I am sure this is the only volume in which Father Coughlin receives equal space to Milton Berle. Unfortunately, there is a very thin line dividing line between critical commentary and celebrity profiles. I realize that line has, at times, been crossed by some of the included writers, but it appeared better to be fairly flexible in my choices rather than rigid and, perhaps, too highly selective.

This book is intended for libraries that do not have a major holding of periodicals from the 1920's through the 1950's and for students and scholars of popular entertainment needing an immediate insight into contemporary commentary on radio and television. It should also be noted that this volume provides reprints of reviews and articles in their entirety, not only from periodicals that are indexed in Readers' Guide to Periodical Literature, but also from many that are not.

Because I have discovered that some librarians and many academics seem unknowledgeable as to just what is and is not indexed in Readers' Guide, it is also worth pointing out that even though some included periodicals, such as The New Yorker, are indexed therein, Readers' Guide does not provide information as to the shows reviewed in the columns by the critics of the indexed periodicals. Therefore, this book can help to provide immediate access to, say, Philip Hamburger's review of an early Milton Berle show in The New Yorker, a review which, Readers' Guide notwithstanding, could otherwise only be located by reading through several years of that periodical. Based on the hundreds of hours spent in combing supposedly indexed journals as well as many that were not indexed, I feel fairly secure in my claim that not one of the reviews of radio or television programs included here can be located through Readers' Guide.

Items in this book were selected from the following publications: America, Catholic World, The Commonweal, Cue, Fortnight, The Forum and Century, Life, Movie and Radio Guide, The Nation, The New Republic, New York Herald Tribune, The New Yorker, Newsweek, Photoplay, Radio Guide, Rob Wagner's Script, Saturday Review, Scribner's Magazine, Script, Time, Variety, and the book With Love and Loathing by John Crosby.

Following each program heading is information regarding the network upon which it was seen and the years it was aired or televised. For more information about individual programs on radio, readers are referred to Tune in Yesterday by John Dunning (Englewood Cliffs, New Jersey: Prentice-Hall, 1976); for those on television see The Complete Directory to Prime Time Network TV Shows, 1946-Present by Tim Brooks and Earle Marsh (New York: Ballantine Books, 1979). A good source for biographical information on radio personalities is this author's Great Stars of Radio in Historic Photographs (New York: Dover Publications, 1982).

ACKNOWLEDGMENTS

For help in the preparation of this volume, I would like to thank Stephen Hanson and David Pierce, and the staffs of the Margaret Herrick Library of the Academy of Motion Picture Arts and Sciences, the Library of Congress, the Los Angeles Central Library, and the Doheny Memorial Library of the University of Southern California.

The reviews by William A. Coleman from America are reprinted with permission of America Press, Inc., 106 West 56 Street, New York, N.Y. 10019. © 1953. All rights reserved.

Reviews from Billboard are © 1939 by Billboard Publications, Inc. Reprinted with permission.

Articles by A.M. Sullivan are reprinted from The Commonweal by permission of Edward S. Skillin, publisher.

PART I

•

RADIO CRITICISM

- RADIO AND THE POET

    The enjoyment of poetry at one time was wholly auditory. Un-
til the advent of the printing press, the poet chanted his poems in
the courts of the kings, or along the roadsides. The pleasure de-
rived through the eye was the complementary delight of seeing the
court bard and his pompous retinue, or the glad smile of the troubadour as he rapped at the gate and offered to say a poem or two for
his supper. The poets were personal salesmen--some clever enough
to win the plaudits and coins of the royal family, others too sharp
of tongue or knavish at heart to share the bounty of the chieftains.

    Such has been the experience of all nations with a culture.
The Homeric bards had no books to circulate, and the king who had
a manuscript counted the parchment with his treasure. The oriental
poets were men of privilege and immunity, and they were also found
in the inner council of the king. The bardic system of the Gaels
has its roots in the eastern culture, and the ollav ranked next to the
druid; the ollav being the poet of great wisdom and technical skill.

    Movable type, invented in the sixteenth century, gradually ef-
fected a change in the sensory enjoyment of poetry. In the poem
that is read aloud the music is dominant, but as use of the printing
press spread, the poet injected philosophy with story-telling, and
mixed wisdom with mysticism. Through leisure provided by Guten-
berg and Caxton the educated person was enabled to give poetic
statement a deeper analysis. Despite the millions of books of verse,
and the vast number of poets who have crowded into classic appraisal
since the making of the first press, there is always an audience for
the poem which is read aloud.

    Radio is ushering back the age of the troubadour. Every radio
station has its staff bard who reads verse without much provocation,
using contributed poems, clips from the newspapers and a shy verse
of his own. Unfortunately, some of these readers are enamored of
their own voices and use poetry as an exhibitionistic medium. They
favor the "home and mother" rhymes which are too syrupy for a dis-
criminating audience. The sentimentalists, however, offer evidence of
of a large following, and are truly indicative of the soft spot in the
heart of the average human, no matter how stunned his imagination
may be.

For a long time the radio station directors have been fearful of the "high brow" program, particularly in poetry. Conjuring in their brain the typical radio listener, they desired to strike an average of taste which would please all. Actually such a policy pleases no one, because there is no typical radio listener. He is as difficult to find as the typical Babbitt. People are selective in their choice of programs, and the dials spin on and off at the whim of the despotic listener. Poetry may have a minority audience, but it is a loyal and appreciative one.

Radio, except for the fine music and the occasional program of some esthetic pioneer, is the sport of the Philistines, who see it as the vaudeville booking agent sees the stage. His method has been to give as much cheap variety as possible and try to please everyone. This has been the accepted formula since Harrigan and Hart were the princes of 14th Street.

The poets deserve a place on the air programs, and they have a solid audience to follow them. Radio is a natural means for giving the neglected poets of yesterday and the poets of today a hearing, but it is important that the function of program arrangement be left to people who have the taste to choose and capacity to enjoy good poetry. It must be directed by men with courage to defy the tyranny of time in studios, so that the atmosphere of calm and leisure be given to the listener and poet. Studio managers will learn that speed is not the essence of esthetic pleasure.

Sooner or later radio will break the shackles of the vaudeville formula, and the creators of entertainment via the ether will understand that they have a totally different agency of expression. This much is certain. The man or woman in the armchair at home are in a different mood than the person who pays $3 for a theatre ticket. Their minds are relaxed and receptive to a more intimate style of social contact. There is no orchestra pit, and no stage. The artist, whether he be poet, singer or humorist, is a guest in a private home and is expected to conduct himself accordingly. He comes in by special invitation and goes out without apology, never knowing that he may have offended good taste. In any event, a touch of the finger will dismiss him, and he doesn't know the difference. Being a guest in a private home is more personal than speaking to the huge anonymity of a stage or concert audience. The radio listener is always singular, and speaking to one person calls for a friendly and casual manner. Those poets whom I have observed in the last two years were most successful who left their platform dignity at home. There is a quality of the X-ray in the loudspeaker, and the voice is a certain index of personality. Sincerity rides on simple statement. It often intrigues a listener who accidentally stumbles on a poetry program, and makes a convert.

The bards of the courts of Babylon and Egypt, the bards who

gathered at the Olympic games to read their poems in the contests,
the bards of Erin who wrote in the elaborate meters of the Gaelic
language and competed for prizes at the annual Feis, were given
great honor; but their listeners were merely a handful compared to
the thousands of poetry lovers who are eager to hear the living
voice of the poet. Spelling-bees, elocution competitions and singing
contests are heard over the air waves now. Why not poetry? There
is no valid objection to a bardic revival with such an instrument as
radio ready to provide a listener for the worthy poet. The little poetry journals are doing a valiant work, but their circulation is a few
hundred in the average, and even Poetry, the first voice to cry out
in the wilderness, has but a few thousand readers after twenty years
of heroic effort. The little magazines have been the trade publications for journeymen and apprentice poets, and radio could be helpful in widening their sphere of influence.

The troubadour is coming back to his own and radio is his
genie. But radio offers little to the poets who have only literary
conundrums to offer. The ear cannot compete with the eye in the
understanding of profound verse. The ear is attuned to music, and
is a tardy herald for difficult messages. The poets who prefer to
mystify their readers, leaving a faint trail and confusing clues, will
have to be satisfied with a small coterie. I suspect that some of
these anchorites of poetry prefer to be misunderstood, and hope
some day to see their poems published with a concordance which explains each cabalistic reference.

Meanwhile, there is a growing audience for good poetry. It
will grow as adventurous listeners, spinning their dials, encounter
a wandering bard here and there, and find in him a prophet, unknown perhaps, but not entirely without honor, when his voice may
probe through vast cubic acres of sky and bring pleasure to follow-
ers of the muse.

--A. M. Sullivan in The Commonweal,
Vol. 21, No. 5 (November 30,
1934), pages 138-139.

• RADIO AND VAUDEVILLE CULTURE

Daniel Frohman's statement that "radio is an instrument of the
gods that is sometimes the work of the devil" might be an appropriate
text for this analysis of radio's responsibility to American culture.

It is less than fifteen years since the studio of WJZ was a shack
at the Westinghouse factory in Newark, and there Graham McNamee
and Milton Cross made their first timid attack on the carbon "mike."
Radio, being a novelty, appealed to the newspapers as a circulation

builder, and during the headphone era, set-building became the
sport of amateurs. The public was hardly critical of the programs,
and were usually satisfied to identify the station call letters. One
listened impatiently through the banjo solo, and then thrilled to
hear, "This is station KOMO, Omaha. Drop us a card if you hear
this announcement." And we gladly obliged.

Then one stormy night in January, 1924, the Shenandoah broke
from its moorings at Lakehurst. The German engineer, Anton Heinen,
pushed the nose of the airship into the gale and his radio called for
compass bearings. Suddenly the throb of the motors was heard
over Newark, and station WOR suspended its programs to direct the
aeronauts. Sitting with headphones on my ears, the writer was one
of thousands who thrilled as the announcers helped to save the big
ship from blowing out to sea. Thus the lusty infant of communication won its spurs in dramatic fashion.

From then on radio broadcasting entered the news agency
field, and his big brother, the press, began to fear him. It was
the battle of the senses--eye against ear. The press had reason to
fear radio, for the people of America got their first lesson in backstage politics at the Madison Square Donnybrook in 1924, in which
Al Smith and McAdoo fought to a bitter stalemate. Radio had learned
to dramatize what the newspapers couldn't. By the time Al Smith
had mustered enough votes to take the nomination at Houston,
broadcasting was a big business, and it was transferred from the
engineer to the vaudevillian.

For the past seven years radio broadcasting has been operated
on the vaudeville formula, and even the ex-booking agents of 10-20-
30 cent circuits recognize that the pattern is getting threadbare. In
their frantic endeavor to get the ear of the average listener they
have shot below their mark and are beginning to suspect that perhaps there is no such person as the average listener. They have
witnessed the upset of many theories about this elusive creature
with the fourteen year old mentality, and find that he likes highbrow
music, editorial chats on economics and politics, and even listens
to poetry by the Pulitzer winners. Now the master minds of radio
broadcasting would like to mend their ways, and they are making
strenuous efforts to reflect a conscience sensitive to good taste and
culture.

But radio got off to a peculiar start. Commercial sponsorship,
which financed its tremendous expansion, also hobbled the program
director. The ideal way to present educational features which are
conceived with some degree of talent for entertainment should be on
a selective "pay as you use" system, as we pay for our gas and
electricity. The idea is not new, but it calls for the use of electric
impulses sent over the power lines of the nation, rather than the
invisible Hertzian waves of the air. Experimental efforts have been
made on this plan in Cleveland by the North American subsidiary

"Wired Radio," and some day soon electric light customers may be
able to purchase entertainment in their homes without the distaste-
ful commercial blurb. Meanwhile, the advertiser's money provides
our radio programs.

According to the U.S. Communications Act of 1934, the radio
station is permitted to sell time by virtue of willingness to serve
"public conveniences, interest, or necessity." There has been an
opinion current that stations are required to devote a portion of
their time on the air to noncommercial features for the common weal,
but there is nothing in the act to support such a belief.

The prime commercial hours are 6 to 11 p.m., and on the
large networks many contractual commitments are made several years
ahead to obtain the premium periods. Electrically transcribed commercial programs are sold to small independent stations all over the
country. Thus, we observe an illogical control of "prime time" by
advertisers.

Perhaps you have heard of the "sustaining" program. It is
an unsponsored program and is usually unsustained by any funds
from the revenue of the broadcaster. It is in the difficult category
of the "sustaining program" that the modern educator hopes to reach
an appreciative audience. The quality of his program is largely a
gamble, depending upon the intelligence of the director, and the
skill and vision of the cultured person who is attempting to appeal
to the esthetic tastes of the American public. It is difficult for the
"vaudeville" trained director to forget that he is dealing with an
"autocrat" at the dinner table, or even in the living room, and not
a typical show audience. Much of his so-called educational features
is the flotsam of amateurs attracted by the novelty of the microphone
and accepted as program fillers because it costs him nothing.

The short history of broadcasting is one of opportunism.
There has been no determined effort within the industry to conceive
a schedule of cultural interests, in which the educator may borrow
the simple talents of the showman. The National Broadcasting Company has created an educational department, which is well staffed.
Columbia has the School of the Air, which makes a definite bid for
school support and interest. But all these departments receive are
the trimmings of the clock, and a cancellation or last minute shift
threatens any scheduled program at the slightest hint of a commercial coming into the spot. Smaller stations, with few exceptions,
make no serious attempt to conceive a balanced schedule of cultural
programs. The open time, not contracted for, is scattered as favors, with the program director attempting to fill the empty quarter
hours with all of the discretion, or lack of it, that he possesses.
Among the exceptions has been such little stations as WEVD in New
York which has consistently attempted to offer a palatable fare of
educational programs. WOR has been considerate to the book lovers
in the quality of its literary interviews, and permits the producer

a fair latitude in his program technique. Scattered among the 650 stations in the United States are 30 weak-lunged independents which are noncommercial voices of creed, cult and school, but they are too weak or too remote for any appreciable influence. It takes a sleuth of the dial to find them and perfect reception to hear them.

While there has been no comprehensive plan within the industry to present a schedule of evening programs that are immune to commercial attack, several outside groups have attempted to help radio broadcasting to mend its manners. Levering Tyson's National Advisory Council on "Radio in Education," with some help from the Carnegie Foundation, has been fighting for more time from the major networks, and has presented a worth-while series of educational programs dealing with civics, health, and related topics. Recently we have seen Philco present the Radio Institute of the Audible Arts with Pitts Sanborn as the director. Philco manufactures radio sets, and must sell them to people who find comfort and entertainment in broadcasting. Its concern about the promotion and recommendation of good programs, sponsored or unsponsored, comes from a motive that is at once healthy and selfish. The Radio Institute of the Audible Arts, which might be more effectively titled the "League for Better Radio Programs," helps the audience to be selective in choosing its audible fodder, though it labors under the handicap of being a lawyer for the defense. Various women's clubs--such as the articulate group of ladies in Scarsdale, New York--have sniped at the children's programs until the thrillers at the dinner hour have been tempered with common sense.

But cultured minorities have exhibited the usual grumbling and disunited front in their critical attack on broadcasting. This was reflected in the hearing at Washington last October when they were put to rout and scorn by the solid and fluent delegates of the opposition. The educators and clerics were called "special pleaders" and "publicity seekers," and their confusion was a sign of guilt. The educators offered no comprehensive plan, and the word "cultural" was constantly confused with "educational." Radio is not, and should not be, a schoolroom, but it has tremendous potentials for the spread of good taste and those delectables of the spirit which cannot be given circulation by the nervous advertiser who watches the clock consume his dollars at the rate of $1,000 a minute on a national hook-up.

While Ford, General Motors and Packard have given us good musical programs, national advertisers are not usually encouraged by their agency advisors to feature arty programs. Only certain advertisers can use radio successfully. Their article or service must have a mass sales appeal, and they are afraid to trim down their potential audience with anything classified as highbrow. The typical advertiser of mass appeal merchandise will audition many programs but eventually chooses a sentimental serial, a popular comedian, or a colossal vaudeville show crammed with tid-bits of opera or musical comedy.

Since the national advertiser is not going to aid the cultural growth of radio, the broadcasters must exhibit a more intelligent attitude toward the "sustaining" features which are presumed to be cultural in character. At the present time the educational program is footballed all over the time schedule, and is always timidly perched on the threat of cancellation. The fault lies directly at the broadcaster's door. He is a tenant of the air, not a proprietor, and the Federal Communications Commission can teach him to behave when he is invited into the parlor. Not that every cultured family doesn't enjoy the radio clowns and wits, or might not prefer Gracie Allen, at times, to Edna St. Vincent Millay, but if Professor Stardust is available for a bona fide series of lectures on modern astronomy, they believe he is entitled to an evening spot without a sponsor, at least equal to Madame Crystal, the astrologer, who deludes the gullible with an advertiser's aid.

It would seem to the writer that the Federal Communications Commission might set up a workable plan within the scope of the present empowering legislation. He would suggest in broad outline the following procedure:

(1) Since the broadcaster is only a lessee of an air band, the FCC reserves at least two hours a day--one in the daytime, one in the evening--for educational purposes.

(2) The commission would create a subsidiary bureau of men and women experienced in the educational and cultural potentialities of radio. They would conceive, direct and produce programs without any station interference. They would be well-paid.

(3) A portion of the gross revenue of each station would be taxed for the support of these hours. A simple method would be to charge one-tenth of the current commercial advertising rate for the time. Thus WJZ would pay about $150 a day, while WHN would pay less than $25. Assuming that 500 commercial stations paid $20 a day for 300 days of the year, a fund of $3,000,000 annually would be available for good sustaining programs.

(4) The subsidiary bureau could recruit the best talent of the educational program builders in radio today, give them a freer hand, pay them better and remove the omnipresent threat of cancellation and change which ruins their morale and destroys their effectiveness.

(5) Free of commercial taint, and uncertainty, the bureau could invite the cooperation of schools and colleges everywhere. Schedules could be published, and distributed through educational systems of each zone.

(6) The bureau could maintain its own Electrical Transcription Department for the preservation of the programs of permanent

value, and distribute recordings to smaller and remote stations where the expense of live programs are not warranted. The electrical transcription of today approaches perfection in the fidelity of recording. The Moser Record can be produced for $50, with additional pressings at $1.50 each, or less.

Broadcasting is too young to have a tradition. Improvements can be made rapidly, if not painlessly. Basically, radio is as important an agency of communication as the printing press, and if the present vaudeville-trained manager doesn't understand the power of the steed he is riding, the day is not distant when he will be tossed off and a rider with a new technique will assume the reins-- perhaps a man with a vision of an armchair instead of circus, stage or classroom.

> --A. M. Sullivan in The Common-
> weal, Vol. 23, No. 7 (December
> 13, 1935), pages 176-178.

• CRITICS AND CRITICISM IN RADIO

Fortunately for the sanity of those who attempt the criticism of radio programs, there is a definite balancing between the verdict of experienced judgment and the realities of popularity. Shows are not hits or flops because criticism either endorses or condemns them. But reasonably expert and plausibly qualified criticism should score .750 or better in calling them correctly. And for that reason alone from a progressive and money-saving standpoint, broadcasting is the loser in that there is so little criticism. And there is very little worthy of the name because:

a. Most publications do not provide the conditions indispensable to criticism.

b. There are no incentives to careful listening. The patience and time required, the boredom that must be endured would gain the average radio editor only trouble.

Radio programs, because they serve the interests of advertising, are commonly considered outside the place. Radio just ain't art. At its best it's good vaudeville. At its worst it's terrible. Nobody much cares. Radio editors, in most cases, correlate the quality of the program in the quality of the Scotch served during the opening night's festivities in the studios.

And most of all, any criticism is rendered slightly ridiculous by the ostrich habit of refusing to mention Jello and Jack Benny together. Some newspapers will allow a mild discussion in personal terms of a radio program, but it's confined to the actors. In all newspapers the title of the show may never be mentioned. Imagine reviewing Alfred Lunt and Lynn Fontaine, but refusing to mention the title of the play because that would be free advertising.

One result of the failure of radio criticism to assume importance is that radio sponsors have become the most guarded, protected and let-down-easy group of entertainment producers in history. A conspiracy to pamper and coddle them exists. Scarcely a hiss reaches them unless they read Variety (and the agencies are very disturbed when they find they do).

General printed criticism would challenge the amateur status of radio's angels. It might burn down the schoolhouse, but it would get sponsors out of the third grade.

Trade paper criticism of radio programs (this publication carries an average of 10 columns each issue) must necessarily devote some attention to "inside" and special considerations that non-trade publications could ignore if, fear of reprisals being conquered, the path were cleared for radio criticism. The result of such a condition (wholly improbable) would be to beam the spotlight of derision on clumsy incompetence. And thus help end it.

For the essence of all the head-shaking is that radio programs continue to perpetrate commonplace, easily-avoided, well-known "mistakes." In the wider sphere of criticism there could be some debate. One man's judgment against another's. But these silly little blunders leave no room for two opinions.

In the past, criticism of radio programs was, in some respects, peculiarly superfluous. In the first place, the businessman made a great emphasis on his credo: "I am not a showman!" (as if he had to tell anybody). It seemed to him that by bravely out-shouting showmanship, by claiming immunity from theatrical standards in the name of advertising he justified anything and everything.

Practically that was pretty nearly the case. A mechanical system of mass communication with cheap and convenient pipelines into the parlors and hall bedrooms of the idle, the immature, and the impecunious, opened up a staggeringly large audience, any fair segment of which constituted a good advertising buy and could be reached more or less automatically by almost any kind of program. So why theoretical sideline blabbering about standards and finesse? It just didn't rate seriously. Volunteer, free style, open field, outside worriers were upset while the persons actually involved, agency and advertiser, seemingly were composed and complacent.

Original idea that any orchestra and any singer would reach the radio audience effectively was followed by the idea that any show composed of big comedians, or, later, big "guest stars," would guarantee big circulation. In both attitudes--first, that the program hardly needed any attention at all; second, that the program needed

only a big budget--the whole concept of "criticism" was laughingly
or irritably considered as outside the arc of the industry's needs.

Criticism is also weakened as an influence of major importance
because each broadcast is a separate production. Sometimes the
premiere is the low, not the high. Sometimes it is a one-time flash.
Thus a formal, detailed review of the premiere broadcast may easily
be at variance with the popularity decision 13 weeks later, when the
option comes up.

Familiar failure of costly shows to be at their best the first
time out is in itself proof that criticism or its lack does and should
play a part. A big show is put together, rehearsed, timed and
brought forward without benefit of criticism, since radio has no
"dog towns" for its pretentious programs to try out on. Basic mistakes escape notice and correction, because no unbiased criticism is
obtained. In its best and practical sense criticism is simply the ar-
ticulation by an experienced eye, ear and mind of the probable reaction of the audience itself.

That is to say, the "normal" audience, for it is certainly
true that the studio audience, swayed by proximity, jollied along by
advance warming up, placed in intimate friendly relationship with the
actors, director, conductor, etc., is the most incompetent critical
guide. It is wholly misleading. In some cases, studio audiences are
deliberately exploited by clever tricksters, actors or agencies, to
make an indifferent broadcast seem like a glowing success. The
sponsor in the soft chairs and the elegant priviledges of his (or
their) position is lulled into thinking everything is hotsy-totsy.

Radio's volunteer worriers, looking on from the sidelines, meanwhile are apt to feel that the sponsor exceeds the lawful limit on
one-man dumbness. But this, of course, oversimplifies the whole
complex question. A sponsor is more often plural than singular,
and not necessarily of the masculine gender. Until quite recently
it was argued that he should get out and let the agency run the
show. Perhaps the best system would be a compromise between the
famous eccentrics among sponsors and the super-dopes among the
agencies.

It is precisely because sponsor-favored "patterns" are forced
on certain agencies that criticism becomes extremely difficult to a
trade paper privy to at least the broad aspects of these embarrass-
ments. Where does critical privilege stop? Should the sponsor be
reviewed?

The sponsor is an unseen Indian fighting from behind trees,
camera-shy, non-quotable, governed by obscure motivations that
frequently justify the original policy. In that case the blame may
ping-pong back to the agency that failed to adequately translate
the idea into entertainment.

In the matter of daytime programs, criticism, of course, collides violently with its greatest dilemma. An arithmetic-verified defense of trash, turned out by manual laborers at typewriters, seems to laugh in the face of standards, scorns the "theoretical" with bales of reasonably exact facsimiles. In the daytime the advertiser gives full vent to the widely held notion that the I.Q. of Jane Q. Public cannot be underestimated.

Making due allowance for the fundamental truth of the low ceiling of discrimination and the incredibly naive unworldliness of millions of devoted listeners, it still cannot be denied that there is a variance between one serial and another. All serials are not equally popular. Some flop quickly and badly. Others are big hits and run for years. There must, therefore, be a question of radio entertainment where it is commonly assumed standards never rise higher than a frog's torso.

However, it isn't the Doctor Trents, Mary Marlins, or Carol Kennedys of the sunlit hours that outrage persons trained in the criteria of the theatre. That's the small time. That's 10-20-30 in Pawtucket. Okay for what it is. Hokey-pokey, laid on with the well-known trowel, geared to low-grade reflexes. Equally, the radio station out in Arabella, Idaho, would be excused its one-tune hillbillies. That, again, is the small time.

Most of the criticism in radio has theatrical antecedents and criteria. Therefore, the thing that flaunts inbred concepts of rightness is the small-timer on the big time. The choice evening spots, nationally known trademark, big names, all combined amateurishly to give birth to a semi-coherent family apology.

The big time in show business, whether vaudeville, legit or cinema, exacts a fairly rigorous standard. The presence on a Palace big-time bill opening matinee of an act that didn't belong was a matter of consternation, not only to the booker and the manager and the other acts, but to show business itself. Such a miscue would be corrected by the evening performance. But radio's clambakes go on indefinitely.

> --Bob Landry in Variety (January
> 5, 1938), page 137

• STEVE ALLEN

Al Jolson last fortnight made Hollywood's newest cult happy. Said he: "I never thought I would see the day a sustaining show was the greatest show on the air." He referred to Steve Allen, on whose CBS midnight program the mammy singer appeared gratis as a guest star. His theatrical exaggeration meant nothing to the

Allen addicts, whose capacity to appreciate their youthful (27),
horn-rimmed Mahatma is vast.

Ordinarily, radio entertainment stops at midnight. That's
when Allen starts, every day except Sunday. A studio audience of
from 150 to 400 persons waits in a midnight line at Hollywood's Columbia Square for a chance to be deftly insulted by the casual, lanky
(6 feet, 3 inches) entertainer. Fans write him they drink black
coffee and set alarms to stay awake for his show. Sample Allen
opening: "If anyone is listening tonight for the first time, there is
something I would like to tell them. Go to bed."

New York born of a theatrical family (his mother was Comedienne Belle Montrose), Allen has acquired a wide following in 10
months of midnight broadcasting. Each morning he spends a few
minutes interviewing people in the studio. To one impudent bobby-
soxer he said: "Thank you very much, dear, and don't come back."
To another of his fans, whose enunciation was nervous, Allen remarked: "Lassie? Oh, Larry. Your r's are rather anemic. Anyway, you look a little like Lassie." He remarked to another member
of the audience: "I'm sorry, I didn't hear you--no, I'm sorry I did
hear you."

Ad Lib. Allen uses no script in his 55 minutes of performing,
but sometimes reads from his mail or possibly from a scratch sheet.
Addicts, some of whom attend his midnight shows regularly, often
give him zany presents--a wilted pretzel or perhaps a horse's tooth.
His attitude is relaxed, loungy and bored. His deadpan voice sort
of a low-winged monotone, expertly underplays his quips, some of
which pass undetected in the night.

Like most of his predecessors, Allen was a disk jockey, did
stints on independent stations (KMTR, KFAC), wrote radio for five
years before joining a network. He did Smile Time for Don Lee
Mutual, joined CBS in 1947. The present midnight show began as a
disk jockey spot, Allen to play records with a minimum of comment.
Gradually his comment squeezed more and more records from the
show until now he promises only to play one, and usually never gets
around to it.

Payoff. Childhood piano lessons paid off for Allen, who is
likely to play at any time for his addicts. He has composed a number
of tunes and once on a bet wrote 50 songs in a week. CBS pressed
him to use more records on his show, but Allen perversely used
more of himself. Said he: "They began letting me alone four months
ago." As the line of addicts lengthened daily and Allen's "mail pull"
climbed, the network became aware that a Hollywood phenomenon was
materializing. A brash young man with unwavering confidence in
himself was turning the first bleak 55 minutes of every day into a
high Hooper, live audience radio property.

This 'n' That. Allen humor is a combination of sophistication and slapstick. He is the kind of an entertainer who inspires
laughs by his mere presence, the kind people are afraid not to
laugh at for fear they may betray their ignorance. The studio
audience banters with him, but seldom tops him. He has brief patience with insolence. Once a husky teenager clamped his foot down
on the cord of the portable microphone as Allen roamed the studio.
The entertainer warned his heckler with inscrutable half-serious,
half-joking inflection: "Take your foot off the cord of I'll punch
you in the nose." Everybody laughed uproariously.

Guest stars have included some of Hollywood's top talent,
many of them (like Jolson) Allen addicts. They never are announced beforehand. Occasionally the studio audience fastens on a
risque interpretation, breaks into gales of sly laughter. Chides
Allen: "I'll tell 'em clean; you can laugh dirty." In a dry satiric
jab at the gullibility of radio audiences, he recently spent several
minutes mentioning various cities and localities while his audience
obediently cheered for each one.

Allen has an explanation for his unusual success. In his
words: "I have a flair for comedy."
                                    --Fortnight (October 28, 1949),
                                    page 14.

• THE AMOS 'N' ANDY SHOW (NBC, 1929-1948; CBS, 1948-1954)

I believe one reason Amos and Andy have lasted so many
years is that they haven't tried to be too funny. (Yes, you can
still get Amos and Andy, and they're a great relief from the rapid-
fire cracks of some of the other and newer comedy programs. Like
"Old Man River," they just keep rolling along, with a great deal of
honest, effortless, somewhat accidental humor. I listen to Amos
and Andy twice a year and see my dentist twice a day. If we were
smarter we'd all go back to Amos and Andy oftener, on and off, and
desert some of the faster, funny scream-lined guys of 1937.)
                                    --Don Herold in Judge, Vol. 112,
                                    No. 2700 (March 1937), page 18.

                          *   *   *

I must rule myself out of court at once as a competent listener to the radio, because of my incapacity to follow the "two remarkable young geniuses," as Brisbane calls them, Amos and Andy. I
have no difficulty in discovering the source of their popularity;
they are combining in a new medium two familiar forms of entertain-
ment--the comic strip and the black-face comedians of the minstrel
show. It seems to me that neither of these is peculiarly suited to

the radio, and I am convinced that the best form of radio entertainment will be one which rises out of the medium itself.
                              --Gilbert Seldes in The New Repub-
                                lic, Vol. 67, No. 859 (May 20,
                                1931), page 19.

• JACK BENNY*

        Not even among comedians is there much argument. Right now
Jack Benny is the funniest man on radio. Back in 1945, after Benny
had been on the air for thirteen rib-tickling years, his program
abruptly skidded. The comedy became dusty and labored. Listeners
demoted him from his customary post among radio's top four or five
shows to twelfth place. The smart alecks whispered that he was
finished. But not Benny. The next fall he clamped more tightly on
his ever-present cigar and paced the floor more nervously--and the
show recaptured some of its old verve.

        This week, after exactly fifteen years in radio, Jack Benny
is back in full stride, as he has been all season. Against the tough-
est competition of his career, the Jack Benny Show (NBC, Sunday,
7-7:30 p.m., EST) has copped the top spot on the bimonthly Hoop-
eratings twice in six months, and week in, week out gives the Bob
Hopes and the Fibber McGees a hard, fast run for the win money.

        Unlike some of his competition, notably Hope, Benny pulls
his radio way almost unaided by outside activities. Of the fifteen
movies he has made, he has had two real hits. During the war he
successfully toured battle zones, but his personal appearances for
home-front civilians have been few. Nevertheless, Benny's potential
draw as a performer on the stage of urban movies houses is such
that this May the radio star and a small troupe move into the Roxy
in New York for a minimum gross take of $40,000 a week. It is the
highest salary ever paid for a theater date.

        For all this Variety in its annual showmanship issue two weeks
ago was moved to give Benny a special award. The cryptic and
critical trade paper said: "The story of Benny is the story ... of
a comedian who, thanks to his own particular savvy, has grown up
with the changing techniques in radio. Variety salutes him because
the program represents the acme in smooth cooperation between
scripters, production crew, and cast."

        It's Hard to Be Funny: At 53, Benny, off mike, looks and
acts like a successful businessman. He is exactly that: a success
at the very serious business of comedy. Unlike the Fred Allens of

the trade, Benny has little natural, spontaneous wit. What gags he ad-libs on the air are those anyone would soak up after 37 years of hanging around professional funny men. In a private gathering of show people Benny is no showoff. He would much rather and usually does sit and listen to others strut their stuff. For them he is a wonderful audience. Even a minor gag can provoke a Benny belly laugh. It is the appreciation of what makes a line laughable that keys his radio program. Benny is the industry leader in the business of manufacturing radio comedy. Like the Henry Fords and the Alfred Sloans, he can't manufacture his product alone. Hence he has surrounded himself with a production team that clicks like castanets.

Benny gives all the credit for his stature to this outfit. "Where would I be today," he asks, "without my writers, without Rochester, Dennis Day, Mary Livingstone, Phil Harris, and Don Wilson?" That he himself hand-picked both the writers and the cast is something Benny never admits. He dismisses lightly the fact that he directs his own rehearsals, down to the last, fine reading of a line. Nor will he ever say part of his success stems from his own sense of timing and showmanship.

This belittling is not new. It was evident in the first words that Benny ever spoke on the air. He said: "Hello, Folks. This is Jack Benny. There will now be a slight pause for everyone to say 'Who cares?'" That was March 29, 1932. Benny was appearing on Broadway that year in Earl Carroll's Vanities. He was a successful graduate of vaudeville and had already hit Hollywood for a couple of movies. Ed Sullivan, the columnist, who then had his own aradio program, had invited Benny to try this new medium. Four weeks later, on a Monday, May 2, Benny opened his own show for Canada Dry Ginger Ale over the old NBC-Blue network. He has never been without a program or a sponsor since then.

The Perfect Fall Guy: Benny's first crack in radio may have been characterized by modesty. But it was never to be so again. The Jack Benny of radio is a cheap, tightfisted blowhard who gets knocked down by everyone and comes right back for more. The balding Benny character of the air let his vanity force him into buying a toupee. The character insists Benny is a violinist--though he has never gotten through more than a few squeaky, sour bars of "Love in Bloom." This is the Benny that is a mirror for a million human foibles--the perfect fall guy. Yet all of this is completely manufactured. The radio and stage Jack Benny is the opposite of the private Jack Benny. And it is a difference which Benny has to fight hard to maintain.

When he was still a kid in knickerbockers in Waukegan, Ill., Benny was given a violin by his father. He learned to play it so quickly that he got a job in the pit orchestra of a local theater before he was in long pants. At 17, calling himself by his real

name, Benjamin Kubelsky,* he went into vaudeville with his violin
tucked under his chin. At home Benny still plays his violin, not
too badly, for his own amusement--and as proof to the skeptics that
he can.

   Though his hair is gray and thinning, Benny is a long way
from being bald. To prove this to the public, Benny rarely wears
a hat and never a toupee except on movie lots. But Benny's worst
fears are that people will take him for a genuine skinflint. He estimates conservatively that it costs him an extra $5,000 a year in
lavish tipping and the like to disprove the nonexistent failing.

   That Benny feels he must disprove his stinginess is, of
course, perfect proof of the success of his radio character. That
character was born on Benny's first regular program in 1932. For
four and a half years Benny worked out the type with his gagwriter,
Harry Conn. How much credit for the idea goes to Conn and how
much to Benny is and probably will remain a moot question. In
1936 Benny and Conn split. Three years later Conn sued Benny
for $65,000, charging that the comedian was still using Conn char-
acters, quips, and sequences. The matter was settled out of
court, and the Benny of the air has continued to grow--and to serve
as the basis for the situations around which the show is built.

   Happy Family: Looking back over old Benny scripts is like
thumbing through a family album. The family group is all there.
Don Wilson, the announcer, fills the same foil role once held by an
earlier Alois Havrilla. Dennis Day, the timorous tenor, is the suc-
cessor to a line of timorous tenors which included Frank Parker,
James Melton, and Kenny Baker. Phil Harris, his bourbon, his con-
summate ego, and his orchestra, joined Benny in 1936, following
Frank Black and Don Bestor. Eddie Anderson, who plays Rochester,
was hired for a one shot in 1937 to play a Pullman porter. But the
public liked him so much that Benny hastily put him to regular work
as his valet.

   Last but certainly not least in the Benny corral is Mary
Livingstone. Unlike the rest of the cast, Miss Livingstone was not
a professional. Benny met her in 1926 when a vaudeville tour took
him to Los Angeles. She was then a 17-year-old clerk in the May
Co. department store. Her name was Sadye Marks--shortly there-
after changed to Mrs. Benny. Five years later on his program Jack
needed someone to read a short poem supposedly written by an

----

*While he was still a smalltime vaudeville violinist Benjamin Kubelsky
changed his name to Ben K. Benny. During a stint in the Navy of
the first world war he worked up a monologue routine to go with
his violin. Shortly after the war, however, the confusion between
the up-and-coming Ben K. Benny and another musician with a sense
of humor named Ben Bernie became too great. Thus Benjamin Kubelsky became Jack Benny once and for all.

addled fan named Mary Livingstone. Sadye Marks Benny stepped
into the bit role--and stayed on as Mary Livingstone to become almost as famous as her husband. On the air, however, she is just
the girl who gets in what is left of Benny's hair.

So thoroughly are these characters established on Benny's
show that this year two of them got their own programs, playing
elaborations of their Benny roles. Dennis Day, whose talents never
get a complete workout on the Sunday program, sings and acts on
Wednesday night in what is one of the year's most promising situation-
comedy shows, A Day in the Life of Dennis Day. Phil Harris, joining forces with his wife, Alice Faye, follows Benny on Sunday with
what is supposed to represent a day in the life of the Harris family.
Unlike Day's, Harris's show is perhaps the year's outstanding flop.
Away from the smart, glib typewriters of the Benny writers, the
Harris radio character fizzles into a boring loudmouth with very few
vestiges of humor.

Behind the Gags: In fifteen years on the air Benny has had
only seven writers. When Conn left, he took on Bill Morrow and Ed
Beloin, who worked for him until 1943 and were then succeeded by
his present staff, John Tackaberry, Milt Josefsberg, Sam Perrin,
and George Balzer.

Benny probably prizes his writers more than any other part
of his organization. They are under exclusive contract to him and
are among the highest paid in radio, with combined salaries totaling
about $5,000 a week. When Benny's program slipped in 1945, instead
of hiring new writers, he held onto his four and trained them even
harder in the Benny ways. Now, he gives them full credit for pulling the show out of the doldrums.

His writers' work begins right after each Sunday's broadcast.
With Benny they sit down and work out the situation for the following week. Some of the ideas come from the writers, but more of
them are Benny's. By Thursday the writers have put together the
script, which goes to Benny for astute editing. On Saturday there
is a cast reading and Sunday morning is spent in loose rehearsal.
Benny doesn't like a final dress rehearsal, saying it spoils the program's spontaneity. Occasionally, this theory backfires, resulting
in fluffs and all too obvious ad-libs.

The most serious criticism of the Benny program has been
that his show seldom changes. The comedian violently disputes
this idea. True, the basic part of each week's humor arises out of
the well-established characters and their well-known reactions to
given sets of circumstances. But the circumstances, Benny points
out, always have an element of surprise. Over the years Benny has
resorted to such diversified gimmicks as a polar bear, a talkative
parrot, a feud with Fred Allen, a museum relic of an automobile,
and the gravel voice of Andy Devine, whom Benny once paid $500
just to say "Hi ya, Buck."

The Lifetime Guarantee: Out of the fact that the Bennys live
next door to the Ronald Colmans in fashionable Beverly Hills, Calif.,
Benny got one of his funniest situations: the socially correct and
veddy British Colmans entertaining the social climbing, inelegant
Benny. Last year the comedian brought the names of three small
Southern California towns into the show. Now the mere mention
of Anaheim, Azusa, and Cucamonga brings a laugh. Jack started
a national nuisance when he got involved wiht a character named
Kitzel who sold him a hot dog with "peekel een the meedle and the
mustard on top."

This year's major contribution to the nation's giggles is
Benny's quartet. He hired them first for laughs and secondly to
help hurdle that necessary evil, the middle commercial. The quartet,
professionally known as the Sportsmen but around the Benny show as
"Mmmmmm," take the middle plug for Lucky Strike cigarettes and
sing or chant it in ridiculous and clever verse. The commercial is
written by Benny himself, with the help of Mahlon Merrick, the show's
musical director.

For comedy reasons, Benny accepts the quartet only as a
major nuisance and recently "fired" them to get a laugh-provoking
situation. Last week the situation had been built up to a temporary
substitute--and extraordinary--quartet consisting of Dennis Day,
Dick Haymes, Andy Russell, and Bing Crosby. In the million-
dollar clambake that followed baritone Bing stumbled on a high note
and nearly broke up the show by ad-libbing loudly "Who the hell
picked this key, Dennis Day?"

Only a Crosby could get away with profanity on a Benny show.
Throughout his radio career, Benny had avoided any off-color, muddy humor. His care to keep his show clean is even greater than his
reliability in coming up with comedy 35 Sundays a year.

For as long as Benny cares to stay in radio, listeners can be
sure they may tune him in on the 7 p.m., EST spot Sundays. In
1941, when it looked as if Benny might move to another network,
NBC made the unprecedented move of giving him a lifetime option
on what is one of radio's most valuable half hours. So long as he
has a sponsor satisfactory to NBC, Benny can use that half-hour as
he sees fit. Two weeks ago he was assured of NBC's satisfaction
for three more years when the American Tobacco Co., Benny's fifth
and current sponsor, renewed his contract through 1950. The terms:
$25,000 a week for the packaged program which Benny owns, plus
$250,000 a year to advertise and publicize the show. Benny will
earn it.

--Newsweek (March 31, 1947),
pages 66-68.

- EDGAR BERGEN

During the past seven years Edgar Bergen has made himself
a national figure largely by talking to himself. He has done this
with the aid of an apparatus called Charlie McCarthy, which has
become an even more popular national figure, and probably more human to a larger number of people than any inanimate object in
world history. It takes only the mildest indulgence in the world of
fantasy to be persuaded that Charlie, a fellow of infinite and raucous wit, is actually alive.

Last week, as usual, millions of U.S. citizens gathered at
their radios (NBC, 8 p.m., E.W.T.) to hear McCarthy confront and
confound one of the nation's names. This time it was Orson Welles.
McCarthy (who, of course, always has Scriptwriter Bergen on his
side) blithely opened up: "Oh, Orson!... Oh, Wellesie!... Where
is old fatso?" Welles came out of the wings at NBC's Manhattan studios, and McCarthy chirped: "Why don't you release a blimp for
active service?" Once before, Welles had taken even worse abuse
from his radio host. That time the actor had asked "the Magnificent
Splinter" what he thought of the weighty Welles efforts on the air.
Said McCarthy: "At first I thought something had died in my radio."

Welles took it handsomely, as do most of McCarthy's targets,
who are invariably delighted to be ribbed by such a super-eminence.
In his wooden insouciance, Charlie gets away with a candid vein of
comment which is unprecedented in radio. Via a small-boy character
(which helps), Bergen manages a titillating form of malice-without-
malice. To judge by his audiences, it is all hugely satisfying to
the U.S. public. Charlie called Gossipist Louella Parsons an "old
blabbermouth," while confiding in an aside that "everything will be
all over town tomorrow." He referred to Emily Post as "a vulture
for culture" and dismissed her with: "It's been a charming evening.
By the way, Miss Emily, you don't have a toothpick on you?" He
asked rippling Paulette Goddard with elaborate sweetness: "Take
away your face and your figure and what have you got?" Of Beatrice ("Advice to the Lovelorn") Fairfax he naughtily inquired:
"Where do you learn all the things you tell the young folks not to
do?"

Magic and Black Art. So irresistible is McCarthy's person-
ality--saucy, lethally precocious and irreverent--that it is all but
impossible for listeners to remember that he is a ventriloquist's
dummy. The instinct to forget it is natural; no such coldly mechanical terms could possibly describe the complex psychological relationship between Charlie McCarthy and Edgar John Bergen.

Charlie has supported Bergen most of his life. He began by
putting Bergen through high school and almost through Northwestern
University, and got him into Delta Upsilon. Charlie was whittled

out 25 years ago by a Chicago barkeep named Mack (price: $35).
He was modeled on a sketch Bergen made of a red-headed Chicago
newsboy. Bergen was then 16, the gawky, moody second son of a
Swedish immigrant named Berggren who had run a retail dairy business in Chicago and a farm near Decatur, Mich.

At eleven, Edgar Bergen had found that he could throw his
voice (his mother was forever answering the door in response to
pleas of mysterious old men who begged to be let in). The boy
was further inspired by Herrman's Wizards Manual, Secrets of Magic,
Black Art, Mind Reading and Ventriloquism (including a chapter on
"how to cut a man's head off and put it into a platter a yard from
his body"). Charlie McCarthy was just what Bergen needed. The
little dummy was such a social success (unlike Bergen alone) that
he lured Bergen from his university premedical studies into vaudeville. For ten years, through the decline of vaudeville, into the
nightclubs of the middle '30s, they made a living, but that was all
--ventriloquists were classed with jugglers and acrobats.

"I'll Mow-w-w-w you Down." The turn in their luck came in
Chicago. Out of work and deeply discouraged, Charlie and Bergen
got a week's tryout at the Chez Paree nightclub. At 3 o'clock one
morning they came on for their final performance. The club was
almost empty. In the middle of their act, Charlie suddenly reared
up, turned to Bergen and said: "Who the hell ever told you you
were a good ventriloquist?"

Bergen blushed, fidgeted, tried to put his hand over Charlie's
mouth. "Don't shush me," Charlie continued. "I'll mow-w-w-w you
down. You better go back to the farm and leave me alone. I'll
get by, but you're all through, brother, all through."

Charlie then turned on the customers and told them they were
a disgrace to civilization. Bergen put him on a chair and backed
away. Charlie went right on giving the customers a piece of Bergen's
innermost thoughts. The management was getting nervous, but the
patrons howled with laughter and pounded the tables. Backstage
later Bergen was saying: "I just had to get that off my chest."

But he was a hit and he stayed on, until Manhattan's lofty
Rainbow Room bought Charlie's raillery. In keeping with this swank
setting, McCarthy appeared in top hat & tails. Then Rudy Vallée
put him on the air. Bergen had finally found his proper medium
of communication: the microphone. Previously, many of Charlie's
asides and much of their patter had been lost to the audience.
Swift give-and-take (mostly give) is the essence of McCarthy's
humor. Now everybody could hear it.

Who Made Whom? The McCarthy-Bergen relationship has often
caught the eye of psychologists who analyze it in such terms as
split personality, inferiority complex, the subconscious expressing

itself. None of their analyses has satisfied Bergen. Says he: "I
will say that Charlie's personality is as opposite from mine as it can
be, and that I envy him. I wish I could walk into a room like
Charlie.... To me it's quite remarkable that this carved piece of
wood ... should be so ... important. He can be invited to the
White House, consulted by OWI, received by the royalty of Europe.... It's ridiculous, even, that my appearing any place without
Charlie is a complete failure. I do think it's a case of the tail wags
the dog.

"But no matter what he says, no matter what he says about
me, I have made him everything he is today.... The public insists
I am a little eccentric. That is not for me to judge. I may be a
little jealous of Charlie. Sometimes it is hard for me to explain why
I have to have Charlie there to get the laughs. But he did a good
show last Sunday and then I liked him."

Edgar Bergen's friends think they know why he has to have
Charlie there. Pink-cheeked, blue-eyed, 41-year-old Bergen, as
Scandinavian as a troll, is as shy as Charlie is brash (Charlie:
"He's an emotional hermit"). He is neat & clean to the point of obsession. He takes vitamin pills, daily exercises, Swedish baths, keeps
fruit handy on a side table. His normal voice is soft and reminis-
cent of Charlie's. His idea of a perfect Saturday afternoon is to go
home alone and pore for hours over his suitcases of old magic tricks.

In public, he can be brilliantly witty--even bawdy, but without Charlie he is more likely to be musing, easily bored, prone to
doze and dream. Charlie McCarthy is his sly vehicle for a set of
highly irreverent opinions on society in general. Charlie has also
been of considerable sentimental aid to the bachelor Bergen.

Their relationship, as profitably aired between them, has long
since become one of the most public of properties. "What would you
be without me?" asks Bergen, and Charlie answers: "Speechless."
They haggle over Charlie's weekly stipend of 75¢. Bergen is sensitive about his balding head, but Charlie isn't. Advised that Bergen
has a girl friend who loves to run her fingers through his hair,
Charlie adds: "Or pat the roots."

Belly-Prophet. Charlie's personality was real to many people
almost from the first time he went on the air. Bergen did nothing
to discourage this. Then the great W. C. Fields joined the program
for a season and railed away at Charlie's vital fabric ("blockhead,
woodenhead, flophouse for termites") with threats of axing him to
death, otherwise treating him as a dummy. Despite such campaigns
as Field's, the illusion that Charlie is a person remains. People
often call Bergen Charlie. When Charlie greeted Eleanor Roosevelt
for the first time, she spontaneously started to shake hands with
him.

Other ventriloquists may be more technically adept than
Bergen, but he has the great illusion-making power which springs
out of imagination, taste and an accurate sense of comedy. He is
a scholar as well as a student of his art, and wrote the Encyclopedia
Britannica's article on it. The Greeks called their ventriloquists
"belly-prophets," and Bergen feels that the art undoubtedly lay
behind the ancient speaking statues and other temple oracles. As
to the requirements, Bergen says: "Ventriloquism is a cultivated
groan. It is as much of a gift as a good singing voice. If you
have the gift and if you are a good mimic, then you have a start
in the right direction. It is something you can learn as you can
learn to be a good singer." But once achieved, the ventriloquial
quality can be lost. Bergen works hard on his vocal exercises,
practicing high notes, keeping Charlie's voice separate from his,
etc.

"He Really Lives There." Charlie lives the life of Riley
now. He and Bergen are not millionaires (their belated success
coincided with high income taxes and Charlie gets no income-tax
exemption), but they are very well off. Chase & Sanborn pays
them $7,500 weekly ($10,000 beginning next January); they now
get $150,000 for a motion picture; and their toys, games, etc.
yield another $75,000 annually.

Charlie travels in style--in a plush-lined trunk. His bed-
room in Bergen's comfortable home on a hilltop outside Hollywood is
just a shade smaller than Bergen's huge one. Bergen's conceit is
to give Charlie a bed, furniture, tile bathroom with built-in shower,
an array of perfumes and toilet waters. Charlie also has a dresser
to get him into his $75 suits (of which he has scores) and $15 shoes
(18 pairs). Among his other appurtenances are his Boy Scout uni-
form, jockey's silks, a grease-monkey's zipper suit, a chamber pot
of the proper size. A dirty shirt hangs over the back of a chair
(Bergen: "To show he really lives there"). Charlie's stationery
bears his motto: E Pluribus Mow 'Em Downus. On his desk is a
letter written, Bergen swears, in Charlie's own handwriting, addressed to his teacher: "Please excuse Charlie for being absent
from school yesterday as he had lara laryn [crossed out] as he attended his grandmother's funeral."

Alter Ego. If Edgar Bergen (with pressagent help) has
made himself a totem, few men have ever had more provocation.
Bergen, who is fond of children, is seldom far from Charlie. He
hires several gagwriters now in order to get some time to himself.
But what they contribute to the show is mainly situations. Bergen
gives the copy his own flavor. With the possible exception of Fred
Allen, he is the most original gagwriter in the U.S. He finds brief
intervals for his workshop, where he builds steam engines; his
desert ranch, where he likes to harvest the alfalfa; a ceramics business, a gold mine, a nonprofit foundation to help girls who want
to study nursing. Says he: "I have to try to convince myself that

I can stand on my own feet without Charlie. That is why I go into these businesses."

Out of challenge to himself, as much as anything else, Bergen created the different character of Mortimer Snerd, Charlie's gap-toothed, appleknocking pal. (Bergen: "Mortimer, how can you be so stupid." Mortimer: "It ain't easy.") His still more recent help-er, Effie Klinker, a lady and bachelor girl ("not an old maid ... she turned down three offers and has an independent income"), came into being for the same reason. There is also a stand-in dummy for "dangerous scenes" in Charlie's pictures. "But," says Bergen, "I have no love or sympathy for him."

Bergen has recently alleged a general restlessness: "I have reached rather an unfortunate time of my life. There is nothing more tiring than looking forward to five or six more years of radio. I am a creative artist and this is routine work now." But it is a reasonably safe bet that his original alter ego will never seem routine to him. Bergen has always been touchy about the backflap through which he manipulates Charlie McCarthy's movements. Once an insen-sitive friend stuck his hand through the flap. Bergen remained im-passive, but Charlie sharply protested: "My God, is nothing sacred?"

> --Time (November 20, 1944),
> pages 54-57.

● THE BICKERSONS (NBC, 1946-1948)

The air lanes are aquiver with the cooings of contented hus-bands and wives (Ozzie and Harriet, Phil and Alice, Ethel and Albert, to mention only a few) but there is one young couple who couldn't have been more thoroughly mismated and who make no bones about it. They are John and Blanche Bickerson, who are heard at the tail end of the Old Gold show, and who are a sort of contemporary Jiggs and Maggie. On second thought I withdraw the reference. Jiggs and Maggie aren't in the same league with the Bickersons.

Blanche, played very capably by Frances Langford, is one of the monstrous shrews of all time. She makes her husband Don Ameche take two jobs, a total of sixteen working hours, in order to bring in more money which she squanders on minks and the stock market. Meanwhile he can't afford a pair of shoes and goes around with his feet painted black. In the few hours he has to sleep, she heckles him all night with the accusation that he doesn't love her. Her aim appears to be to drive her husband crazy and she succeeds very nicely. The harassed John's only weapon is insult, at which he's pretty good. I have here a sample of John and Blanche's

conversation culled from a couple of scripts. Bear in mind that this
is 2 a.m. and John is trying throughout to get to sleep.

BLANCHE: You used to be so considerate. Since you got
married to me you haven't got any sympathy at all.

JOHN: I have too. I've got everybody's sympathy.

BLANCHE: Believe me there's better fish in the ocean than
the one I caught.

JOHN: There's better bait too.

BLANCHE: I don't see how you can go to bed without kissing
me good night.

JOHN: I can do it.

BLANCHE: You'd better say you're sorry for that, John.

JOHN: Okay, I'm sorry. I'm sorry. I'm sorry.

BLANCHE: You are not.

JOHN: I am too. I'm the sorriest man that ever was born.

BLANCHE: Did you take care of the cat?

JOHN: No.

BLANCHE: Why not?

JOHN: Cat can take care of himself.

BLANCHE: Don't be funny. What about the goldfish and the
canary? Were they hungry?

JOHN: Starving.

BLANCHE: What are they eating?

JOHN: Each other. Why don't you let me sleep, Blanche?

BLANCHE: All you have to do is give me a civil answer.
Just tell me what you gave the goldfish to eat.

JOHN: Eggs! Fifteen poached eggs. And the cat had the
same.

BLANCHE: Where did all those eggs come from?

JOHN: The canary laid 'em. Please, Blanche, I've got to
get some sleep.

BLANCHE: Male canaries don't lay eggs and ... How is the
canary?

JOHN: I haven't seen him since I vacuumed his cage.

BLANCHE: John Bickerson!

JOHN: Oh, don't blow your top. The canary's fine!

BLANCHE: Did you give him his bath?

JOHN: I gave him his bath. I powdered his tail and I plucked his eyebrows. What do you want from me, Blanche?

BLANCHE: I'll bet you didn't let the cat out tonight.

JOHN: I'm sick of playing nursemaid to a broken-down alley cat!

BLANCHE: He's a beautiful cat and I love him.

JOHN: I hate him.

BLANCHE: You wouldn't feel that way if you got a little friendly with him. Why don't you bring him something to play with?

JOHN: I'll bring him a dog in the morning. Good night.

BLANCHE: Is there any milk for breakfast?

JOHN: No.

BLANCHE: Then you'll have to eat out.

JOHN: I don't care. I've been doing it all week.

BLANCHE: What for? I left you enough food for six days. I cooked a whole bathtubful of rice. What happened to it?

JOHN: I took a bath in it.

BLANCHE: Why didn't you eat it?

JOHN: I've told you a million times I can't stand the sight of rice.

BLANCHE: Why not?

JOHN: Because it's connected with the saddest mistake of my life.

Just how pretty Miss Langford contrives to transform herself so convincingly into this venomous witch is her own little secret. She nags with the whining persistence of a buzzsaw, a quality that can barely be suggested in print. Mr. Ameche responds in accents of tired loathing which could hardly be improved on, though they may well cost him the women's vote.

At the risk of losing the women's vote myself I'd like to go on record as saying I think the Bickersons very funny. In a medium which strives so desperately to spread sweetness and light, in which every wife is an angel of tolerant understanding and every husband dumb but lovable, the bickering Bickersons are a very refreshing venture in the opposite direction.

> --John Crosby in New York Herald
> Tribune (May 25, 1948).

• NORMAN BROKENSHIRE

Here is a voice which can be greatly amusing with its deliberate, hearty overexaggeration of the broad-A type of announcing.
He has developed such a host of inept imitators that in self-
protection he should have a law passed.

--Cyrus Fisher in The Forum and
Century, Vol. 88, No. 2 (August 1932), page 127.

• ABE BURROWS

This is a comedian-type story, as Abe Burrows would say.
And it's all about Burrows.

Funniest of the New York Burrows, unless you count Brooklyn, Abe is heard Saturday nights over CBS (9 p.m. PST). The
time choice may be strategic. This way they can keep him a secret,
so other networks won't lure him away.

Abe sings his own song creations. Songs about life and
love and grain speculation ... atom bombs, birds and bees ...
Lana Turner. He sings them, largely to his own erratic piano
accompaniment, in about Nelson Eddy's key, with Andy Devine's
tonal purity, and the diction of Ed Gardner's Archie. His delivery
is as smooth and effortless as that of a hippopotamus having twins.
Following a recent attck of laryngitis, Burrows assured his doctor
that his voice was all right again. "How can you tell?" the medicine
man puzzled.

The format of the Abe Burrows Show is magnificent in its
simplicity. Solid Burrows, with a short pause, fore and aft, for
Burrows identification. Sandwiched in are two brief commercials
and a musical number by Milton DeLugg's instrumental quartet.
This gives Burrows a chance to recover should his voice lapse into
human utterance.

Opening the program, announcer Bob LeMond says, "Here's
Abe Burrows." Then Abe's voice, warm and vibrant as a burned-
out bearing, "I'm Burrows like he said." From there, CBS and its
listeners gather 'round the piano while radio's answer to the Cherry
Sisters covers some monumental themes in song and story.

Tin Pan Alley blubberings inspire his uncluttered versions
of songs of our time. "Now I'll do a love-type song," he advises,
"entitled 'Morning Becomes Electra But You Look Better at Night.'"
Or he will do a political-type song, like this one dedicated to

President Truman, "Now That White Shirts Are Back, Maybe He'll
Go Back to Missouri."

Not all of Burrows' lyrical brain children reach maturity.
Some die a-borning, the monstrosity of their conception too much
even for their author to tackle beyond the title. Like the one
about Minnie the Maid-mer, a girl whose upper half looked like a
fish.

Unlike the Henry Morgan school of radio satire, Burrows
approaches the commercial with respect and some dignity. With ad-
mirable restraint, he permits his announcer, Bob LeMond, to give
the Listerine pitch, permitting himself only an occasional subtle jab
like, "I've found the Listerine plays an important part in nutrition.
If you don't buy it, Burrows don't eat." Working on a jingle for
his product, Abe's first try came out, "Try a tube of Listerine
tooth paste, it's very high class and not an uncouth paste."

Radio reached into its hip pocket, where it keeps its gag-
writers for its newest and brightest comedy star. Rudy Vallee's
show, Duffy's Tavern, Fred Allen, the Dinah Shore show, and
many other big-time airers have known one touch of Burrows.
Until last month he stroked the Joan Davis crew of laugh-makers.
Before getting around to radio, Abe was a bank runner, a Wall
Street board boy, an accountant, and a salesman. At NYU and
CCNY he majored in Latin.

A fair gagster herself, Nature abandoned Burrows, in the way
of appearances, at the accountant stage. Although slightly hefty, he
still looks like a bookkeeper. His shoulders droop dejectedly and he
blinks uncertainly behind his glasses. He has no moustache and
hair to match.

Despite a decade in radio, it was a hobby that finally pushed
Brooklyn's new Sinatra in front of a microphone. His hobby was,
of all things, being the life of Manhattan and Hollywood parties.
No one misses a tony shindig once it's known that Abe will be there.
His fans include such show-world intelligentsia as Nunnally Johnson,
Groucho Marx, Danny Kaye, Clark Gable, Ira Gershwin, and Norman
Corwin. Not to mention John Steinbeck and Sinclair Lewis, who
we'll throw in here for ballast.

On such an occasion, the likely spot to look for Burrows is at
the piano, the four-legged love of his life. Here, surrounded by
kindred spirits, he pursues his own shady muse, gleefully and dis-
cordantly pulling the wings off some of Tin Pan Alley's most delicate
butterflies. In his rhyme scheme, "love" pairs with "shove," "moon"
with "baboon," "jestin'" with "intestine."

Taking a line ... any line ... like "It's Only a Shanty on
Roxbury Drive," Abe pounces on it, mangles a warm-up chord or

two, and he's off. The result, spontaneous and lyrical as a hiccough,
is a raucously touching nostalgic-type song.

Pried from the piano stool, Burrows becomes a spell-binding
monologuist who can and does hold the floor for an hour at a time.
He is very self-conscious about this social breach and, once aware
of it, hastily concludes his discourse with some completely irrele-
vant insanity.

To listeners of the Abe Burrows show, the picture of Abe as
a philosopher and student will come as a shock. But it's the same
kid, all right. In his role as a parlor Baruch, he never sullies
his beautiful Brooklyn brogue with the muck of the King's English.
Talking like a Manhattan truck driver and thinking like a Nicholas
Murray Butler are his Bronx cheer for the pompous and the crooked
pinkie. A broad intellect doesn't require a broad A, the man says.

Burrows finds this relaxed social attitude a great giant killer.
A stranger to the Burrows scene, coming on Abe standing in the
middle of a friend's living room, with a salami sandwich in one hand
and a glass of Irish whisky in the other, is apt to underestimate
his new acquaintance. Frank Loesser, the song writer and Burrows'
good friend, takes a terrific beating. Recently he entertained Dr.
William Howard Schumann, probably No. 1 man among contemporary
American musicians, head of the Juilliard School, composer of five
symphonies, and knighted by Pulitzer. With such an accredited long-
hair in tow, Loesser felt that at last he could vindicate his lowbrow
Tin-Pan Alley antecedents.

"Ya know somethin', Schumann," Burrows croaked on being
introduced at Loesser's home, "you're the first guy ever came into
this house that could read notes."

When Abe decided to pack his parlor tricks and make a radio
show of them, his close friends discouraged him. He was too sophisticated for the dialsiders. "They won't get it," he was touted. But
he didn't believe it.

"People ain't as dumb as poeple think they are," he philos-
ophizes. "You take the average guy who spends an hour a day on
the bus, back and forth to work. What does he do? He reads.
He ain't got money for night clubs and shows. What does he do
for entertainment? He reads. So he knows what's goin' on ...
more than people in show business.

"I'm a serious guy. The stuff I write is stuff that I think
about. It's not just jokes ... it's about something that's going on
... that people are interested in. That's what they like about the
show."

"But what makes them laugh?" you want to know.

"Well, that I can't explain exactly. You might say I'm a kinda Coney Island mirror. I reflect by distortion. I see things funny and that's the way I point 'em out to the people."

Seeing her head gag-man dying on the vine because he wanted to act was more than Joan Davis could bear. One night last spring, she persuaded Abe to try on her studio audience for sleeve length. Taking a deep breath and a firm grip on his wonderful homemade repertoire, the Brooklyn-type calypso singer plunged in up to his cactus-coated voice-box.

"My first line was, 'I'm a singer,' " Burrows recalls. "That's all I said ... and they laughed. Then I knew I was in."

Fan mail is a new and awesome experience for Abe. He carries choice tidbits in his pocket, flashing them like a gold-starred report card.

"I gotta show this one to the sponsor. It's a Listerine carton turned inside out. They made a post card out of it. All it says is, 'Dear Abe Burrows: Need I say more?' "

Sartorially, Burrows is as uninhibited as he is conversationally. At the moment, he is passing through a turtle neck sweater cycle. "Good for my throat," he explains. And to the further dismay of his friends, his current new look also features a baseball cap.

His opinions cover every subject conceivable, from presidential candidates to rye bread. "The Kinsey report," Abe contends, "has done more for sex than anything since the invention of the cocktail party by Sir Andrew Cocktail."

A gourmet of the delicatessen school, Burrows can lick his weight in pastrami, swiss cheese, or dill pickles. In line with his reputation as a great thinker, he has a definite theory about delicatessen rye. "When you order rye bread in a delicatessen, always tell 'em from the middle. The ends either get dried out from standin' or they're soggy from leanin' in the potato salad."

With or without his turtle neck sweater and salami sandwich, Burrows is certainly destined to be one of radio's men of distinction. He's the only gag-writer who ever slipped his leg-irons to stand shy and trembling, but free, before a microphone.

--Mary McSkimming in Script
(March 1948), pages 28-29.

- CANDID MICROPHONE (ABC, 1947-1948)

And now the gift the giftie gie us to hear ourselves as others
hear us. It's all done, not with mirrors, but with a microphone.

The candid microphone, like its inspiration, the candid camera,
aims to catch the victim in a moment of unflattering informality.
Now, along with the visual enjoyment of a soul-revealing newspaper
photo of Sir Stafford Cripps picking his teeth or Mme. Peron tugging
at her girdle, you can flip your radio dial to get similar second-hand
audeo thrills. You can hear the mating call of a lovelorn plumber,
the diatribe of a stymied landlord, or the verbal whimsey of a Manhattan traffic cop running his quarry to the curb.

Principal weakness of the candid microphone, compared to
the candid camera, is the anonymity of the performers. Piquancy
and meatiness of the candid camera shot vary with the recogniza-
bility and news worth of the subject. A lady midget cozy on the
lap of an unidentified fat man would stir a mild flicker of risability,
but a lady midget dawdled on the hallowed knee of J. P. Morgan
was the squat heard 'round the world.

It was the prospect of gems like that which undoubtedly led
to expecting too much from the new A.B.C. program, Candid Microphone. But even using unnamed subjects, it could have been a lot
more fun than it turned out to be. To a born eavesdropper, the
anticipation of wallowing in secretly recorded conversation is intriguing. If you've never lingered before replacing the receiver on a
busy party line, if you've never unconsciously leaned backward or
sideward to catch the tête-à-tête at the next table, you would dial
past this show fast.

The name Candid Microphone is a good two-word description
of the show. If developed as specified in the announcer's introduction, the program presents a terrific production job. The person
being interviewed is unaware of the fact, so this calls for hiding the
mike on the reporter ... up his sleeve, under his cravat, lower
plate, clavicle, or toupe. The wire from the mike is supposed to
run "inconspicuously" to an engineer manning a wire recorder some
distance away.

Now there's a feat for you. On a show where everyone is
supposed to know what's going on, it's conceded to be a full-time
job for an engineer to keep people from tripping over the parapher-
nalia. Stretching a wire, even an inconspicuous one, a hundred feet
or more on a busy street sounds more like a Hallowe'en stunt. Of
course, if the interviewee spots the wire running out of the A.B.C.
man's trouser leg and ad libs a few inappropriate remarks, the jig
is up.

When you stop to think, very few conversations heard in a day's walk could be aired without fumigation. But, of course, erasing the naughty words is easy for the wire recorder. In fact, a three-minute segment may have a hundred splices holding it together.

A recent program in the series teed off with a conversation between the Candid Microphone reporter and a locksmith hired to saw a padlocked chain off the leg of the former's secretary. The locksmith, although viewing with askance his eccentric chore, didn't make very good radio out of the situation, evincing only a mild reaction to unshackling a live female gam. This got the whole show away to an artificial start. And that was unfortunate because the basic idea depends upon a natural situation as well as spontaneous lines. Staged spots like that one have a People Are Funny flavor.

Other Candid Microphone vignettes on the same line-up featured a visit to a barber shop for a youngster's first hair cut ... a heart-to-heart talk with a used-car dealer, promising much and revealing nothing ... and a look-in on a group of children playing sidewalk games. Not exciting, not even intelligible on the outdoor sequences because of noise interference.

The pièce de résistance had its setting at Ebbets Field. Through the offices of the British Consulate, Allen Funt, the show's producer, snared a long-time Brooklyn resident who had never seen a baseball game. They put him in the bleachers next to a highly articulate Dodger fan complete with a rich Brooklyn brogue. He and his Canarsie cousin took it from there.

Mr. Funt, fathering a good idea in Candid Microphone, seems to have let it bog down before getting far off the ground.

It's too bad, too. There are so many wonderful places you could plant a candid microphone. Say, for instance, in national Republican headquarters a day or so after Senator Taft made so many friends mad and influenced so many people with the new diet plank in his presidential platform. We plug in our candid mike:

"Honestly, Bob, whatever made you say a thing like that? Can't you be more Lincoln-like?

"Lincoln-like? Why, we Tafts are Cadillac men. And besides; I didn't say...."

"Well, whatever you said, that's the way it came out. Tell 'em to beat their wives ... tell 'em not to pay their income tax ... but, man, never tell 'em not to eat. Eatin's a habit those Democrats got 'em into and you can't talk 'em out of it."

--Mary McSkimming in Script (November 1947), pages 42 and 44.

- CAPTAIN HENRY'S SHOW BOAT (NBC, 1932-1937)

    Favorite old and new tunes and good singing and perhaps the
worst black-face team in existence [Molasses and January].
                                    --G. W. In Life (April 1935),
                                       page 46.

- BOAKE CARTER

    A man of a few thousand words, every one of which is elo-
quent, dramatic and spell-binding. And darn wearisome, too!
                                    --Don Herold in Judge, Vol. 112,
                                       No. 2703 (June 1937), page 22.

                          *   *   *
    Radio's nerviest commentator who pulls no punches, and the
sponsor who leaves him be. Excuse his growl.
                                    --Don Herold in Judge, Vol. 113,
                                       No. 2705 (August 1937), page 22.

- THE CHESTERFIELD SHOW (CBS, 1938)

    Debut of George Burns and Gracie Allen under the Chester-
field banner last Friday [September 30] marked the beginning of
their seventh consecutive year on American networks. It's their
fourth commercial, with each change having been accompanied by a
substantial boost in salary. What they've got still represents one
of radio's choicest pieces of entertainment property. Team's initial
program was a darb from every angle. It was saturated with stock
laugh material, smartly rounded out with the high level of musical
fare that goes with Frank Parker and Ray Noble and adroitly riveted
together with good production sense. In the past production has
been one of B & A's short suits.

    Routine remained unchanged. Gags for each occasion have
a flashback theme (the opening one dealing with a trip to Honolulu)
and they're all fashioned to fit Miss Allen's screwball personality.
Noble is back, doubling with his Piccadilly accent and joke interpola-
tions, while Parker's stooge innings are founded upon his embarrassing encounters with blind dates. George Burns takes as much pains
in piloting these side comedy episodes as he does with the passages
between himself and Miss Allen.

    Parker, successor to Tony Martin on the show, has all that

it takes to make the femme addicts of the B & A entry look forward
to his vocal interludes. His selection of numbers was uniformly
sound.

Until the show goes west the plug dishing assignment will be
Paul Douglas. The copy oozes with luxury phraseology. They're
rich and aromatic. They make smoking a delightful pleasure.
They're more soothing than any tobacco you've ever smoked; and,
to say the least, they're refreshingly mild.

--"Odec" [Ben Bodec] in Variety
(October 5, 1938), page 30.

• FATHER CHARLES E. COUGHLIN

Too many radio talkers make the fundamental mistake of
thinking of themselves as talking to fifty million people. They
ought to think of themselves as being in a room with just one or
two other people. They ought to think of that and tame down.

I've always resented oratory and exaggerated intonation.
"Public speaking" in its worse sense is a relic of barbarism. (Yet
they even teach it in colleges, still.) I don't like to have anybody
try to "sway my emotions" with the tune of his voice. That sort
of thing is to be classed with tom-toms. If any subject is at all
vital, gimme the words without the music. As I say, convince me
if you can--but don't try to sway me.

Now I'm never quite sure what it is that Father Coughlin
wants or is trying to say, but I'm always pretty sure it is something
pretty fishy or pretty trivial, because he says it with such passion-
ate intonation. He hits every syllable as if it were a bass drum. He
must be afraid of his subject matter or he wouldn't work so hard at
his delivery.

This Economist-with-a-Pipe-Organ has the lushest line of fur-
lined words on the air, and I haven't the slightest idea what it's
all about.

The other night, the Father's announcer offered to send anybody a handsome pocket crucifix for the asking, and a few minutes
later Father Coughlin was tearing at Roosevelt's Supreme Court plan
like a tiger at a wheelbarrow full of raw meat. I don't get the connection.

Every few minutes, the Father would drag in "a living annual
wage for the working man." Well, I'm in sympathy with that in spite
of Father Coughlin, but as an ex-proprietor of a sliver of U.S. Steel,
I resented a crack he took at the Steel Company. He said that U.S.

Steel raised wages and prices the same day, so that the working-men would practically have to pay their own raises--that is, in the ultimate higher prices of the automobiles they buy.

Now, I happen to have bought a couple of shares of U.S. Steel at 250 a few years ago and to have held them a few years without a cent of dividends and to have sold them at 80 a few months ago, and I don't call that a living annual wage for Mrs. Herold and the kiddies. Yet F. Coughlin expected us steel guys to raise wages and simultaneously lower prices after a few years like that. I mean, there are some sad aspects to both sides of these pictures.

But I am against oily hypnotism on either side of the fence. I am against it in priests, politicians, labor leaders or capitalistic spellbinders, or in radio announcers peddling their toothpaste. Just say it, boys, and leave off the grease.

Incidentally, I've been amused how Father Coughlin, when he gets hot, makes "o's" of nearly all of his vowels--porpetrated, porchasing power, the forst shall be last, nineteen thirty-seven, borning zeal, opathy, foctories, copitalism, annivorsory and cortain doom.

Radio right now is where the drama was a hundred years ago. It is full of practices as naive and elementary, for example, as the "asides" of the old-time speaking stage. Remember how the villain used to come down to the footlights and talk to the au-dience? I believe it was Ibsen who first conceived of the stage realistically as a room with one wall removed. We had to have cen-turies of artificiality in the theatre before anybody thought of that. And that put, or should have put, a definite end to stomping and stalking on the stage, and to such phoney practices as "asides."

I believe that the reformation of radio will come with the general conception of radio programs as going to one or two persons sitting in a room ... rather than as going to millions of people in a vast auditorium. Oratorical hypnotism and announcer goo which might get over to a theatre full of people seem ridiculous when spilled to one or two people at a fireside. Would Father Coughlin call me up on the telephone and go into such orgiastic raves? Would a Packard salesman call me up on the telephone and give me all that gush? Well, what is a radio, but a telephone in a box?

A tip to all radio speakers and performers: treat me as if I were one person. I resent being addressed as if I were an audi-torium full of morons.

--Don Herold in Judge, Vol. 112,
No. 2702 (May 1937), page 22.

                                    *   *   *

     The fact that Father Coughlin is a minister of the gospel has
nothing to do with the case.   There have been priests and ministers
in politics before.   Monsignor Seipel was dictator of Austria in the
years after the war.   Cardinal Innitzer is perhaps the most important political figure in Austria today.   Bishop Cannon, of another
faith, had great influence in this country during prohibition.   What
is important, however, is that Father Coughlin is a political menace.
Anyone who has studied the rise of Fascism in Italy and Germany is
faced with alarming parallels between Father Coughlin's program and
the programs of Mussolini and Hitler.   The deadly resemblance has
been pointed out most clearly by Wilfred J. Parsons, S.J., in the
columns of the Catholic periodical America.

     Hitler's appeal was to the middle classes and the small mer-
chant.   Father Coughlin's strength comes from the same sources.
Hitler's party was the National Socialist party; Father Coughlin's is
the National Union for Social Justice.   Hitler's program was extremely radical until he got into power.   It demanded distribution of
wealth, a curbing of the great bankers, protection for the small
merchant against the chain stores, nationalization of the land.
Father Coughlin has equally hard words for the bankers, defends
the wage earner, calls for printing press money to pay the bonus
and threatens the end of capitalism by the ballot box if capitalism
fails to solve its problems.

     The bankers of Germany were never disturbed by Hitler's
rantings; instead they supported him while he built up his following
by the use of radical slogans.   It is an old trick of demagogs
practised earlier by the ex-socialists, Mussolini and Pilsudski.   Once
in office, Hitler forgot his liberal policies.   He smashed the labor
unions, protected the chain stores, failed to nationalize the land and
failed to bother the bankers, including the great Jewish bankers who
had financed him on the way to power.

     Father Coughlin, the professed friend of the common man,
built his new church in Detroit with non-union labor.   Belaboring
the iniquities of Wall Street, he himself secretly gambled in silver
futures while filling the air with demand for the nationalization of
silver.   His social program, if carried out, will inevitably lead to
Fascism, as Father Parsons has pointed out.   You may care nothing
for the rights of labor, but you may care for your own freedom.
You may not care to be Hitlerized even by a man who seems as
kindly intentioned as the sage of Detroit.   There are various pied
pipers of discontent seeking to divert the minds of the masses with
tales of the promised land--the Longs, the Coughlins, the Town-
sends, the Sinclairs.   They point out many genuine evils; their
solutions are fantastic.   Like the others, Father Coughlin's generali-
zations are broad, beautiful and meaningless.   He declares that his
National Union is not to be another political party.   How, then, is

he to lead us out of the wilderness? By working through the Democratic and Republican parties to vote capitalism out of existence?
That is comparable to working through the Vatican to vote Christianity out of existence. It is nonsense. It is Coughlinism.

--K. S. C. in Life (July 1935),
page 24.

*   *   *

When the announcer on Father Coughlin's program went on the
air on February 4 and, in a series of cryptic and intriguing announcements, said that Father Coughlin would not appear to speak
and intimated that dire and sinister forces were at work to prevent
his addressing the radio audience, this writer went to Detroit to
seek out the reason behind this strange occurrence. Inasmuch as
Father Coughlin refused to see him or make any statement despite his
persistent efforts to reach the priest, the writer then checked
every agency and force powerful enough to censor Coughlin from the
air.

His investigations showed that neither WJR nor the Coughlin
radio network had censored Coughlin's address. Neither had the
Catholic Church nor the Federal Communications Commission. The
inescapable conclusion to be drawn, therefore, is that Father Cough-
lin--and Father Coughlin alone--was responsible for the weird performance after exhorting, through his announcer, all listeners-in to
telephone their friends and get them to their loudspeakers. But
why? Why should a man of Father Coughlin's stature resort to an almost stagelike trick mystery to attract listeners? Let us look at the
Coughlin ambitions.

After all, what are Father Coughlin's ambitions, judged in
the light of his own words and actions? Banned from the presidency
by Canadian birth, does he burn to become an American Hitler? Is
the Coughlin-inspired Christian Front--with seventeen members already indicted for conspiracy to overthrow the U.S. Government--an
embryo Storm Troop ready for revolution? Does the Thunderer of
Royal Oak, shouting his love of nazism and fascism across the free
American airways, dream of the day when our Constitution is dead
and his proposed "Corporate State" stands in its stead? Is anti-
Semitism to become the same rabble-rousing weapon of revolution here
in America that it was and is in Germany?

Father Coughlin, by his every word and act, admits ambition.
Once his ambition was to be known as a maker of presidents. In
1932, no louder voice was raised on behalf of Franklin D. Roosevelt
than that of Coughlin, and his talks following the election were filled
with what "the President said to me and what I said to him." Then
something happened. Differences began to grow up between the two
and, almost before the victory celebration was ended, there was an
open breach. The same voice that shouted "Roosevelt or ruin!" was

now shouting--and as loudly--"Scab President" and referring to that "great betrayer and liar, Franklin Doublecross Roosevelt." Differences over monetary policy were one cause of the breach, and Father Coughlin took to the air.

"The restoration of silver to its proper value is a Christian concern." Father Coughlin thundered. "I send you a call for the mobilization of all Christianity against the God of Gold." This exhortation was followed by the Government's amazing revelation that Father Coughlin was the holder, through his secretary, of more silver than any other person in Michigan--500,000 ounces. It was at this period, too, that he was urging the expulsion of the moneylenders from the Temple and condemning Wall Street gambling. It was then revealed that the priest had been playing the stockmarket. "I just made an investment," he said, forgetting that this was the very answer offered by those he had condemned.

Father Coughlin's ambition to be a maker of presidents was undimmed by his first sad experience, and the next time he tried-- in 1936--he did not repeat the mistake of climbing on another's bandwagon. This time he chose his own candidate--William Lemke-- who was so unmistakably labeled with the Coughlin trade-mark that there could be no renunciation in event he won. In the bitter campaign, Father Coughlin made a promise: "If I cannot swing 9,000,000 votes to Mr. Lemke, I'll stop broadcasting educational talks on economics and politics." Mr. Lemke polled 891,858 votes, less than one-tenth of that number, and Father Coughlin, cornered for the moment, said:

"I am withdrawing from all radio activity in the best interests of all the people. I am doing this without attempting to offer one alibi, thereby proving that my word is better than my bond."

A year before, in 1935, Raymond Gram Swing had written: "More nearly than any demagogue in America, he (Father Coughlin) has the formula for a fascist party...." Now, in his quiet retreat at Royal Oak, far from the madding crowd, with no radio broadcasts to prepare, Father Coughlin went to work on ways and means of making his "fascist" party come alive and breathe--of making it a vital, a dominating force in the land. When Father Coughlin again returned to the air he was no longer the maker of presidents but the advocate of a new era in America.

The Father Coughlin who returned to the microphones in 1937 made no bones about his love for nazism and fascism. Nor did he conceal his contempt for democracy. On November 6, 1937, he contemptuously denounced the "magic of numbers." Discussing the French Revolution, he said, "A new king was set upon the throne of Notre Dame in Paris--the king symbolizing the magic of numbers; the king which said, 'Mankind is king and the majority shall prevail'." This magic of numbers--we call it Democracy--he blamed

for having kept religion out of government, ignoring with a fine
disdain that freedom of religion and separation of church and state
is a cardinal principle of the American way. In the same vein,
Father Coughlin's Social Justice declaimed: "Democracy! A mock-
ery that mouths the word and obstructs every effort on the part of
an honest people to establish a government for the welfare of the
people."

Nor did Father Coughlin long leave his listeners in doubt as
to what he proposed as an alternative to our present form of government. Flatly he came out with a proposal that we scrap our Congress, abolish our representative form of government and set up in
its place a fascist creation he labeled "The Corporate State." His
address of March 13, 1938, dealt exclusively with this "Corporate
State," expounded fourteen points as its essentials, which were but
re-echoes of the twenty-five-point nazi program as expounded by
Dr. Frederick L. Schuman in "The Nazi Dictatorship."

The militant return to the air of Father Coughlin marked more
than an attack upon the American government. It marked the employment by the radio priest of every nazi technique in effecting his
purpose. At his enemies he shouted "Jew!" and "communist!" He
revived, in Social Justice, the discredited "Protocols of Zion,"
papers purporting to show a Jewish conspiracy for world domination
which, time after time, have been shown to be spurious and forged.
Later, he said that, while the protocols might not be authentic, they
were "factual." And in the face of all this, Father Coughlin's Social
Justice carried this amazing statement: "The only source of truth is
Father Coughlin!" That is a position even the Pope does not take
in the Roman Catholic Church.

The American reaction was one of incredulity, at first; then,
horror. Nazi atrocities were too fresh in the minds of liberty-loving
Americans for such seed to take root. Radio stations banned him.
The Nazis were jubilant. Hitler's newspaper, Voelkischer Beobach-
ter, ran a picture of Coughlin with a caption saying "in Free America, he (Father Coughlin) had to undergo censorship because of the
embarrassing truths he spoke." The New York Times reported:
"The German hero in America, for the moment, is the Rev. Charles
E. Coughlin."

But in America, the Coughlin reception was different. Where
once Father Coughlin had boasted 15,000,000 listeners, now his
audience was declining by leaps and bounds. Before his mysterious
stunt broadcast of February 4, according to figures released by one
of the forty-seven stations still airing Coughlin, his audience had
dropped to a mere 3,000,000.

Events now moved with a tragic swiftness for the once powerful Thunderer of Royal Oak. Seventeen Christian Fronters were
arrested on conspiracy charges. Coughlin at first denied any connection with them, a few days later espoused their cause. United

States Department of Justice then announced that it planned to investigate the priest on charges, among others, of using the mails
to defraud.

Now, assailed on almost every side, Father Coughlin needs a
wide radio audience, a wide following to stem the tide which has
turned against him, and he finds his listening audience at its lowest
ebb. So, on February 4, the Coughlin announcer said to an astonished audience. "Call all your friends by telephone and tell them
to listen to this program." And again, later in the program, after
an interlude of music: "I am instructed to say, 'Pay no heed to
idle rumors which will be circulated this week. Be assured, Father
Coughlin knows what he is doing. Probably events transpiring this
week will enlighten you.'"

Nothing happened in the following week. Neither did Father
Coughlin give any explanation of the strange announcements to an
audience which had been greatly augmented by the news stories
which followed the February 4 broadcast. Was it a deliberate trick
to entice listeners back to his program? What other reason could
there be? Surely, none is obvious.

Failing to get an interview with the priest, this writer addressed a registered letter to him, asking him to state his side of
the story. Social Justice for February 12 had denounced the American press for its failure to permit Father Coughlin to speak in its
columns, for telling only one side of the story.

Father Coughlin's letter in reply to mine--and signed by a
secretary, C. Smith--said, in part:

"He (Father Coughlin) wishes me to inform you that he has no
worth-while information to disclose to the public at this time...."

The one conclusion which is logical and inevitable is that the
mystery and melodrama which shrouded the Coughlin broadcast of
February 4 was a planned and deliberate attempt on the part of a
frustrated and ambitious man to gain a listening audience--regard-
less of the cost.

If there is any other reason, only God and Father Coughlin
know of it. And Father Coughlin isn't talking.

> --Francis Chase, Jr. in Movie and
> Radio Guide, Vol. 9, No. 23
> (March 16, 1940), pages 15 and
> 57.

- THE CUCKOO HOUR (NBC Blue, 1930-1932)

Apart from the occasional appearance of a fine artist like
Heifetz, or the broadcasting of a new opera with Mary Garden, or
the reception of events not specifically prepared for the radio, my
greatest entertainment is due to Mr. Raymond Knight, who broadcasts at ten o'clock on Saturday evenings from WJZ, without any
perceptible commercial backing. Mr. Knight provides a complete
burlesque of radio broadcasting, a sort of Jimmy Durante and Joe
Cook event of the air. He insists he is broadcasting from station
KUKU to the "great unresponsive radio audience (the voice of the
diaphragm enunciating)," and his orchestra of fifty-four-and-a-
half pieces, each man a musician and each musician a man, has
learned to play by correspondence, so that the burlesque music occasionally breaks off waiting for a special-delivery letter to bring
in the end of the composition. The musical director's commentary
is an entertaining parody of other directors, and the historical notes
inform us that Mendelssohn's "Spring Song," for example, was recently discovered in manuscript form by a stray dachsund which
brought it to the professor, and the latter, recognizing its true
value, sold it for wastepaper. With his helpers, Mr. Knight also
conducts a Personal Service for Perturbed People, a Poetry Hour,
and Uncle Ambrose's Hour of Detachment with the Kiddies, not to
mention a Missing Person's Bureau and a brief News Summary--
all of it completely cockeyed--and one of those uplifting domestic
hours in which the cooing sentimentality of the morning periods of
the radio is beautifully taken off.

> --Gilbert Seldes in The New
> Republic, Vol. 67, No. 859
> (May 20, 1931), pages 19-20.

- WALTER DAMROSCH

Darling Mr. Damrosch:
        I have been meaning to write you now for a couple of years
and tell you how much I enjoy your Saturday evening programs
which are broadcast through WJZ and Heaven only knows how many
other stations. But you know how things are. When there is paper
in the house, there is no ribbon on the typewriter. And when there
is a ribbon on the typewriter, there are no stamps.

        Anyway, you get a lot of letters. What is one more from just
poor little me? You get letters from sheep-herders who are knocked
cold by the Siegfried "Waldweben." You get letters from old ladies
made young again by Strauss' "Tales from the Vienna Woods."

        What can I say? Only that I think you are swell. That

sounds pretty dumb compared with your other letters, which are mostly from people who live forty miles from a five-and-ten-cent-store.
I am here in New York where symphony concerts are as plentiful as
taxicabs and where there are as many guest conductors as there are
traffic cops.

Let's get down to the compliments: you have an ingratiating
voice and a charming way of announcing your selections. You can
get your listeners as much steamed up over Brahms as they are over
George Gershwin. You can make them think that the William Tell
overture is an exciting novelty. You can make the old warhorses of
symphony music sound as though they were frisky colts.

As a conductor, you are something of a missionary--but you
do it in a nice way. People who go around telling others what books
they ought to read or what music they ought to enjoy are usually
pests. You get away with it. Personality, that's what it is. And,
confidentially, don't you get more fun playing for an unseen audience than facing the same old gang of Sunday subscribers week
after week?

This plan of giving you an orchestra to broadcast concerts
to school children is a big-hearted gesture on the part of the RCA.
Why not go all the way and form a symphony orchestra just for the
air? Most of the concerts from Carnegie Hall sound as though they
were broadcast from the Times Square subway station. With the
merger of the Philharmonic and New York Symphony, a lot of musicians are lying around looser than usual. Surely, Mr. Damrosch,
with your persuasive ways, you can get them together and form a
permanent radio symphony orchestra.

--Agnes Smith in Life, Vol. 91,
No. 2375 (May 10, 1928), page
29.

*   *   *

We have chosen to devote our editorial page this week to a
tribute to as worthy a gentleman as these eyes and ears have beheld.
Who among us has not heard the National Broadcasting Company's
Music Appreciation Hour? Who has not heard the high but kindly
inflection of the dean of that eleven-year-old program, Mr. Walter
Damrosch?

This program, as well as Doctor Damrosch's participation in it,
is designed to give to those of us who have not had the advantage
of a musical education all we need to know in order to enjoy and
understand opera and symphony. In consequence, it has come to be
employed in thousands of schools and home-study groups. How many
of us realize, as we sit listening, just what we have got in that program.

Consider the music student of the last century. He traveled miles over pitted roads, across frontiers, to the home city of the great music-master. Then he worked at any task he could find while he studied and practised and studied again. Sometimes the master would not have him. Often he could not get together the means of reaching the master's side.

But now the master comes to us in our parlor. Make no mistake about it, Walter Damrosch is a master. Schoolchildren listening today cannot be expected to appreciate their great fortune, for that is not the way of children, but some day they will learn that their teacher was one of the musical giants of his day.

Walter Damrosch's father was a well-known conductor in Europe when Richard Wagner was conducting at Bayreuth. In 1870, he brought his family to America at the invitation of a German choral society. Three years later, Walter was singing in the newly organized Oratorio Society just formed by his father. Four years later, the same auspices founded the Symphony Society, and then the elder Damrosch began to conduct German opera at the Metropolitan Opera House.

By now, Walter was eighteen. Though tender, of years, his ability was already so recognized that he had become conductor of the Newark Harmonic Society, while at the Met he was an unofficial assistant. Then, in the midst of the season, the elder Damrosch sickened swiftly and died. Because no one else understood German music, Walter Damrosch became the principal conductor. At the age of twenty-three, he took the Metropolitan Opera Company on tour. One month later he conducted his first performance of the New York Symphony Orchestra, and was acclaimed so highly that he was elected permanent conductor. So many other honors followed that they placed him on a musical pinnacle that no other conductor in America has reached.

Under his baton Tschaikowsky's Sixth Symphony was heard for the first time in America. And many others. He wrote an opera, then a magnificent Te Deum inspired by Dewey's victory at Manila. When he played it, both President Theodore Roosevelt and Admiral Dewey were in the audience. Every year brought new triumphs, new achievements, and new understanding of his amazing world.

Think of that the next time you hear his voice. Remember that there labors a man who, in the last century, would have been feted by kings and dukes, whose instruction would have been reserved for children of royalty or those other fortunate ones who could afford to find their way to his studio.

There labors a man whose distilled experiences, from his witnessing the immortal Richard Wagner conduct to his intimate association with every great musical event in America for three-quarters

of a century, are at the disposal of us and our children for the
mere flip of a switch.

To say that such a privilege is another miracle of radio is to
sound trite and stuffy. We do not mean to sound that way. But
say it we must, for in our opinion nothing that broadcasting has
ever done is of greater importance or of more lasting benefit than
the work of Walter Damrosch and his NBC Music Appreciation Hour.
                              --Curtis Mitchell in Radio Guide,
                              Vol. 8, No. 21 (March 11, 1939),
                              page 1.

● JESSICA DRAGONETTE

When Jessica Dragonette looks about the new NBC studios
and thrills at their magnificence, she says to herself and means it,
"I must try to be as marvelous as this equipment, I must really
try."

That may be, she thinks, the secret of her success. She
loves radio, she believes in it, she never gets over the miraculous
wonder of it, she is proud, deeply proud to be associated with it.

To little Miss Dragonette, whose pretty face and wide blue
eyes light up when she so much as thinks about radio--radio is not
a stepping stone to a stage career nor a springboard to Hollywood,
no. It is an end in itself. When, eight years ago she went into
radio, it was by deliberate choice. She had been the voice in The
Miracle, she had played in a road company of The Student Prince,
she had capered in The Grand Street Follies, but she gave all that
up for radio.

No one knew about radio in those days. It was an uncharted
sea. If she remained in the theatre, she knew she would only be
following a tradition--but in radio she could build her own technique.
As a matter of fact, she'd have to. There was no radio technique.

Now she looks back on those early days of radio, remembers
the pitiful inadequecy of the carbon mikes she used to sing into,
and is ever so grateful for the experience. Just because the equipment then was so inadequate, she was compelled to experiment, to
perfect in spite of the handicaps, a radio technique. What she
learned then stands by her today--although nobody must think that
she's stopped learning.

That's what's so wonderful about radio to Miss Dragonette.
Everybody in it is still pioneering. They haven't begun to use the
facilities available, she believes. "We're playing with a miracle," she
says. "The whole trend of music will change. It will be better

music. Even now, nobody turns on his radio and lets it play all
day. Today people select a program."

If, as has been rumored, most sopranos are poison on the
air, Miss Dragonette counters with the thought that most sopranos
are poison anywhere. There are so few good ones.

Good ones realize first of all that they must not make their
audience nervous. They should sing with so little apparent effort,
they should be so easy that their listeners say to themselves, "Why,
I could do that. There's nothing to it." The good ones know that
radio technique requires more intensity of thought and feeling to
put themselves across, that they must ignore their visible studio
audience and think only of the millions outside waiting to catch their
notes. There is something that Miss Dragonette, tapping her forehead, calls "Radio psychology," which is the basis of all of it. You
acquire radio psychology, she feels, if you're really sincere about
radio.

Miss Dragonette just knows she is sincere. She is always
thinking of her fans, wondering what will please them, trying so
hard to do what they would like her to. Though she admits visible
studio audiences disturb and distract her, she wouldn't think of
refusing them admittance. They wait so long for tickets, they come
from so far to see her. They are, after all, her public, always
foremost in her consideration.

Because of them she turns down personal appearance offers.
If she accepted a stage job, she might destroy the illusion, she
fears. Pictures, though; that's different. She might do a picture,
if it were a charming one. But for Miss Dragonette, radio is an end
in itself. She wants above everything else to be worthy of radio.

                                        --Cecelia Ager in Variety (Novem-
                                           ber 28, 1933), page 38.

• THE EASY ACES (CBS, 1931-1934; NBC Blue, 1935-1943; CBS,
  1943-1945)

Mr. Goodman Ace's conception of home life made easier by
frequent resort to the bridge-table appeared last year throughout
the Middle-West and into the East. Easy Aces was originally an
instructional series for bridge and contract addicts. In order to
attract a greater audience the series was enlivened by the conversa-
tional mewings of "Mr. Ace" and "Mrs. Ace," portrayed by the author
and his wife [Jane], who, oddly enough, possess the same names.

The characters and plot gradually ran away from the original
educational idea, as has frequently happened with other similarly

specialized radio offerings. Regionally, this may have passed un-
noticed. Nationally, there are other bridge programs which depend
upon expert instruction instead of dramatic interest to hold an audience. Dramatically, Easy Aces creeks painfully when the card-
table atmosphere glues up the action. Most national dramatic strips
now seek expert acting talent. Both Mr. and Mrs. Goodman Ace may
be bridge experts. They would not qualify as expert actors.

> --Cyrus Fisher in The Forum and
> Century, Vol. 88, No. 6 (Decem-
> ber 1932), page 383.

● W. C. FIELDS

The best fun on radio since Marconi invented static. I
thought W. C. Fields died a year or two ago. If he did, somebody
ought to shoot all the other radio comedians.

> --Don Herold in Judge, Vol. 113,
> No. 2704 (July 1937), page 22.

● FRED ALLEN'S BATH CLUB REVUE (CBS, 1932-1933)*

This is a dismal hodge-podge of music and cracks by Fred
Allen and stooges. A few men's locker-room jokes have been diluted
to a bathroom atmosphere. The usual guest artists come and go with
varying ability. An organ plays. There is nothing here which has
not been made considerably more amusing by other radio programs
now on the air.

> --Cyrus Fisher in The Forum and
> Century, Vol. 89, No. 1 (Jan-
> uary 1933), page 64.

● GENE AUTRY'S MELODY RANCH (CBS, 1940-1956)

Our tin ears grabbed a load of Gene Autry's first radio venture for the gum-chewing sponsor [Wrigley's] and at first blush we
felt inclined to note that the effort was simply cowboy stuff with a
wild studio audience that wasn't applause-broke. Radiops will be
golswanged and horn-swoggled (it's the rhythm of the range in us)
if it don't play hell with a program to have that damn studio applause
cracking eardrums wide open every minute or two.

---

*Also known as The Linit Bath Club Revue.

We listened to Tom Brenaman's "Spelling Bee" on KNX Sunday and there was applause after every word the contestants spelled. We're just plain stubborn, folks, we think that's goin' too durn far and we're ag'in such moronic goin's-on.

As for Mr. Autry and his ether-effort, if you like cowpoke music and wal-I'll-tell-ya-boys conversation, this is a good piece. Autry gets $1,000 for his part of the thirty minutes, but we can't make up our mind if he sounded like $1,000 worth of talent.

--Dale Armstrong in Rob Wagner's Script (January 20, 1940), page 24.

• NILS T. GRANLUND

Introducing just the busiest, happiest and most enthusiastic man in all this wide world. He is Mr. Nils T. Granlund; and ever since Station WHN has been pumping the noises of Broadway into the most sedate homes, N.T.G. has been the head man at the microphone and the boss of the works. I suppose WHN has other announcers; I have heard them for a few brief minutes, when Mr. Granlund was jumping from studio to cabaret in a taxicab and in the swift completion of his appointed rounds.

But WHN is Mr. Granlund's playground; it's his life, his work, his love, his all. No other announcer has succeeded in making his station so completely identical with his own personality. The result is that you either love WHN and Mr. Granlund or you dial past their wavelength as you would skip past a talk on Our Fur-Bearing Friends.

For enduring popularity, N.T.G. is the Abie's Irish Rose of the air. And, shocking as it may seem, this Dream Prince of the Bronx is the purest of Nordics. Mr. Granlund is a Danish boy who landed on Broadway with such a scant supply of English that he immediately became a motion picture press agent.

The late Marcus Loew saw in Mr. Granlund something bigger and finer than a mere sender of News Notes for Sunday Release. Mr. Granlund proved to be a good picker of vaudeville talent and a perfect master of ceremonies at the opening of the new theaters. Because of his abilities as a glad-hander, Loew intrusted his infant radio station to his care.

Mr. Granlund comes from a race of Viking adventurers and the zeal for discovering is strong in his blood. Mr. Granlund doesn't bother with new continents but he does make a specialty of finding talented chorus girls and promoting them to be prima donnas in

cabarets or "singles" in vaudeville. The evening's program of WHN
is enlivened by Mr. Granlund's past discoveries or future hopes.
Talented girls just happen to drop in on Mr. Granlund and Mr.
Granlund urges the reluctant artistes before the microphone. When
some of the artistes sing as if they were having their teeth straight-
ened, Mr. Granlund softens the blow by telling you what gorgeous
girls they are and how easy on the eyes.

Mr. Granlund is at his best when he takes you to the Silver
Slipper, which is "not a night club, but a place for the whole family
with a chorus of twenty-eight of the most glorious, the most whole-
some girls on Broadway." With complete artlessness, Mr. Granlund
confesses to being more than an announcer to the Silver Slipper; not
only does he stage the show, but he supplies the kitchen with eggs
from his own farm, eggs as pure and as fresh as the chorus girls.

Yes, Mr. Granlund runs a farm, in addition to handling one
of the most arduous jobs on Broadway. Over in New Jersey, he
raises cows and chickens and runs a rest home for weary chorus
girls. His interest in chorus girls is sincere; he married one.

Most of the material which Mr. Granlund has to sponsor is
pretty much tripe. WHN boasts few de luxe or pretentious programs.
Nevertheless, N.T.G. has kept it on the map, merely by the strength
of his own personality. In all his years before the microphone, he
has managed to keep clear of that terrible church usher pompous-
ness that falls on even the best announcers.

There are two pretty little Broadway legends that concern
Mr. Granlund. One is the story of an actor who was out of work
and broke. He was bemoaning his terrible luck to a friend. "Put
on skirts," advised the friend, "and borrow fifty dollars from Nils
Granlund." And the other story is to the effect that N.T.G. sometimes grows sick of it all--even of the Silver Slipper--and leaves
Broadway flat. He ships on Scandinavian sailing vessels as a common
seaman and disappears beyond the horizon where there is no couvert
charge.

> --Agnes Smith in Life, Vol. 91,
> No. 2379 (June 7, 1928), page
> 27.

• HAMLET (CBS, July 12, 1937)

It's a pretty good bet that the nation as a whole would trade
in John Barrymore and Burgess Meredith combined for Jack Benny's
version of Hamlet. It's also pretty clear that neither Columbia nor
NBC is thinking of listeners, but of that vague value known as
"prestige."

Burgess Meredith does remarkably well. He goes from walk
to canter to gallop and reverses. His progress as an actor is mani-
fest throughout. It'll do him good. And it's a bit of a success
story that three years after Beechnut's Red Davis juvenile serial
the young player should be chosen by CBS to window-dress its
flyer in culture.

But apart from the career impetus for Meredith as an individual what is the net result of this newest Hamlet four weeks after
NBC donned black tights?

CBS will have scrap books full of publicity, tie-ups with
English teachers (with schools not in session), comments from stuffed
shirts, and a flurry of admiration which will possibly be followed by
a sudden jolting realization that only in summer, when it doesn't in-
terfere with biz, would the networks indulge in such artistic capers.

Entertainment? Good Shakespeare? Starting something or
elevating production standards in radio? CBS' Hamlet, like NBC's,
is indifferent entertainment, obscure Shakespeare and workaday
mike technique. Whole scenes in both versions were shady and
hard to follow. Voices were not uniformly set apart by tone.

Educational value may, of course, be advanced. Fortunately,
in the east the heat spell broke, else few would have had the
physical stamina to stick out the hour. Like all Shakespeare, the
archaic free verse is aurally bumpy.

Of the supporting cast in the CBS version no objections can
be cited. Bill Brady was a tomb-like basso playing the ghost.
Grace George was a believably tormented mother and wife as the
Queen. The King had sock, as miked by Montague Love. They
were all essentially interruptions in the long monolog of Meredith.

There is this to be said for the CBS Hamlet. Meredith
made a better impression than Barrymore, and the editing seemed a
bit more intelligent. So what?

> --"Land" [Robert J. Landry] in
> Variety (July 14, 1937), page
> 49.

• "THE HAPPINESS BOYS"

At last an old wrong has been righted. Billy Jones and
Ernest Hare, formerly confined merely to a local broadcast through
WEAF, have been turned on the country at large and are progress-
ing from New York popularity to national celebrity just like Al
Smith. The Happiness Boys are now also the Flit Soldiers and you

may hear them through WJZ and its sister stations at half-past ten on Monday nights. I commend them to your attention. If you don't like them, you need never speak to me again.

I have loved Jones and Hare ever since the days when they sang "Jump, Fritz, I gif you liver." I can even keep some feeling for them when they sing ballads like "Wife of Mine" or tell jokes that I seem to have read somewhere before.

Don't tell me that they are just a vaudeville team with "a merry line of songs and patter." Any minute they are apt to break into "While strolling in the park one day, in the merry, merry month of May." Nevertheless, the Happiness Boys are one of radio's meager contributions to history and sentiment.

Jones and Hare are the oldest feature on the air. Back in October, 1921, when the lower half of the Mississippi Valley was still part of the Gulf of Mexico, when lizards as big as trucks roamed over the New England streets and when there was only one speakeasy to the block, Jones and Hare made their radio début over WJZ. There were only two stations then in existence, WJZ and KDKA.

Jones and Hare went over to the Westinghouse factory in Newark, N.J., in a coach. The journey took three days. Billy Jones wore side-whiskers, and Ernest Hare had a long beard, in those days considered very natty. Newark was then a larger city than New York, which was just a sleepy little Dutch village.

To give you more comical details about those funny old days, Jones and Hare were asked to sing for one hour and a half without stopping. The station was making experiments; it wanted to see how far it could push the public. Jones and Hare sang thirty songs without stopping; they earned their money.

Before their radio début, Jones and Hare had been teamed up in vaudeville and had been making phonograph records. Hare had been understudy of Al Jolson in Sinbad at the Winter Garden. Sometimes when you thought you were hearing Jolson, it was really Ernie Hare who was bending the knee. Billie Jones had been a choir singer in his early days. Combine an understudy with a choir singer and you get a star radio team.

Now for the art of Jones and Hare: as the Happiness Boys they have been mingling tears and laughter for years. Their jokes prey on our national weakness for puns. Their sentimental ballads are divided as solos between them. Billy Jones, the tenor, sings all the pieces that represent a young man in search of love. The selections of more mature feeling fall to Ernie Hare, the baritone, who represents the man who has discovered that there are Other Things in Life, such as mothers and wives. Their comic songs are the best things they do. And they manage to get the new ones while they are still fresh.

As the Happiness Boys, they are assisted by Dave Kaplan at the piano, he being the Dormouse of the party.

The Flit Soldiers are more pretentious because they have an orchestra to accompany them.

But either as sponsors of chocolates or as patrons of something to massacre mosquitoes, Jones and Hare are worth your kind attention. To my prejudiced mind, their imitators should suffer the same fate as the imitators of Charlie Chaplin--oblivion and ignominy.

> --Agnes Smith in Life (July 12, 1928), page 16.

• BOB HOPE

Bob Hope, now approaching his 20th week on the air, has reached that point where you suddenly realize they're signing off and the half hour is over.

Hope's show seems to be based on speed and informality. If the quality has been uniformly good then, perhaps, his low point to date was the program of Jan. 10. That one was really bad. But allowing that the outfit kicked it that time, they bounded right back the next week (17) when Patsy Kelly was the guest. The crossfire between Hope and the comedienne was so good and fast as to create doubt that he could follow it. Yet the boys rolled out a burlesque drama based on a tune, "Get out of Town," and held the momentum. Maybe it was faster than it was funny, but if Hope has a mania for tempo he's not wrong either. Nor do they make a blacking back out of the commercials. A pretty good program, what with one thing and another.

> --Variety (January 25, 1939), page 34.

• TED HUSING

A pretty parcel of posies for one Ted Husing, who broadcasts a football game as she should be broadcast. One of the best radio picturing of gridirony was produced by Mr. Husing last Saturday when Ohio State and Cornell tangled. These ears have never heard Husing do a better job. He was able to convey suspense, excitement, animation--and without ranting, screaming, running verbally amok, or any display of hyper-thyroid hysteria. He painted an accurate word-picture of the proceedings on the field without fumbling for words, there weren't any stutterings or stammerings sending the listener into a frenzy of frustration.

> --Dale Armstrong in Rob Wagner's
> Script (November 4, 1939),
> page 24.

• IPANA TROUBADOURS (NBC, 1933-1934)

There are six minutes of a lively orchestra, six minutes and a half of bang-up choral harmony, about twelve minutes of guest stars, and five more minutes given to the adroit introduction of next week's artists. Usually such a program starts off great guns and winds up with an animal act. Miss Helen Hayes, conniving with Mr. John Beal, and capably serving a rewarmed section from her latest cinematic vehicle; "Doctor" Rockwell, sporadically entertaining monologist; and the comic-opera star, Miss Fritzi Scheff, shoved the two opening programs above the passing mark.

> --Cyrus Fisher in The Forum and
> Century, Vol. 90, No. 6 (De-
> cember 1933), page 384.

• THE JELLO PROGRAM (NBC, 1934-1942)

What stood out in Jack Benny's re-entry in the 1938-39 C.A.B. steeplechase last weekend [October 2] was the novel way he introduced himself and the members of the cast. Each was sketched as hurriedly getting ready for the opening broadcast, and the whole thing added up to an unbroken fusillade of sock laughs. After that it was nip and tuck.

Most of the exchanges carried the usual Benny wallop, but there was one interval that sounded as though the troupe was taking time out to toss a hot potato. But even this doubtful interlude was compensated for. That came with the reading of a wire from Fred Allen, which said he had heard the Benny program and that motion pictures would continue to be his best entertainment.

Benny had apparently elected to limit the participants to his permanent payroll for the opening installment. In addition to Mary Livingstone, Kenny Baker, Phil Harris and the salesman-stooge, Don Wilson, there was the blackface valet, "Rochester," and the perennial door-rapper with the quick rib. Among the nifty touches in the

script was the foundation laid for Kenny's British-imported valet.
Kenny also contributed added underpinning to his status as one
of radio's choice interpreters of romantic ditties. His voice and
style are still making strides upward.

--"Odec" [Ben Bodec] in <u>Variety</u>
(October 5, 1938), page 30.

• JOHNNY GOT HIS GUN (NBC, March 9, 1940)

        If you're the ostrich type--you know, the type who buries
his head in the sand at the first sign of danger or trouble and
keeps it there until the storm-clouds have blown over ... or struck
--you won't want to tune your radio to Arch Oboler's play this
Saturday night. It's an ugly, sordid piece--<u>Johnny Got His Gun</u>--
and it'll have no pantywaist handling from Oboler or from James
Cagney, who'll star in it. It'll make your stomach roll over and
over. It'll keep you on the edge of your chair, and when it's all
over and you try to dismiss it with a snap of the fingers or a toss
of the head, you'll keep on remembering it. You'll always remember
it.

        That's why <u>Johnny Got His Gun</u> should be required listening
for every man, woman and child old enough to understand its impli-
cations. Stripping war of every vestige of romance and glory, this
gripping drama bares it for the horrible and gruesome business
war really is, and it isn't done in the broad generalities of politicians taking an anti-war stand to garner votes nor in the impassioned
pleas of statesmen with axes to grind or isms to promote. No, here
is Joe Bonham, a simple American boy, who tells his story. Slowly,
in dots and dashes made by the thumping of his head against his bed
in a veterans' hospital, he talks. It's the only way he can talk and
it took him years to find it. It's the only way you could talk, too, if
your mouth and your nose and ears and legs and arms had been shot
away in a war you didn't know anything about and cared less.

        <u>Johnny Got His Gun</u> was written by Dalton Trumbo last year
after he visited a veterans' hospital. "I found horrors there that
the average man in the street had long forgotten," he said. "I
thought that if all those youngsters with fire in their veins and all
the politicians and warmongers who shout about saving Democracy
would visit these places and see the real fruits of war, then there
wouldn't be any more war. Here war ceases to be a matter of battles
won and people conquered and becomes a matter of what can--and
does--happen to the 'you' and the 'me' who fight those battles.
Since people don't visit veterans' hospitals any more, I tried to bring
the hospitals home to them."

        His book is a living, breathing biography of a man who lies

among the living dead. He has made the pitiful wreckage of Joe's
body and life come vividly alive, and the lasting impressions he made
upon his readers' minds was testimony to the success of his effort.
And yet he felt that somehow he had failed; that the message he
had for the world was going to only a few of the millions he wanted
to reach. How could he bring Joe Bonham to the millions of other
Joe Bonhams.

Radio was the answer. One Saturday night he heard a broadcast of an Arch Oboler play. "I'd like that man to do the dramatization of my book," he thought. "As a matter of fact, had he set his
mind to it he might have written it." Both Oboler and Trumbo deal
with the inner consciousness of characters, use the technique known
as the "stream of consciousness" technique, in which the inner
thoughts of characters are presented. Also, Oboler was something
of a crusader against war, and in several broadcasts had written
drama which bitterly condemned war and dictatorial policies of government which, he felt, made for war.

At almost the same time Oboler--who is one of the most daring
and original writers yet developed by radio--had read Johnny Got His
Gun, and the idea of dramatizing it strongly appealed to him. A
call to Trumbo readily brought the author's permission, and he set
to work to recapture, for his listeners everywhere, the bitter plea
for peace and good-will contained in the book.

This far along, NBC then started searching for a star capable
of handling the difficult part. Their search led them to the New
York stage, to the ranks of radio actors, and to Hollywood, where
officials found Jimmy Cagney working in a picture, The Fighting
69th. Tough-skinned but tender and sensitive inside, Cagney was
the man for the part, they felt, and negotiations led to his engagement.

Cagney will play the part of Joe Bonham, an American boy
who might have lived next door to you or me. If we'd kept out of
the last war, Joe probably would have been one of those listeners
who'd tune in his radio to this play next Saturday, and when it was
over he'd say to his wife, Kareen: "That's not for us, Kareen. We
have our work and our family and we're happy. War's not for us."
Only Joe doesn't have any ears now, so how could he listen to a
radio? And he couldn't talk because his mouth has been shot away,
along with his nose and ears and arms and legs--shot away in one
violent explosion in a shell-hole of France. That's why Kareen is
still his sweetheart--in dreams--and not his wife. He didn't want
to go to war. He and Kareen were about to be married and he
didn't have a quarrel with anyone. But the draft got him. That's
why he's lying now in this war among the living dead, one of them.
He's a prisoner. He's a prisoner within the confines of his own
body. There, locked in from all others because he cannot talk,
cannot smell, cannot see or hear anyone, he lies in his silence for

days, months, years. Then suddenly he hits upon a way to release himself from this prison. He'd use the Morse code, which he
had learned as a child. He'd thump his head against the bed--dot-
dash-dot--until they answered.

Only, the nurse doesn't understand what he's trying to do.
She believes he is in pain, gives him morphine. Each time, when
the sedative wears off, he tries again--dot-dash-dot--S-O-S. Days
pass, months pass, and he knows now that getting someone to understand him, someone to whom he can talk, is the most important thing
in his life. And at last a relief nurse does understand what he's
trying to do, listens. This time he is understood.

Then, after years of silence, what can he say? He'd found a
means of coming back, a little way, into the world of the living, but
what was there to say? In his silence he thought of many things
he'd say, but now that he was able to talk there was nothing to say.
He was like Lazarus, he thought. No, he was like Christ--a messiah
of the battlefields, for he did have something to say. He would
say, "As I am now, so shall you be." He'd go out into the world
and he'd say that to everyone he met, shoving his twisted, agony-
wrought body in front of them so that they could see it. He was
... The Future. He was a picture of what all men would look like
if war came again. So, they wouldn't let him out. They'd keep him
here in the hospital forever because if men could look upon him,
listen to him and understand that he was their picture when war
came again, there'd be no more war. And because those in high
places had plans for another war, he must stay, always, hidden
from the living, whom he might warn.

Stark, harrowing realism in its most naked form is Johnny
Got His Gun. It will do much to prevent our entry into other wars
if we'll listen instead of burying our heads in the sand, for what
Joe Bonham has to say to you and to me and the thousands of
other Joe Bonhams of America and to their sweethearts and wives
and mothers makes war the sordid, horrible thing war is and will
be, and strips it, without mercy, of the white banners, bands
and catch-phrases with which the politicians and generals invariably
disguise it.

> --Howard Long in Movie and Radio
> Guide, Vol. 9, No. 22 (March 9,
> 1940), page 15.

• AL JOLSON

Al Jolson's show returns to the air-waves after a summer's
hiatus in its last season's cast lineup, with, of course, the exception
of the guests. Tee-off stanza [September 20] had a strong name in

"Wrong-Way" Corrigan, it being the trans-Atlantic flyer's first commercial air shot. Otherwise, as is often typical with name variety shows returning to the air after a seasonal layoff, and not yet in stride, it was pretty much of a clambake.

Jolson's show in the past was always a problem child so far as comedy is concerned. Situation is unchanged, the laughs still being few and far between. Script handed Corrigan for by-play with Martha Raye, Parkyakarkus and Jolson was only fair at best. One hearty chuckle in the lesson to Corrigan on making love coming at the bow-off, when he "mistook" a window for the door. Actually Corrigan had little to do and little to say for the $3,500 he received for the guest shot. A couple of gags anent his flight were okay.

Comedy brunt still falls on Parkyakarkus and the Greek dialectician is still giving out with those puns, anemic comedy at best. Otherwise, the entertainment was held down to a minimum due to the excessive greetings amongst the performers on their reunion. Martha Raye sang but one song, a duet of "A Tisket" with Jolson, while the latter's solos consisted of "Walking Stick" and "At Long Last Love." On the straight music side, [Lud] Gluskin's orch delivered "I'm Going To Lock My Heart" expertly.

Commercials are hardly the believable sort; a sketch insert between two femmes, one of whom suffers from something her best friend won't tell her about, but the personnel manager will. A bath in Lifebuoy is all you need, honey, etc. and et cetera.
                                        --"Scho" [Joe Schoenfeld] in
                                        Variety (September 28, 1938),
                                        page 30.

• LASSIE

The most versatile actor in radio by all odds is that phenomenal dog, Lassie, who, as every one knows, is a he-dog, not a she-dog. In addition to playing the opposite sex, Lassie has been about every breed of dog there is.

Not long ago, on his radio program, Lassie, by nature a collie, was an Irish setter, the property of a young married couple who, while very much in love, quarreled violently. The marriage would have gone to smash but for the dog, whose gentle nature so shamed them they became the most sweetly dispositioned couple in town.

That's one of the least of Lassie's feats. Generally, he is required to do far more difficult things. Just last week Lassie was called in on a case of psychosomatic medicine, a rather new branch of the medical profession about which much is still unknown (except to Lassie). This one featured a crippled boy whose ailment was all in his mind. Lassie's owner, a physician, had despaired to getting the lad out of his wheel chair and called in the dog as a last resort. Lassie turned on his charm, of which he has a great deal, and had the boy up and around within seven minutes. (Lassie has to work fast. It's only a fifteen-minute show, much of it devoted to the sale of dog food.)

That particular program was rather unusual in that Lassie played his own breed, a collie. He generally scorns the collie role as being much too easy. He has played a German shepherd, a Doberman pinscher a boxer, a great Dane, a cocker spaniel, a St. Bernard, a coon dog and a French poodle. He has been cast as a young puppy and as an aged dog, barely able to walk, and he has been both a male and a female.

His acting style, it must be admitted, doesn't change a great deal, no matter what he is. His bark is pretty much the same whether he's a Doberman or a cocker. Still, as dogs go, he runs the full gamut of expression. He has one bark for simple animal spirits, another to inform the stupid humans around him: "Take it slow and easy, kids; the murderer is right over there, hiding behind a tree." He can sound heartbroken, deeply hurt or--when the commercial comes on--just plain hungry. He also whines very expressively, indicating to his masters that if they'd just pay attention to him he'd point out where the loot is hidden.

He has solved some remarkable crimes. A week or so ago he broke a million-dollar bank robbery. This was a particularly difficult case for Lassie because the robbers made their foray by speedboat, and even Lassie's nose is not sensitive enough to track a scent in a river. He has solved almost as many murders as The Fat Man.

Unlike The Fat Man, Lassie is frequently accused of committing the murders. No dog, possibly no human, has been unjustly accused of so many crimes. Once, while playing a Doberman pinscher, he was accused of killing his wealthy mistress, conceivably for her money, an unfair charge to level at a pooch whose material wants have never extended much farther than Red Heart Dog Food. He had to break the case to beat the rap.

On another occasion Lassie was accused of killing lambs in his owner's sheep herd in Montana. Once, playing a particularly benevolent St. Bernard in the Swiss Alps, who'd devoted his life to the rescue of fallen travelers, he was indicted for killing baby goats. He was cleared of both charges, largely through his own sleuthing.

One thing about Lassie that marks him off from all other radio entertainers. You never know what he's going to do next.

With Jack Benny or Arthur Godfrey or Boston Blackie, you know
pretty well what's coming--jokes or murders or whatnot. But Lassie
will solve a $1,000,000 holdup one week; the next he's an expectant
mother who adopts a motherless baby coon.

> Could Clark Gable, another M-G-M star, do that?
> --John Crosby in New York Herald
> Tribune (March 27, 1950).

• LEAVE IT TO THE GIRLS (Mutual, 1945-1949)

Love can be beautiful. It can also be exhilarating, lost,
strayed, stolen, mistreated, and monotonous. It can be hot or cold,
or just around the corner. You find this out by listening to Leave
it to the Girls, Mutual-KHJ, on Wednesdays at 8:30 PDT.

"The Girls" juggle delicate enigmas, such as, "Do sweaters
help a girl hold a man?" On this, the consensus was, I'm sorry to
report, "If a girl has the necessary points, it'll help. But he'll
pull the wool over her eyes."

The program is manned, which seems hardly the word, by a
glamorous board of experts on Romance. Its three permanent members, Constance Bennett, Binnie Barnes, and Robin Chandler, are
aided weekly by an equally decorative and articulate guest, usually
a movie star.

Miss Bennett always looks like a movie star, which is only
fair to the fans, who have a right to feel cheated when the Exquisite
Creature they wait hours in line to see often shows up in a wrinkled
dirndl, dark glasses, and yesterday's mascara. The day I saw the
broadcast, Miss Bennett was handsomely coiffed and expensive-
looking in a black summer sheer and a wide-brimmed black straw
hat which trailed a gossamer black lace veil. Seated on her left
was Binnie Barnes, a shade less formal but elegant in dark blue.
Both were wearing the same hair-do, and their having hit upon the
same tint must have been as disconcerting as meeting another woman
wearing the same dress. Robin Chandler, next on the panel, is a
former Vogue editor and a charter member of the original New York
program. She is now a Californian, the wife of movie actor Jeffrey
Lynn, and recently rejoined the show when Sylvia Sidney yielded to
the lure of summer stock in La Jolla. Miss Chandler, a striking ash
blonde, also wore black that day, but was hatless, with her hair
smoothed simply into a low chignon. Guest-star Ann Rutherford
was looking properly girlish in an emerald-green ensemble.

To balance all this glamor, each session of Leave It to the
Girls features a fugitive from the men's locker room. This unhappy

fellow, The Man Who Strikes Back, is almost invariably a movie or
radio personality. Rudy Vallee, Gene Raymond, George Jessel,
Nigel Bruce, Richard Ney, and Walter O'Keefe have sat, more or
less uneasily, in the forum's chair of applied male psychology.
Reginald Gardiner appeared the same week that his wife Nadia was
one of "The Girls," so that he had a friendly skirt to hide behind.
Kirk Douglas had the temerity to show up shortly after he publicly
announced that he believed woman's place was in the home.

There is also a referee, male, who puts the questions and
attempts to keep proceedings on a fairly civil basis. This job was
recently assigned to Mike Frankovich, a former All-American football hero and the husband of Miss Barnes.

Originating in New York, Leave It to the Girls was brought
to Hollywood not long ago by its author, Martha Rountree, who is
also the mother of Mutual's Meet the Press, which keeps her in
New York while Jean Wright steers "The Girls."

Re-setting the scene of the show in Mutual's impressive new
Hollywood home and refurbishing the cast with movie "names" undoubtedly steps up "The Girls'" sponsor appeal. Although it's been
a scintillating weekly half-hour in radio for almost three years, and
many buyers have flirted, none has been lured to sign a contract.
This is a situation which Mutual and Miss Rountree hope to remedy
at any moment now.

Unlike anyone else we've heard of, "The Girls" did not perk
up and bloom with increased radiance on being transplanted to California soil. It certainly can't be our lush climate and casual outlook
that discourage freestyle ad libbing. No, if the Hollywood panel is a
little slower on the uptake, more apt to weigh words than its Manhattan sister, it's probably because movie stars, with the exception
of Binnie Barnes and one or two others, just don't feel free to ad
lib. Not without a quick check on how the quip will echo in (1) the
box office, (2) the front office, (3) the gossip columns.

Questions, which provide the program material, are sent in by
listeners and paid for, when used, at $10 each. For clients past
the courting stage, there is no marital quandary, animal, vegetable,
or mineral, that "The Girls" will not tackle. But, of course, the
most popular poser submitted can be boiled down to, "How can I
get married so that I, too, can have marital problems?"

Another frequently recurrent situation on which counsel is
sought concerns the handling of teen-age daughters. "Take her on
trips, give parties for her friends," Miss Bennett advised on a recent
broadcast. Or, as we say in Hollywood, "Money. What's money?"

In rebuttal, as the girls sound off, the intrepid male defender
may interrupt his protagonists at any point. He simply bleats one

timid bleat on a small horn, his only mechanized equipment, and that theoretically dams up the conversation long enough for him to take issue with the current feminine view being aired. Gene Raymond brought this discussion to earth with a recommendation that the father "take a hair brush and apply it on the part of the dress that fits the tightest."

In another problem, of a young daughter who used too much makeup, Miss Bennett suggested the use of Constance Bennett cosmetics, with which, she said, it is impossible to use too much makeup. This phenomenon was never explained, but it does illustrate how in a spot like this, business acumen can fill an awkward pause.

Naturally, not every problem that confronts "The Girls" can be solved with a jar of cold cream. For the more complex issues, it is well to have on hand a double-threat glamor girl like Vanessa Brown, who is a combination movie starlet and Quiz Kid graduate, and, for good measure, an authoritative psychologist like Dr. John W. Gregory.

Both appeared as guest experts on the same show when Worried Wife sought advice about her husband, who posed as a single man when away from home on business trips. Married twenty-three years, she wanted to know if she should suffer in silence or confront him with his duplicity. The diagnosis went something like this:

VANESSA: Well, I don't think she should worry too much about it. She says they've been married twenty-three years ... that means he's getting along and should be stopping this monkey business soon.

BINNIE: As long as she's put up with him for twenty-three years, she might as well stick with the deal. She should go on a couple of these trips with him. That'll put a crimp in his curlers.

DR. GREGORY: What does she think he is doing as a single man that he wouldn't do as a married...?

BINNIE: What do you think, Doctor?

CONSTANCE: I don't see why she worries, either. He's been coming back to her for twenty-three years, married or single. What does she care if he poses, as long as he comes home?

It was Vanessa, too, I think, who helped solve the case of the seventeen-year-old baby sitter who brought her boy friend along on the job. Her employer wanted to know if this was proper. "Yes," Vanessa approved, "I think this could serve as a sort of an indoctrination period for him. If she plans to marry him, the girl could see how he reacts to children ... if he likes them, or if they'd have to dance all the time. It seems to me like a good idea."

Another note of frankness was struck by Florabel Muir, the magazine writer, when she guest-starred on the show. She led a discussion brought up by a young man who complained about never getting beyond the first date with a girl. The recommendation for him went like this:

FLORABEL: Well, it's easy to see what his trouble is. Doesn't he ever read the ads in the magazines?

BINNIE: I agree. It's obvious that he has B.O. He should talk frankly to his girl friends and ask them if he has.

SYLVIA SIDNEY (Discreetly): Well, after all, if his best friends won't tell him, why should we?

Studying these unfurled samples of ad libbing, Hollywood style, perhaps it's just as well to confine it to rare occasions; it shows, though, that "The Girls" are bravely pushing back social frontiers that Beatrice Fairfax never dreamed existed.

--Mary McSkimming in Script
(August 1948), pages 48-49.

• LITTLE JACK LITTLE

For over a year John Leonard, calling himself "Little Jack Little" (I don't know why), has been delighting a cross and sleepy audience every morning [on CBS] with his tinkly piano playing, foolish little tunes, and inconsequential chatter. He is a one-man sustaining program that has gradually pushed itself across the continent without any great publicity build-up, without any excited fanfare from a sponsoring organization. Put him on some morning instead of the dish-washing, happy-time exercises. He is an amusing personality; the nicest morning pickup I know of.

--Cyrus Fisher in The Forum and
Century, Vol. 89, No. 1 (January 1933), page 64.

• THE LONE RANGER (Mutual, 1934-1941; NBC Blue/ABC, 1942-1955)

This show had been on the Michigan network out of WXYZ Detroit, as key station.* Recently the program has been adopted by the Gordon Baking Company of Chicago for the commercial good of its Silvercup bread. Original plan of the bakery was to reproduce

*The Long Ranger was not heard nationally until 1934.

the show in Chicago and New York with local casts. It was audi-
tioned as such in Chicago by WGN, but the finale saw AT&T string-
ing wires in from Detroit, the bakery figuring that line charges are
cheaper than another bunch of salaries. Show thus comes into Chicago with the final tag of "this is the Michigan network." Nothing
yet set about the New York show. Will probably be local cast,
again figuring the relative costs of cast as against wire charges.

Ranger is a sort of low-grade Zane Gray material. Commercial copy is aimed at the adult audience and even at the better brack-
ets, the copy plugging the fact that the Gordon Bakery's Silvercup
bread is more expensive than ordinary bread. Show is running rather
late to be considered a kid show, hitting at 7:30 p.m., though the
story and treatment is fine children fodder. It is on three times
weekly for 30 minutes per program. And all counts doesn't figure
as particularly suitable for its potential customers.

Plug is aiming at the femmes as the buying portion of the
public. Women won't even be near this station for this program
and will rarely be around to hear the plug. They'll be listening
to something without Silver, the wonder horse, Indians and down
Cimmaron way.

From all appearances the Gordon Baking company is approaching its sales problem backwards. It won't get the women with this
program. But it will get the children. WGN is admittedly a big kid
station in this territory. Probably kids buy more bread, than their
mothers. It's up to Gordon Bakery to merchandize, not the femmes,
whose ear they're not going to get, but the children's, whose ears
they'll have 100% and who will coax that extra coin from their moms
to buy Silvercup bread if the bakery puts a sound commercial hook
into this program.

Typical story concerns the westward trek to new lands in the
early days of the 1880's, the battle with Indians, the separation of
man and wife, and the birth of a child. The passing of 20 years
and the reunion of the long-lost son and father. Its sub-story of
wheat-hoarding and misanthropy is somewhat adult in nature, but
may be okay for the older children.

Plugs are inserted between episodes, clean-cut but distinctly
to the adult buyer. Program and plug clash. They aim at different slices of the population.

--"Gold" [Herb Golden] in Variety
(December 12, 1933), page 38.

• MAJOR BOWES' ORIGINAL AMATEUR HOUR (NBC, 1935-1936;
  CBS, 1936-1946)

The Major [Edward Bowes] is, I believe voted the most

popular item on the air today, and I suppose I should, in view of
the Major's renown and my comparative oblivion, pipe down. But
popularity often proves nothing. The Major is popular, but so is
a sick horse. Most people, in short, don't care what is happening,
just so something is happening. They'll go to any movie that moves,
they'll gawk at any electric sign that flickers, they'll stop and watch
a steam shovel or a drunk man or a sick horse, and they'll listen to
amateur hours.

My own feeling is that most professional entertainers are bad
enough. I've always gone miles out of my way to avoid amateur
theatricals and amateurs of all kinds in the show world, and here
comes Major Bowes and a half dozen others making a big business out
of bad entertainment. A bad solo on a saw is a bad solo on a saw,
even if it is played by a man who drives a milk wagon in the Bronx
and has five children and an aged mother and Broadway aspirations.
Give me professionals and give me only the best of professionals.

One of the silliest outbreaks of radio is this practice of rubbing cities the right way. Major Bowes slops over on the subject of
St. Louis, and St. Louis, in return, naturally makes him honorary
City Superintendent of Sewers, gives him a gold watch and a pair of
handsomely monogrammed ear muffs, and votes him a gelatin key to
the city.

> --Don Herold in Judge, Vol. 112,
> No. 2698 (January 1937), page
> 21.

• THE MARCH OF TIME (CBS, 1931-1936; NBC and NBC Blue,
1937-1945)

More fun than reading a newspaper, more exciting than a
newsreel.

> --G. W. in Life (April 1935), page
> 46.

                              *   *   *

There are two especially sickening vogues in radio. One is
radio's habit of "acting things out." A speaker leads up to an incident, pauses, and a cast of actors put on a little play to give you
the incident. Almost every second spoken program on the air today
employs this tiresome technique. I believe The March of Time went
in for these little re-enactments. I, for one, could never listen to
these charades, and always wondered how an organization as adult
as those Time guys usually show themselves to be could stoop to
these juvenile skits. I much prefer an intelligent, rational description of an event.

--Don Herold in <u>Judge</u>, Vol. 112,
No. 2702 (May 1937), page 22.

●GRAHAM McNAMEE

Six years ago, he was a baritone out of a job. And being a
baritone out of a job is just an octave more desperate than being a
tenor out of a job. In an economic pinch, a baritone is always first
to get the axe. When anyone wants to save money, the first thing
he cuts out is baritones.

So picture, if you can, the terrible plight of Mr. Graham
McNamee in the summer of 1922. Mr. McNamee had come from Min-
nesota and hoped to establish himself as a concert baritone, although he did not disdain musical comedy or even the Metropolitan
Opera House. But that was in the snooty days before the Metropolitan allowed local Chambers of Commerce to select its stars.

In the course of his wanderings around concert bureaus, Mr.
McNamee heard of strange and magic doings then being conducted at
195 Broadway. In the same spirit that prompted out-of-work stage
stars to take a fling at the movies in a shamefaced way, Mr. McNamee applied for a job at WEAF to tide him over the dull summer
months.

The man was almost an instant success. He was the first
announcer to pronounce the names of foreign composers and selections correctly. In those early days, when most of the announcers
spent their brief moments on the air apologizing for what was going
on, Mr. McNamee introduced a touch of culture and refinement, a
hint of the Better Things in Life, and a <u>salon</u> atmosphere. Love-
starved women, who had hitherto looked upon the radio as an unmitigated nuisance, found something beguiling in the way Mr. McNamee
said: "Good evening, ladies and gentlemen of the radio audience."

However, enough of these musings; let us consider the Graham
McNamee of today. Although the offices and <u>ateliers</u> of the National
Broadcasting Company swarm with announcers, it is easy to see that
Mr. McNamee is the star of the outfit. He is Grover Whalen on a
national scale. No aviator has really arrived until he has been introduced to the public by Mr. McNamee. No football game is really important unless Mr. McNamee tells you about the scenery, the weather
and (now and then) the plays. More persons remember Mr. McNamee's part in the last Democratic Convention than could tell you the
name of the Democratic candidate in 1924.

There are purists who tell you that Mr. McNamee's style is
far from perfect. He wanders too much; he is sometimes inaccurate

and his wit is far from penetrating. Nevertheless, he has the in-
gratiating habit of working himself up into a lather of excitement.
The excitement is genuine. Mr. McNamee is one of those sandy,
blue-eyed, choleric gentlemen who are never casual about anything.
Even when broadcasting so unthrilling an opera as Samson et Delilah,
Mr. McNamee can take a burning interest in the plot.

Mr. McNamee has become so much a symbol of something or
other that broadcasting is now only a part of his life. All his time
is booked solid for over a year. Certain advertising hours have
stipulated in their contracts that Mr. McNamee must officiate as
master of ceremonies. He is in constant demand at conventions. He
is sure-fire at Oratorios and he sings at several concerts a week.
He also goes in for literature.

Who says that there is no place for a hard-working baritone
in our national life?

                                   --Agnes Smith in Life, Vol. 91,
                                   No. 2380 (June 14, 1928), page
                                   15.

                         *   *   *

Before the opening of the football season and before election
night, something should be done about radio announcers. My suggestion is that the stations fire all the ex-tenors, baritones and
basses and hire a gang of good reporters without regard to how
their voices register. And I also suggest that these reporters work
under the direction of a news editor and that they be held as responsible for the accuracy and clarity of their reports as the reporters for the big news services.

Radio announcing is no longer a question of being able to
stand before a microphone and say, "The next selection by Jazzbo's
Jazzmaniacs will be 'Old Man Sunshine'." For most persons the
broadcasting of news events is the most important function of the
radio. And these particular broadcasts are the ones that are most
conspicuously manhandled.

Suppose, for instance, that you read a newspaper account of
a football game like this: "Guffis carries the ball around right end
--no, it isn't Guffis, it is McFeely. Yes, McFeely carries the ball
around right end to the twenty-yard line. Wait a minute, McFeely
didn't go around right end. Just a minute, now, and I'll tell you
what is going on down there. Yes, that's it. It was a forward
pass and McFeely--no, it was Guffis--caught the ball on the ten-
yard line. Wait a minute. It was an uncompleted forward pass and
Tate was penalized fifteen yards for holding.... Believe me, folks,
I wish you could see how beautiful the sunset looks from the stadium
here. We can see the setting sun beyond the roofs of the Freshman dormitories... Just a minute.... What's that, Joe?... Oh--Joe

tells me those aren't the Freshman dormitories--that's the Medical
School.... Well, Joe, you're the doctor! Ha, ha!... Oh, wait a
minute.... Something's happening... I think it's a touchdown...."

This sort of thing passes for good reporting on the radio.
You may say that a newspaper reporter doesn't have to give a running account of a game; that he has time to sit down, marshal his
facts and correct his copy. But as a matter of fact, football and
baseball games and prizefights are telegraphed directly to the office
from the grounds. Moreover, the radio announcer has an observer
at his side to report the plays for him. And it wouldn't hurt anyone's feelings if he waited a few seconds and got his facts straight,
before he mangled the account of a good play.

Unfortunately, the radio announcer--and I am pointing directly at you, Mr. McNamee--is all steamed up on the idea that he
must be ingratiating, witty and a devil of a fellow. He thinks of
himself as a cross between a movie star and an after-dinner speaker,
which is a horrid thing to say. He has, alas, His Public to think
about. He sets his personality between his audience and the game
and his account is mostly close-ups of himself. And Mr. McNamee
is pretty well aware that he is more important than the event he is
announcing. No matter how many stalwart stars are out there on
the field, dying for dear old Yale, the real All-American hero of
the battle is always Graham McNamee.

So Mr. McNamee gets, and deserves, all the blame for the
growth of the star system in radio announcing. Moreover, rightly
or wrongly, he is made accountable for the sins of his imitators.
The chief sin of the McNamee school is the belief that you can turn
any blah comment into a witticism simply by laughing at it yourself.

> --Agnes Smith in Life, Vol. 92,
> No. 2394 (September 21, 1928),
> Page 18.

• LES MISERABLES (Mutual, 1937)

Orson Welles is an excellent actor; Les Miserables is an excellent novel; WOR has managed a pretty good radio version of it
(Welles did his own adaptation) and it was pretty well staged. But,
like the CBS Shakespeare series, or like the NBC Shakespeare series,
it was just plain dull. And what are you going to do about that?
It may be good for you, like classics were in school, but where's
the chocolate coating?

WOR claims it isn't trying to follow in the footsteps of its
competition with this new slab of culture; it seems it thought up
this idea all by itself long before anyone stuck a copy of Shakespeare
into the eager mitts of the big chains. Maybe, and if so, so what?

Welles is going to do the Victor Hugo novel in seven installments, of which the half hour hunk Friday night [July 23] was the
beginning. Maybe there'll be someone left to listen to the finish six
weeks from now and maybe not.

The way it's done is supposed to be something new. Welles
narrates the yarn and it fades in and out, in dramatized hunks.
Hard to tell what's new about that. Or which chunks are better--
the acted-out ones, or the Welles-narrated ones.

Welles is an excellent actor, that has been noted before; let
it be noted again. He gets good support from Whitford Kane, Martin
Gabel, Alice Frost, Frank Readick, Ray Collins and Will Geer. But
it's still Welles who counts. For 10 minutes it's a pleasure to forget
the program and listen to his voice. For a half hour? Well, that's
asking quite a lot, isn't it?

> --"Kauf" [Wolfe Kaufman] in
> Variety (July 28, 1937), page
> 42.

• mr. ace and JANE (CBS, 1948-1949)

Goodman Ace, one of the few genuine wits in radio and one of
the veterans, is back in business again with a new show called
mr. ace and JANE, an arrangement of capital and lower case letters
which spells out pretty well who ranks whom in the Ace family.
The new program differs from the old Easy Aces in about the same
manner as the new and old Amos 'n' Andy programs. It's once a
week, half hour, streamlined up to date, and very, very funny.

Jane Ace is another Dulcy, another Irma, another Gracie
Allen, another Mrs. Malaprop, though in her defense it ought to be
added she got there ahead of most of them. She is a woman of sun-
ny amiability who takes an extremely literal and subjective view of
everything around her. This makes life very easy for her and extremely difficult for everyone else. When, for example, she is told
she is to be a member of a jury, she declares heatedly, "I'll say
he's not guilty, whoever he is. If he's nice enough to pay me
three dollars a day to be his jury, the least I can do is recuperate,
doesn't it to you?"

There are a lot of Malaprops in radio but none of them
scrambles a cliché quite so skillfully as Jane. In fact, many of
Jane's expressions are great improvements on the originals. "He
shot out of here like a bat out of a belfry," "The coffee will be
ready in a jitney," "I'm really in a quarry," "this hang-nail expression," "the crank of dawn"--those are a few of her improvements.

In most other respects Jane is a rather difficult conversation-
alist because she is either three jumps ahead or three long strides
behind the person she is conversing with.

"Hi, Jane," an acquaintance will call out. "What have you
been doing?"

"Just fine, thanks," says Jane.

Goodman Ace, the brains of this team, tags along behind his
wife acting as narrator for her mishaps in a dry, resigned voice (one
of the few intelligent voices on the air) and interjecting witty comment. The couple's conversations are usually masterpieces of cross-
purpose.

"Dear, I've just done the most terrible thing I've ever done
in all the years we've been married and seven months," his wife is
likely to tell him. "I was talked into it by someone I should have
known better. In other words yes."

While most of the action revolves around the scrapes Jane
gets into, Ace, who writes the scripts, uses his program to take a
few pokes at radio, the newspapers and the world in general. He's
particularly sharp on the subject of radio, a field he knows intimate-
ly. Once, playing the role of an advertising man, he asked a prospective sponsor what sort of radio program he had in mind. "How
about music?" asked Ace.

"Music? That's been done, hasn't it?" said the sponsor.

In addition to the Aces there are a number of other strange
people hanging around, each with his special obsession. Bobby, a
young newsboy, has stopped handling The Sun because he disagrees
with its editorial policy and refuses a career in radio because he
doesn't want to boost a competing advertising medium. (Bobby,
I suspect, pretty well sums up Ace's ideas on all newspaper men.)
Jane's brother, Paul, hasn't worked for twelve years "because he's
waiting for the dollar to settle down," and primly objects to the use
of four-letter words in front of his sister, especially "work."

There's also an announcer named Ken Roberts whose function
is to kid all the commercials on the air. Here's a sample of a Roberts commercial: "Fifty years ago Blycose began selling the public
its high-quality products and today, just as it was fifty years ago,
it is March 20."

The real sponsor for the Ace show is the United States Army
recruiting service and after President Truman's message to Congress
urging re-enactment of the draft, Ace remarked blithely that he was
the only comedian in radio for whom the President did the commercials.

--John Crosby in New York Herald
Tribune (March 29, 1948).

• MORAN AND MACK

Picture me writing this with a breaking heart. Make it a
talking picture, if you like, and listen to the sound of sobbing.
For I would rather be boiled in oil than break the sad news that
Moran and Mack, broadcasting on Sunday evening over the Columbia
System, are not so hot. In fact, to me, they are both cold and wet.
Hard words, indeed, but facts are facts.

All heroes, actors and public figures of any sort who make
a sudden and unique success should be mercifully done away with
as soon as that first edge begins to wear away. Only bores like
Elsie Dinsmore can go on forever. The Two Black Crows go before
a radio public who hope to capture the first fine fervor of their
early records. It can't be done.

Moreover, the comics are barred from repeating any of their
best lines. Anyone breaking into a conversation with "What's your
idea in bringing that up?" is instantly thrown out of the window.
The Black Crows are paying the penalty of their own popularity.
They would no more dare tell why white horses eat more than black
horses than Ethel Barrymore would dare appear in a play containing
the line, "That's all there is. There isn't any more."

The idea at the back of the radio sketches of the Two Black
Crows is a swell one, but the way it works out sounds as if a
dozen Hollywood supervisors and two dozen gag-men had been putting
their best brains to it. Moran and Mack are a couple of colored
brethren who get mixed up in the World War. So far the doings
have been confined to a small Southern town. Unfortunately, instead of remaining strictly Octavus Roy Cohen, they have permitted
someone to inject a lot of the most objectionable so-called white characters that ever annoyed an audience.

The radio is making a mistake which the movies have only
just begun to outgrow. All sketches are supposed to have a love
interest. The love interest of the Two Black Crows is furnished by
the rivalry of Lieut. Davis and Steve Reinhardt, a German-American,
for a half-witted girl called Mary Jane. Just to show how broad-
minded we are and how far we have progressed towards international
peace and good will, the lieutenant is the villain and the hyphenate
is the hero. You have to listen to this trio of mistakes court and
scrap in old stock company fashion, while you are waiting for Moran
and Mack.

And there are times when the waiting isn't worth while. One
of those times, on a recent program, was when Mack, the head
Black Crow, got involved in a tongue-twister about Esau saw the saw.
Anyone over ten years old who can get a laugh out of one of those
"Peter Piper picked a peck of pickled peppers" is hereby advised
to join a school for retarded children.

By way of being constructive and helpful, I suggest that the
Black Crows go in for a minstrel show. Nobody expects new jokes
in a minstrel show; in fact, if anyone ever heard one, he would
have to be carried out and treated for shock.

Once again, I apologize for letting you down and if you really
do enjoy the new sketches of the Two Black Crows, and aren't just
carried away by sentiment and dreams of old times, you are entitled
to call me names. But before you get nasty, I urge you to recall
those terrible five minutes about Esau who saw the bucksaw.

--Agnes Smith in Life, Vol. 92,
No. 2395 (September 28, 1928),
page 18.

• NOAH WEBSTER SAYS (NBC, 1942-1951)

It takes a better-than-par I.Q. to have fun with just words.
You know, words. Like malediction, odiferous, comedian. So it was
quite heartening to learn that Noah Webster Says, Haven MacQuarrie's Thursday night radio show starring the dictionary (NBC, 9:30
PDT), has reached, at times, a Hooper rating of fifteen, and at
present is coasting along on a comfortable ten-point plus.

The announcer's introduction of Mr. MacQuarrie on the air
as "your genial, jovial master of ceremonies" is one of radio's biggest
exaggerations. His voice is a ponderous and booming reminder of by-
gone theatrical days when microphones were unknown, and his delivery is about as friendly as that of a truant offficer with tired
feet.

In selecting the contestants for his weekly fun-with-words
game, Mr. MacQuarrie's technique could be described as the iron-
hand-in-the-velvet-glove method, except that there is no sign of
the velvet glove. Culling the studio audience in a lengthy warm-
up, he finally picks six civilians and two servicemen. In the process,
he glares at them, growls at them, and shoots a district attorney's
forefinger at them when their replies falter. You get the idea that
they all need $50 desperately or he would have frightened them
speechless before getting them onto the stage.

Getting down to the business of outsmarting the dictionary,

"your genial and jovial host" intones the one-dollar, the two-dollar,
the five-, and the ten-dollar words, and finally the fifty-dollar
topper. As Mr. MacQuarrie defines a word, the announcer writes
it on a blackboard behind the contestant's back but visible to the
studio audience. This places the studio visitors in the confidential
position of knowing all the answers, while the contestant tries to
guess the correct word.

Despite his stern demeanor, Mr. MacQuarrie has a soft heart.
A loser on Noah Webster Says is rare. If the contender fumbles.
the philanthropic quiz master quickly tosses him a clue. If he fails
again, a second and broader hint follows. It may take six or seven.
But in the end, Mr. MacQuarrie usually succeeds in forcing the $50
on his dazed guest. In a final desperate shove across the finish
line, Noah Webster's front man will unhesitatingly reach across the
microphone and twist the contestant's head squarely around to see
the answer on the blackboard.

To give the program an authentic academic background, a real
educator, Charles Frederick Lindsley of Occidental College, corrob-
orates each definition.

Mr. MacQuarrie's unorthodox approach and formal courtroom
manner have an understandably hypnotic effect on his subjects.
Once, an elderly man en route to the coveted cash award, broke
down and volunteered on the air that he had once committed a murder. This brought Noah Webster Says a fine front-page coast-to-
coast news break.

An old-time Orpheum and Keith trouper, Mr. MacQuarrie has
always been fascinated by words and their meanings. Noah Webster
Says was his idea from the start, although he did not personally
emcee the show when he sold the idea to NBC seven years ago. He
chooses all the word categories used on the show from thousands of
lists sent in each week. Often he uses only one word of a submitted
list and selects companion words for it. While most of the words
featured are in everyday usage, he enjoys unusual ones. Sometimes
the definitions of these are hilarious to radio listeners.

"Define 'ululate,'" he once asked a dignified middle-aged
lady.

She couldn't.

"Do you have a dog?"

Yes, she had a dog.

"Tell me, does your dog ululate?"

Doubting her ears, but brightening perceptibly because she

thought she could guess the definition, she said yes, her dog did.

"When was the last time your dog ululated?"

Oh, shortly before she left home, she thought, stammering a little.

"How many times a day," coaxed Mr. MacQuarrie, "does your dog ululate?" After a pause she answered, "About eight times a day."

"Very well. Now define the word, 'ululate.'"

The dignified lady swallowed hard, and was silent.

Fixing her with his best third-degree eye, MacQuarrie solemnly barked twice.

"To bark," she gasped, and reached limply for her $50 bill.

The program offers little booty to the contestant. There are no mink pipecleaners, platinum plumbing ensembles, or paid-up annuities. A plain old $50 bill is the reward for trouncing the team of Webster and MacQuarrie.

What makes it click, then? Obviously, it isn't the vicarious thrill of hearing a fellow-Rotarian or an unknown but kindred spirit from your old home town stagger away from the microphone loaded to the ears with loot. It isn't the magic spell of thinking that any minute your phone will ring and you'll guess Mr. Hush. There are no pleasantly sadistic touches such as bashing the studio stooge in the face with a custard pie or sending him out into Vine Street to sock a policeman. No, Noah Webster Says offers the listener just what the title suggests, an opportunity to enlarge his vocabulary. The listeners are invited to send in lists of words which if used bring only $5 per set. To word-lovers, money appears no object. Mr. MacQuarrie's mail is interesting in another respect which may bear out the inference that the dialside I.Q. is higher than previously suspected. The bulk of fan mail received by most programs is written on pencil-tablet paper and penny postcards. Most Webster-MacQuarrie correspondents use good bond paper. It is not uncommon for erudite fans such as university presidents, lawyers, or writers to phone in after a program to argue about the pronunciation of a word, proving that while they may not see eye to eye with Webster, they do listen to MacQuarrie.

In many public schools along the West Coast, English students are given extra points for listening to Noah Webster Says, and recently the Los Angeles County School Board wrote to tell its quizmaster that recordings of the program are played back as part of the regular English curriculum.

Which brings this story to its finis, as Noah Webster says
... and according to Mr. MacQuarrie, mispronounced by millions.
It's "fie-nis" ... with a long "i," please.

--Mary McSkimming in Script
(July 1948), pages 47-48.

● ONE MAN'S FAMILY (NBC, 1932-1959)

Have you ever witnessed a good tent performance of Uncle
Tom's Cabin, played straight and in earnest by a group of tent-
show actors? Probably not. Most of the real tent-show troupers
have retired. But if you ever saw Uncle Tom's Cabin played com-
petently and with deadly seriousness, I'll wager when little Eva went
to Heaven it wasn't such a funny bit of business as you had been
led to believe. One Man's Family is a loosely knit, sentimental saga
of family life. It could be the most obvious claptrap on the air if it
were not for two elements:

First, One Man's Family is written and produced by an expert
craftsman [Carlton E. Morse]. There's no better writer of authentic
homespun radio serials in the country. Secondly, the members of
the cast--excepting Mr. J. Anthony Smythe, who consistently over-
acts as the father--work together as if they had been born and
brought up under the same canvas. I know that I should dismiss
the whole lot of them as study hoaxers; they all belong in a tent
show. Well, there used to be some pretty robust drama in tent
shows.

--Cyrus Fisher in The Forum and
Century, Vol. 90, No. 2 (August 1933), page 127.

● AL PEARCE

This is by somebody who doesn't know one radio program
from another, or one station from another, or who is hot in Duluth
but cold in Detroit.

Or anything like that I don't know.

But a radio guy named Al Pearce came through here (La
Jolla, California) with some friends about a year ago, and in an off
moment while at my home said what I needed was a barbecue.

"Sure I do," I answered.

"Well, I'll get you one," he said.

"That's fine. Thanks." And I let it go at that. For if all
the off-moment promises were taken seriously and placed in a heap
the heap would still be there, I for one not even bothering to light
a match to it.

We know how this incident ends, of course, because I'm still
pondering about this guy Al Pearce. And I certainly wouldn't have
had if I had not seen him again. The barbecue came, as I say, and
so did he. But what the devil for, I can't explain, since I have
never danced before the crowned heads of Europe nor played so
much as an ocarina for the Queen. There's nothing of the theater
connected with me.

Yet the more we talked by my ocean here (sure, it's my
ocean), the more startled I was to discover how even a fellow in the
broadcasting business knows more about real life on the outside,
whether farming or repairing telephone wires, than I--who prided
myself on such things--ever could hope to know even if I had continued trying right up to now.

As a kid I had been a Montana ranch kid. Sure. And had
thought I had seen one tough time of it, what and all with wearing
gunnysacks for shoes. But guess what? We began comparing notes,
and he did not even wear gunnysacks. They were the symbol of
an aristocrat where he came from, his farm in Santa Clara County,
California. Al Pearce went barefoot up till he went to high school.
And so it goes.

His jobs included milking, door-to-door selling, repairing
electrical wires in Sacramento Valley for the light-and-power company. Everything, really, until he organized an orchestra--long,
long ago. But from that point on I don't care. For I don't like to
write about successful fellows. Generally they bore me, their sentences being too filled with "I," "I," "I" and more "I's."

And yet I find myself writing about Al Pearce, and this is
because when around him I find that I am the one doing all the "I,"
"I"-ing. Nor can I make the reason out, except that he's just that
way. Al least when on my ocean here, which is the only criterion
I have to go by.

And there's another thing which bewilders me. The other
night some young fool took his girl (or at least a girl) riding in a
car on the beach. These birds should be shut up in a cellar until
they know better, for not only can the salty sand ruin a mighty
fine car but such drivers also can scare ten years onto the surf
fishermen fishing there in the darkness of night. So I was glad,
really glad, when this young fool finally got stuck in the sand,
and stuck badly. I would have left him and his car there forever.

But this Pearce fellow would have none of it. He worked for
two hours, maybe longer, digging and rocking the car, digging into
sand and rocking the car--until the young fool finally was released.
Why? Perhaps because Pearce remembers only too well when he himself was young. Or maybe he's still young. Maybe that's it.

Anyway, anybody with comprehension like that--and all done
without benefit of klieg lights--sure, anybody like that surely wins
my money whether or not I know anything about a radio.

And I have a hunch that anybody like Al Pearce is just Al
Pearce--plain and unadorned--when he broadcasts just like when he's
on my ocean. Fact is, they say he's got the same comprehension
when it comes to his radio program and that's why it goes over so
big with people who are fed up on temperamental canaries and show-
offs and such like.

I think I'll listen to him after this. And there's another
reason, too. He likes to fill his fishing-boat with kids who otherwise could not go fishing. I know this for a fact, because at least
a half-dozen youngsters I suggested have all had one whale of a
ride.

> --Max Miller in Movie and Radio
> Guide, Vol. 9, No. 19 (February
> 17, 1940), page 14.

• THE PEPSODENT SHOW (NBC, 1938-1950)

That small speck going over the center field fence is the four-
bagger Bob Hope whammed out on his first time at the bat for Pepsodent. If he can keep up the pace he'll get as much word-of-
mouth for 1938-39 as Edgar Bergen got for 1937-38. He sounded
like success all the way.

Hope must have been trying, because the script showed
plenty of thought. But it's his particular gift not to seem to be
trying. And that's a great psychological aid. It suggests wearing
qualities.

Hope has one knack--even when he introduces a "plot" or a
"situation" he never takes either seriously and never gets tangled
up with anything that is merely plot and not gag. Let him show
over a period of time that he can duplicate and the other comics
will be lending a jealous ear. Those situational boys have tended
with the passage of time to back themselves into the machinery.
They don't run the plot, the plot chases them.

Or, maybe, we're neglecting the writers. Whoever he or them
is/are, house rules allow an extra bow.

Jerry Colonna, who is making a career out of being terrible, is off-buying for Pepsodent as Hope's chief stooge. He's an artist at being inartistic and his prolonged high note falsetto as he staggers full tilt into "Mandalay" and what-not may catch on. Particularly with the kids.

Constance Bennett was the lady in the case for the opener. She was strictly for gagging. And it was amusing flippancy. Feather-light and pushed by a breeze.

Commericals were intelligently integrated with the program and Hope was deferential with that kidding-the-one-we-love trick of the funnymen. It was modern in self-mocking, but never so engaged in mirth as to forget that keeping the breath scented with Pepsodent is a serious matter (see minutes, Board of Directors).

Musical tie-togethers nicely done. Although there was one bit of singing that historically rates as serious, but seemed at the time to be working up to a comedy break-down. Maybe it's best not to go into that. It was a good radio show.

> --"Land" [Robert J. Landry] in
> Variety (October 5, 1938),
> page 30.

* POT O' GOLD (NBC, 1939-1941)

There has been so much gab about the Pot o' Gold program in which Horace Heidt's dance-banditry is briefly sandwiched between thick slices of dull chatter about a glorified giveaway. The lawyers finally switched on the green light for this show* which is based on the simple act of calling some telephone subscriber in the U.S. and, if he's home, giving him a grand note. If he isn't home, he gets 10 per cent--a $100 bill.

On paper, the idea is brighter than a zircon, but this department predicts the show won't kick the present leaders out of their positions in the Crossley ratings. Bob Landry, able radio editor of Variety, says it this way: "A brainwave whereby entertainment is subordinated entirely to a giveaway ... a case of making the giveaway the whole show ... dish-night on the kilocycles ... one winner and umpteen losers."

Looking at it this way, you can see it's an 11,000,000-to-1 chance with one winner (there being that many phones). The Irish Sweeps is a 4,000,000-to-1 shot with many winners. At those odds

---

*At this time, the networks had a ban on radio programs featuring lotteries.

you're not going to get me staying home Tuesday nights to sit
through Heidt and those mountains of gab.

> --Dale Armstrong in <u>Rob Wagner's
> Script</u> (October 14, 1939), page
> 30.

- THE RADIO GUILD (NBC, 1929-1938)

Something to make Sunday afternoon worth living through.
Broadway stage hits and very fine stuff.

> --G.W. in <u>Life</u> (April 1935), page
> 46.

- THE RUDY VALLEE SHOW (NBC, 1929-1939)*

Rudy Vallee celebrated his 500th broadcast for Standard
Brands last week, compiling a record that is likely to stand for some
time. For the occasion program offered two of the stars Vallee's
show has launched, Edgar Bergen and Frances Langford, together
with Cliff Arkette, Dr. Lee DeForest and Lionel Barrymore. It was
by no means a sock show, certainly not the sock show that was to
be expected in view of the occasion. If anything dominated the program it was the plugs; they were insistent and frequent and showed
that the entertainment standards of the series are far ahead of the
sales.

A line break broke up the opening medley of tunes identified
with Vallee, getting the show off to an awkward start. Charlie
McCarthy had a bit of patter before Dr. DeForest, inventor of the
vacuum tube which makes radio possible, partook of a short interview. To show that he still can toot the sax, Vallee played a piece
by Rudy Weidoft and did it okeh for a fellow who hasn't played in
some time.

The dramatic sketch starrring Barrymore was an old piece of
flannel, about the Civil War veteran who tells his grandson Baron
Munchausen stories and then tries to destroy the kid's ideas of war's
glamour by extolling peace. Barrymore, as usual, pretty porcine.

Miss Langford did two numbers, one a solo and the other a
duet with Vallee, and again raised the question in this reviewer's
mind as to why she is a star. No less disappointing was Bergen's
version of <u>Robinson Crusoe</u>. Neither his lines nor the dummy's were

---

*Also known as <u>The Fleischmann Hour</u>.

up to snuff. Cliff Arkette does an old man routine and, as heard,
belies the wisdom of selecting him as one of those to be touched by
the Vallee wand. Program was completed by hit tunes Vallee has
done since he started.

Altho the program disappointed as a show, it held a considerable sentimental appeal, built around the performer who not only became a star but stayed up there and brought others to the top.
> --J.F. [Ferry Franken] in The
> Billboard (May 27, 1939), page
> 9.

• THE SAL HEPATICA REVUE (NBC, 1933-1934)

In a smooth and merciless satire on all high-adventure programs and two specifically, The Sal Hepatica Revue--quite a title in
itself--presents Mr. Fred Allen as an explorer seeking the East
Pole. His voice, bland beyond all belief, totally devoid of feeling and
respect for the higher pursuits of life, casually emits remarks concerning his barefoot boyhood and other touching subjects in a manner
which will make explorers of radio programs squirm with admiration
and certain other explorers squirm with something less than admiration.

At intervals he switches on the radio placed in his good ship
--and you must hear him to appreciate the blistering irony possible
in "good ship." The pleasant fiction of turning on the radio offers
a convenient excuse for Mr. [Ferde] Grofé's orchestra to come in
with its usual brilliant constructions. If I have not been overly
kind in the past to Mr. Allen it is because until now he has been
struggling in productions unfitted for his satirical enterprise. Let
me finish and make amends for possible neglect by repeating what
is, to date, the best line of 1934. There is an unearthly roaring
noise, presumably one of Mr. Lord's waves, coming through the microphone, and Mr. Allen pauses, asks: "Who's that? The sponsor?"
and imperturbably continues to pour vinegar over the high seas.
> --Cyrus Fisher in The Forum and
> Century, Vol. 91, No. 3 (March
> 1934), page 191.

*   *   *

In the latter, longer and better part of Fred Allen's inaugural
program [January 3], which was typically, whoopingly and rollicking-
ly Allenesque the laughs came fast and comic ideas tumbled over one
another in rich profusion. In the opening few minutes and intro-
ductory session, getting the revue onto the air for the first time,
the results were less successful. But the brilliant comedy tempo of

the imaginative rubberneck tour of New York City squared and
erased the non-Allenesque beginning.

Allen's great advantage for radio is the twist he gives things.
His comedy has a tinge of the intellectual about it. But never esoteric. It's the smart patter superimposed upon familiar Americana
that at once renders him and his stuff capable of pleasing the hoi
polloi simultaneously.

Music of Ferde Grofé is good music and the singing of the
Four Songsmiths and others is good singing, but essentially the
Sal Hepatica Revue is Fred Allen plus interruptions, comment, and
cross-fire from Portland Hoffa. Incidentally the comic's wife has
developed a singing-talking style of delivery that's excellent. It
has an Alice-in-Wonderlandish quality of dementia.

Some doubt as to the comercial copy. It seems a trifle too
explicit and graphic. Hard to know just how a laxative can get its
message over and stay within the limits of what, rightly or wrongly,
the canons of refinement bar from polite conversation. Sal Hepatica
doesn't bother being subtle.

Allen's type of comedy wears well and grows. Comic writes
most of his own stuff and his inspiration seldom lags. His ear for
droll expressions and phraseology is as acute as his genius for topsy-
turvy thinking. Obviously he is the kind of comedian who has to
be given a free rein. At the same time there is a minimum of need
for supervision of his material because he is too clever ever to have
to be off-color.

Presence of Allen and comedians of his high grade of humor
on the air will gradually make it pretty tough for the phoney comics.
                                --"Land" [Robert J. Landry] in
                                Variety (January 9, 1934), page
                                32.

• THE SCREEN GUILD THEATRE (CBS, 1939-1948; NBC, 1948-
   1950; ABC, 1950-1951)

This reviewer has always regarded radio broadcasts as he
does ptomaine--something to look out for. But hereafter he intends
to spend Sunday afternoons at the El Capitan where the first Screen
Guild Show (Gulf Oil pays the bills and the Guild will use the money
to erect a home for the industry's unfortunate)* was a complete success, something to watch as well as hear.

---

*What became the Motion Picture Country House in Woodland Hills
on the outskirts of Los Angeles.

I don't know how the show sounded on your radio, and this isn't a formal review, but I must congratulate Mitch Leisen who directed the half hour, must compliment the sponsors and their dignified spokeman for their reticence, must record my admiration for the performers, the music, and a streamlined show unusual for its tact and grace and wit. With all the talent of Hollywood to draw from, the Guild elected to be modest instead of striving to be overwhelming, and I hope the public was as pleased as the first audience, a complete edition of Hollywood's Who's Who.

The invited guests enjoyed serveral treats which stay-at-homes were denied, such as Jack Benny's breathless arrival (sirens blowing) from his own show; his Don Juaning with Joan Crawford, who swooned into a chair and was so breath-takingly lovely, both in appearance and voice, that I won't rest until she does a stage play; and Reginald Gardiner, with a broken arm, whose gifted mimicry of trains--domestic and foreign--was more amazing when one could watch how effortlessly he did it.

The whole show was so intimate and such fun that I wish director and writers could have been on the stage to share the sincere applause. This Sunday (though C.B.S. won't thank me for urging you to obtain tickets) Ernst Lubitsch directs a musical comedy with Fred Astaire, Franklin Pangborn, Loretta Young, and others. It ought to be grand, and if you want to meet all your friends, without bothering to tempt them with a Sunday buffet, just do the smart thing, which for a number of months will be dashing off to the Screen Guild Show, the best news of 1939.

> --Richard Sheridan Ames in Rob Wagner's Script (January 14, 1939), pages 16-17.

• SHERLOCK HOLMES (NBC Blue, 1939-1943; Mutual, 1943-1946)

Basil Rathbone is not on the radio every Sunday but Sherlock Holmes is.

This is the contention of a friend of mine who was talking the other evening about varous art forms. We had just seen William Saroyan's Across the Board on Tomorrow Morning, which world-premièred at the Pasadena Playhouse.

It isn't my department to go into discussion of Mr. Saroyan and his provocative pen but I would like to say that had his play finished with the originality, wit and clarity with which it began, he'd really have presented a minor masterpiece.

But about Basil. When I argued with my friend that Mr.

Rathbone could be heard on KFI each Sunday at 5:30 p.m., as well
as over KECA the same day at 9:30 p.m., he still insisted, "I know,
but it isn't Rathbone; it's Sherlock Holmes."

In Radio (my friend said), if an actor does a good job, the
listeners see him as they want him to be. Out of his voice alone
they build in their minds his appearance, his costume, even the
locale in which he, at the moment, is living. And if the actor does
not do a good job, the dial is usually twisted to another station.

In motion pictures, for instance, if the actor wears a short
tunic with pearl buttons, a top hat and an Inverness cape, that is
precisely what you see. No matter what his voice is like, you still
see the tunic, the hat and the cape. And you see the actor himself.
But in Radio, this isn't so. Radio gives the tuner-inner a superla-
tively better chance to see the character rather than the actor.
And to the extent the actor is able to paint pictures in your mind
with his voice, to that extent will you allow the character to live.

So my friend insisted, adding that because of this, the
actor who can paint pictures with his voice gets a better break on
Radio than he does in pictures or on the stage.

All of which brought us back to a consideration of Basil
Rathbone and Sherlock Holmes. Because Rathbone is a fine actor,
having made a great reputation in the theater as well as in pictures,
he is able to create word-pictures with his voice. He is able to
project the character he is portraying and not himself; an art, sadly
enough, neglected too often by the player.

In his performance each Sunday for N.B.C., Rathbone brings
Sherlock Holmes to life in many, many forms. To those who have
seen him as the master-sleuth on the screen, he comes through
their ears in that guise; to those who have read the Conan Doyle
stories and conjured up the appearance of Holmes out of the prose,
he sounds like that identical picture; and to those who meet the
greatest of all English-speaking detectives for the first time via
Radio, Basil is not Basil but Holmes--and Holmes as the listener
wants him to be.

Some time ago, Rathbone told me he liked Radio very much.
Primarily, I think he said, because Radio was like the theater in
that it permitted the actor to give a sustained performance. Unlike
pictures, there is only one "take" in Radio. The actor gets ready
to do his job from start to finish without interrruption or repetition.
And any actor used to the theater prefers that method, I'm sure.

So much for that. It's a viewpoint with which you may agree
or disagree--and in either case, I'd be interested in your slant.

--Dale Armstrong in Rob Wagner's
Script (February 22, 1941), page
28.

• KATE SMITH

Here perhaps is the season's best opportunity to point out
that radio runs are lengthening into radio careers. Kate Smith is
going into her eighth year. In that time she has grown from a
single singer into an organization with shares, staff, sidelines,
by-products and legends. And coincidental with the picking up of
the threads after the summer layoff, her autobiography has just
appeared in book form.

Present at the re-christening last Thursday were old standbys
and fresh items. Accent the fresh when mentioning the character,
Henry Aldrich, adolescent protagonist of a George Abbott hit, who
is brought to life on stage and in the air by Ezra Stone.* This
male brat, on the threshold of an electric razor, is a champ annoyer-
at-large. With natural, homey, familiar dialog the Aldrich series of
domestic caricatures should fit in nicely with a radio program selling
things to put into cakes and biscuits. Was heard previously during
the summer on the [Rudy] Vallee show. Cornelia Otis Skinner, who
is booked quite frequently for the variety line-ups, did her Anne
Boleyn with that richly embroidered detail that builds such strong
illusion. It was an interlude of distinction.

There was a lot of voltage-harnessed Kate Smith singing, a
program tempo that was crisp, the nut stuff of Abbott and Costello
(who are building) and a choir that reflected in its ultra effects a
willing-to-rehearse history. Eddy Duchin made the keyboard glow
as soloist. Jack Miller was the baton-wielder as usual.

And this was one opening night that was "ready." Nobody
had to squirm in sympathy with the performers. It had been cut,
edited, paced and laid out to get its results starting immediately.
                              --"Land" [Robert J. Landry] in
                              Variety (October 5, 1938), page
                              30.

• THE STANDARD HOUR (NBC, 1926-1956)

The notion appears still to persist in New York that all territory west of the Hudson River is wasteland, occupied only by
Indians and buffalo. Witness: when Lowell Thomas on Oct. 4, 1950,
celebrated his 20th anniversary as a newscaster, he said that his
was the oldest continuous program in the history of radio. Either
his history or his arithmetic is wrong.

---

*The Aldrich Family became a long-running radio series from 1939-
1953.

Thomas began broadcasting in 1930. Four years earlier--
1926--a program was inaugurated in California which has continued
without interruption to this day. Moreover, it was the first program
in the US to employ a network of stations, called then by another
name--"simultaneous broadcasting." (That combination of stations
became the nucleus for NBC's Western network.) It came to be and
still is known as The Standard Hour.

Standard Oil of California got into the business of radio broadcasting more or less by accident, well ahead of any other sponsor of
like size employing radio as an advertising medium. At the time,
the late Alfred Hertz was conductor of the San Francisco Symphony
Orchestra. The supporting committee in San Francisco had run into
some trouble raising necessary funds for the season of 1926-27, so
Standard agreed to sponsor a first broadcast to help the campaign.
Its success was so outstanding as to prompt Standard to continue
the broadcast purely as a good-will building enterprise. Since that
time it has been heard every week.

During its 24 years The Standard Hour has presented many
of the world's greatest artists and conductors. It has been the
starting point for a large number of young California musicians,
many of whom have taken their places among today's top-flight
artists. Its programs have been of a high standard. It has brought
good music into thousands of Western homes through a network that
now includes 25 stations.

Since its inauguration the winter season has been divided
equally between the San Francisco and Los Angeles orchestra with
occasional concerts by those of Seattle, Portland and the Janssen.
The summer season provides popular programs by the Standard
Symphony Orchestra (65 players selected from the two major organi-
zations) while the autumn period is occupied with broadcasts by the
San Francisco Opera Company.

Can It Go? At first there was doubt among Standard executives as to the value of the enterprise, but its success was so spectacular as to convince the doubters that here was something the
public wanted and something which could do immense good for the
company in the field of public relations.

That prompted Standard to set up a companion program which
it called the Standard School Broadcast and which provided schoolchildren with music education and music history. That program, now
in its 23rd year, plays weekly to an audience of literally hundreds of
thousands of youngsters throughout the West.

Big Investment. A conservative estimate of the cost to
Standard Oil of California, not including the School Broadcast, has
been six and a half million dollars--a pretty tidy sum for an industry
to spend on music with no hope or intent of selling a product. It

is notable that the programs never had been bedeviled with slam-
bang commercials. Recently, a modest amount of time has been devoted to institutional advertising but not a single effort to sell merchandise.

Has this program and policy paid off? Well, The Standard
Hour consistently has enjoyed one of the highest ratings among musical programs in the territory where it is heard. It never has fallen
below third place among similar programs coming into the area from
Eastern cities. It has continually been rated higher as to listening
audience than the New York Philharmonic in the seven states where
the program is heard. Estimated audience at present is three quar-
ters of a million.

Incidents. The Standard Hour has not been without its moments of travail for producers and announcers. There have been
times when these gentlemen might willingly have indulged themselves
in a bit of bloodletting. Vagaries of conductors and artists have on
many occasions been responsible for premature gray hair. One such
was during a concert being conducted by Sir Thomas Beecham and
broadcast from Hollywood Bowl. The various numbers had been ac-
curately timed at rehearsal, but when the concert got under way
Sir Thomas was so determined in his deliberately slow walk to the
podium and the long waits between numbers that he lost a total of
five minutes, which made it impossible to include the final number.
Fortunately the announcer had prepared for such an eventuality and
signed off from the offstage booth. Another cause for fingernail
chewing was when a famous violinist refused to go through a rehearsal with the orchestra, making it impossible to time the concerto to
be played. The announcer did get the timing from a recording, but
a different cadenza was to be used than was recorded. The can-
tankerous artist even refused to play the substituted cadenza for
timing, assuring the producer that it would take exactly four minutes. Everything went well until it transpired that the artist had
played the cadenza in exactly two minutes, thus leaving the frantic
announcer with two minutes of dangling "dead air"--the nightmare
of all producers and announcers. The only thing to be done was to
read and reread the closing announcement until sign-off time.

While Eastern radio networks and sponsors are cutting down
on serious musical programs Standard of California has no notion of
abandoning its Standard Hour.
                                          --Fortnight (January 22, 1951),
                                          page 18.

• BILL STERN

Bill Stern has been on the air at the same time, on the same

network (N.B.C.) for eleven years, ten of those years for the
same sponsor (Colgate). Over the years he has created his own
little world of sportsdom, where every man is a Frank Merriwell,
every touchdown an epic feat of arms, and coincidence stretches
like a rubber band to fit every conceivable situation.

In fact, N.B.C. has received so many comments concerning
Mr. Stern's casual attitude toward facts on Sports Newsreel that
the program is now prefaced with the admission that Stern's stories
are partly fact, partly hearsay.

Even the word "hearsay" is a rather generous description,
implying, as it does, that Stern's stories have reached the stature
of legend and therefore are beyond the irksome confines of journalism. This is misleading. Many of the most lurid of Stern's "legends" originated in the teeming brains of his writers and started
on their way to legend only after Stern put them on the air to his
devoted audience which runs well into the millions.

You can start an argument in any saloon where sportswriters
congregate by picking out any Stern story as the weirdest he has
ever told. Stern has told so many fantastic yarns that it's pretty
hard to pin down any one of them as deserving the superlative.
However, there is one story that bobs up more often than any other,
the Stern version of Abraham Lincoln's dying words. As the great
emancipator lay dying, Stern related, he sent for General Abner
Doubleday, the man who is supposed to have invented baseball.

"Keep baseball alive," said the dying President to Doubleday.
"In the trying days ahead, the country will need it." And he fell
back on the pillow and expired.

Whether or not this deserves the accolade as the most flabber-
gasting story Stern ever told, it is typical of all of them. It links
a great name and a historic occasion with a sport. And it is totally
true. (Lincoln never regained consciousness, as every school child
knows.) The Lincoln tale is also illustrative of the Stern philosophy
that every American worthy of the name puts sports ahead of all
other considerations, including the Civil War.

There is hardly an American of renown who has not been
thrust by Stern, completely unsupported by the facts, on to a football field, a baseball diamond, a prize ring or a tennis court. Thomas
Alva Edison, for example, would have been greatly surprised to hear
that his deafness was the result of a pitched ball that hit him in the
head when he was a semi-pro ballplayer, which he never was. (Edison's deafness is pretty generally attributed to a conductor who
boxed his ears when he was a candy butcher on trains as a boy.)
The pitcher who threw that ball, according to Stern, was Jesse
James.

Stern's method of delivering these whoppers is in many ways even more startling than the stories. He tells them in short, declarative sentences, bristling with exclamation points. After every other sentence or so, a studio organ delivers what in radio parlance is known as a "sting," a chord or series of chords which are the closest musical equivalent to an elevated eyebrow. Stern generally keeps the name of his hero a secret until the very last line and then reveals him by means of a sentence that has become a Bill Stern trademark: "And that man was ____." Then the name.

One of Stern's former writers has confessed that he frequently left the last part blank to be filled in at the last moment by whoever happened to be prominent in the news--General Eisenhower, Jackie Robinson, the late President Roosevelt, anyone at all. Stern's writers, of whom he has had many, view him with a mixture of admiration for his audacity and total cynicism. One of them summed up his feelings recently by confessing that he had written a lot of utter malarkey for Stern. Then he added belligerently:

"But look here, it ain't easy to dream those things up."
                              --John Crosby in New York Herald
                                 Tribune (November 24, 1949).

• LEOPOLD STOKOWSKI

Compare Mr. Leopold Stokowski's ritualistic approach to a symphony concert, before an audience, to his zeal for bringing good music to all over the air. In the concert-hall applause between sections of a work is frowned upon, and if you are one minute late, you may be kept outside the auditorium for a half hour or more while the orchestra plays four movements of a symphony, ranging from the tragic to a gay dance, some of it no more significant than the music one hears over the discreet rattle of a restaurant; whereas Mr. Stokowsky, a genuine enthusiast for radio, knows that during his broadcast people talk and read and play bridge, and still hear music.
                              --Gilbert Seldes in Scribner's Maga-
                                 zine, Vol. 100, No. 4 (October
                                 1936), page 79.

• THE STORY OF MYRT AND MARGE (CBS, 1931-1942)

Starting over two years ago as a fast, glittering superficial memodrama of the chorus girls' end of the showbusiness, Myrt and Marge has veered toward more blood and thunder and less amusing tinsel. Miss [Myrtle] Vail--motivating power house for Myrt and

Marge--has amply demonstrated that she is acquainted with all the
sure-fire lures ever used in the theater to attract paying customers.

At present the locale is in South America. Here Miss Vail is
busily redecorating her successful formula of two girls--one beautiful
and helpless, the other not so helpless but who also has her feminine moments--constantly pestered by worse than death and lack of
money. The strenuous adventures are made credible by a slick and
varied cast. Until Miss Vail misplaces her atlas, or radio audiences
grow up, there's no apparent reason why Myrt and Marge should
not continue to run on like the brook.

--Cyrus Fisher in The Forum and
Century, Vol. 91, No. 2 (February 1934), page 125.

• DEEMS TAYLOR

Of all the musical people that I hear discussing music,
Deems Taylor comes nearest to winning my confidence. For me, he
offsets thousands of the bluffers and poseurs that I believe to exist
in the musical world. Sometime I'm going to visit Deems Taylor for
two hours and give him $50 and have him psychoanalyze me musical-
ly, and see if he can find out if my mother was, just before I was
born, frightened by a long-haired chautauqua piano-player.

I believe Deems Taylor would be tender with my musical
stupidities, instead of scathing in his condemnation of them. He
would take me gently by the hand, I'm sure, and lead me into some
sort of appreciation of the simple forms of more complex music.
In my next reincarnation I hope to get an early start with Deems
Taylor and find a way to enjoy music. I'm afraid it's too late to try
in this life.

Next winter when Deems Taylor comes back with the New
York Philharmonic Sunday afternoon concerts, I think I'll stay home
and listen. Some gasoline company ought to pay Deems Taylor and
the New York Philharmonic to stay off the air on Sunday afternoons,
because they're so much better than Sunday afternoon motoring ...
with anybody's gas.

--Don Herold in Judge, Vol. 112,
No. 2703 (June 1937), page 22.

• ARTURO TOSCANINI AND THE N.B.C. SYMPHONY ORCHESTRA

The late William J. Henderson was the only first-line newspaper music critic one could read with respect in recent years, but

there was one subject on which his emotions got the better of his mind. He was irritated by the commotion over Toscanini: the New York Philharmonic-Symphony Orchestra and the music of Bee-thoven and Brahms, he insisted, would remain when Toscanini had gone. He was irritated because the commotion was made by people who could not themselves have distinguished Toscanini from any other conductor, good or bad, and who knew his greatness only from ceaseless public proclamation of the fact. And his irritation led Henderson to contend that it would have been better not to proclaim Toscanini's greatness, and to have a less great conductor at the head of the Philharmonic-Symphony--which was as absurd as to contend that since many people pretend to admire Cézanne only because of what other people have said about him, these others should not have said it, and he should not have painted.

Henderson, we may assume, would have been irritated by the renewed and greater commotion over the recent Toscanini broad-casts. He would have insisted that among the countless listeners only a few really could appreciate what in Toscanini's performances the excitement was about. He would have been aware that N.B.C.'s objective was not to benefit our musical life--not "to enrich musical appreciation," not "to encourage the support of local symphony orchestras"--but to benefit N.B.C. in its competition with Columbia. He would have pointed out that in accomplishing its objective N.B.C. had in fact damaged the orchestra of the country: by scheduling the broadcasts on the night when these orchestras gave their principal series of concerts it diminished their audiences, and this after luring away some of their best players. And he would have proceeded to a conclusion justified to a degree by the damage but not by the false pretensions. For the fact is that we have rarely got the good things in art for good reasons and under good conditions; and it would be folly to reject them when they come for bad reasons and under bad conditions--to reject the performances of a Toscanini, as Henderson and others would have us do, because we owe them to the fact that they serve the ends of N.B.C., or Mr. Sarnoff, or Mr. Chotzinoff, or because they provide an occasion for phony pretentions and other imitating forms of human weakness. What Henderson wanted done the Philharmonic-Symphony Society finally did--with the result that a year later we still had, true enough, the Philharmonic-Symphony Orchestra and the music of Beethoven and Brahms, but these as conducted by [John] Barbi-rolli, which Henderson did not like very much (and we had them, incidentally, not for good reasons).

N.B.C. having set out to bring Toscanini's performances to the ears of radio listeners, we do best to ignore motives and consider results; and I would say the undertaking was only partly successful. One hundred per cent transmission would have been defeated in varying degrees by the inadequate reception in many homes; but even one hundred per cent reception would have been defeated by the losses in transmission. The shape that Toscanini gave a work in time was completely transmitted; the correlated shape in tone was often altered by monitoring in the control room: as Toscanini built up a tonal mass the monitor cut it down; when he reduced it below a certain point the monitor built it up. What, moreover, Toscanini made distant, the monitor brought near; what he veiled, the monitor made clear and bright--which wrought havoc with things like Debussy's "The Sea" and Berlioz's "Queen Mab."

But there were losses even before the loss from monitoring. Privately made records exist which testify to the fact that these broadcast performances originating in the acoustically dead N.B.C. studio lacked the richness of sound of broadcast performances origin-ating in resonant Carnegie Hall. Moreover, to hear the broadcast performance of the Overture to "Semiramide" after the performance of the work recorded by Toscanini with the Philharmonic-Symphony two years ago--to hear the absence in one of the miraculous con-tours and colorings of the other--was to realize how far the N.B.C. Symphony Orchestra was from being able to produce all that Tos-canini could imagine. And for some time the performances gave evidence of lack of inner repose and ease in Toscanini himself--most strikingly in the nervous, tense performance of Mozart's G Minor Symphony at the first broadcast, and again at the first Carnegie Hall concert in the tense, hurried, drive performance of Beethoven's Ninth, in which even the strings that are the glory of the N.B.C. Symphony sounded dry and harsh. But at the second Carnegie Hall concert one could infer equilibrium inside Toscanini from the performance of Verdi's Requiem outside--its controlled flow, controlled intensity, controlled power, its plastic perfection, its loveliness of sound (one noted, however, occasional deficiencies in woodwinds and brass). And here, for the first time, what his unique powers created one heard in its entirety.

In this series, as always, one was appalled by Toscanini's waste of those powers on things like Martucci's "Tarantella," Tom-masini's "Carnival of Venice," Saint Saën's "Danse Macabre," or even Brahm's Serenade in A. That, one comes to realize, is some-thing one must take with Toscanini; other things are the unctuous voices of announcers, their pretentious mouthing of foreign names, the rubbish they are given to speak about the music.

--B. H. Haggin in The Nation,
Vol. 146, No. 12 (March 19,
1938), pages 338-339.

• THE TOWN CRIER (CBS, 1933-1943)

The town crier's bell tinkles. A soft, precise voice--either concealing a peppermint lozenge or a lisp--says, "This is Woollcott speaking." The voice rises when it encounters an anecdote and may even pass on to a second anecdote before springing the nub of the first, pattering along about it's owner's experiences, about people

and events the owner has met. You're suddenly surprised to find
yourself smiling. The voice is saying, surprised too: "Oh dear,
that was a joke, wasn't it?" You grow accustomed to the embryonic
lisp or the occult peppermint lozenge long before the voice ends with:
"This is your oral correspondent of the air" and retires, and you
want more of it. Perhaps one of these days, when the voice is so
shamelessly betraying its owner's confidences, we shall learn whether
it is a peppermint lozenge or a lisp. Either, when assisting Mr.
[Alexander] Woollcott, would be sweet.

> --Cyrus Fisher in The Forum and
> Century, Vol. 90, No. 5 (No-
> vember 1933), page 320.

* VIC AND SADE (NBC, 1932-1944)

Here is another toiling camp follower in the wake of the
continued serial type of program popularized by Amos 'n' Andy
and Myrt and Marge. Arthur Van Harvey has a few moments of
life as "Vic" but the other two principals, Bernardine Flynn's
"Sade" and Master Billy Idelson's "Rush," freeze the action and
destroy the sense of actuality. The program is parsimoniously
produced. There is much shouting over fences at neighbors who
don't reply because they don't exist.

> --Cyrus Fisher in The Forum and
> Century, Vol. 89, No. 5 (May
> 1933), page 318.

* THE WAR OF THE WORLDS (CBS, October 30, 1938)

The mass hysteria that broke loose on the night of October
30 when Orson Welles broadcast H. G. Wells's War of the Worlds
with variations is almost as disturbing to any thoughtful person
as the attack of the Martians was terrifying to those who took it
literally. By now the editorial writers and columnists have listed
all its more obvious causes: the psychological carry-over from the
days and nights of the European crisis, when the listening mass was
in a constant state of excitement at the incredible happenings in
Berchetsgaden, Godesberg, and Munich which turned out to be real;
the compulsive force of the human voice issuing from the upper air;
the mass attitude toward the wonder workings of science, which has
become quite as credulous as that of the Dark Ages toward religious
miracles.

These are the main immediate causes, but all of them stem
from a deeper source--the sea of insecurity and actual ignorance

over which a superficial literacy and sophistication are spread like
a thin crust. In a world where everyone knows the latest news and
few understand its meaning, it is perhaps not surprising that the
broadcast of an imaginary catastrophe only a little more fantastic
than some of the major events of the past few months should have
causes this undertide of conscious and subconscious fear to burst
forth in all its foolish and pathetic and terrifying manifestations.

These manifestations, too, have been thoroughly exploited by
the press, and they were not confined to the uninitiated. One
Southern newspaper summoned its staff to get out an extra; it is
reliably reported that an N.B.C. executive, inadvertently tuning in
on a C.B.S. station, nearly fainted at the thought that his own
system had been scooped on a story so colossal that neither system
could exist long enough to relate it.

It is easy to point out that if casual listeners casually turning
the dial--and their names seem to be legion--had stopped to think
they would have discovered their error at least within a few minutes.
The fact that they did not is what makes the mass flight from mythical monsters not merely a funny story but a significant social phenomenon.

One of the dangerous results of the whole occurrence was
the automatic suggestion of radio censorship, but fortunately the
FCC shows no sign of taking the proposal seriously. For the rest,
it provided a new insight into the power of radio. The disembodied
voice has a far greater force than the printed word, as Hitler has
discovered. If the Martian incident serves as even a slight inocula-
tion against our next demagogue's appeal for a red hunt or an anti-
Semitic drive it will have had its constructive effect.
                                --The Nation, Vo. 147, No. 20
                                (November 12, 1938), page 498.

*   *   *

All unwittingly Mr. Orson Welles and the Mercury Theater of
the Air have made one of the most fascinating and important demon-
strations of all time. They have proved that a few effective voices,
accompanied by sound effects, can so convince masses of people of
a totally unreasonable, completely fantastic proposition as to create
nation-wide panic.

They have demonstrated more potently than any argument,
demonstrated beyond question of a doubt, the appalling dangers and
enormous effectiveness of popular and theatrical demagoguery.

They have cast a brilliant and cruel light upon the failure
of popular education.

They have shown up the incredible stupidity, lack of nerve
and ignorance of thousands.

They have proved how easy it is to start a mass delusion.

They have uncovered the primeval fears lying under the thinnest surface of the so-called civilized man.

They have shown that man, when the victim of his own gullibility, turns to the government to protect him against his own errors of judgment.

The newspapers are correct in playing up this story over every other news event in the world. It is the story of the century.

And far from blaming Mr. Orson Welles, he ought to be given a Congressional medal and a national prize for having made the most amazing and important of contributions to the social sciences. For Mr. Orson Welles and his theater have made a greater contribution to an understanding of Hitlerism, Mussolinism, Stalinism, anti-Semitism and all the other terrorisms of our times than all the words about them that have been written by reasonable men. They have made the reductio ad absurdum of mass manias. They have thrown more light on recent events in Europe leading to the Munich pact than everything that has been said on the subject by all the journalists and commentators.

Hitler managed to scare all Europe to its knees a month ago, but he at least had an army and an air force to back up his shrieking words.

But Mr. Welles scared thousands into demoralization with nothing at all.

That historic hour on the air was an act of unconscious genius, performed by the very innocence of intelligence.

Nothing whatever about the dramatization of the War of the Worlds was in the least credible, no matter at what point the hearer might have tuned in. The entire verisimilitude was in the names of a few specific places. Monsters were depicted of a type that nobody has ever seen, equipped with "rays" entirely fantastic; they were described as "straddling the Pulaski Skyway" and throughout the broadcast they were referred to as Martians, men from another planet.

A twist of the dial would have established for anybody that the national catastrope was not being noted on any other station. A second of logic would have dispelled any terror. A notice that the broadcast came from a non-existent agency would have awakened skepticism.

A reference to the radio program would have established that the War of the Worlds was announced in advance.

The time element was obviously lunatic.

Listeners were told that "within two hours three million people have moved out of New York"--an obvious impossibility for the most disciplined army moving exactly as planned, and a double fallacy because, only a few minutes before, the news of the arrival of the monster had been announced.

And of course it was not even a planned hoax. Nobody was more surprised at the result than Mr. Welles. The public was told at the beginning, at the end and during the course of the drama that it was a drama.

But eyewitnesses presented themselves; the report became second hand, third hand, fourth hand, and became more and more credible, so that nurses and doctors and National Guardsmen rushed to defense.

When the truth became known the reaction was also significant. The deceived were furious and of course demanded that the state protect them, demonstrating that they were incapable of relying on their own judgment.

Again there was a complete failure of logic. For if the deceived had thought about it they would realize that the greatest organizers of mass hysterias and mass delusions today are states using the radio to excite terrors, incite hatreds, inflame masses, win mass support for policies, create idolatries, abolish reason and maintain themselves in power.

The immediate moral is apparent if the whole incident is viewed in reason: no political body must ever, under any circumstances, obtain a monopoly of radio.

The second moral is that our popular and universal education is failing to train reason and logic, even in the educated.

The third is that the popularization of science has led to gullibility and new superstitions, rather than to skepticism and the really scientific attitude of mind.

The fourth is that the power of mass suggestion is the most potent force today and that the political demagogue is more powerful than all the economic forces.

For, mind you, Mr. Welles was managing an obscure program, competing with one of the most popular entertainments on the air!

The conclusion is that the radio must not be used to create mass prejudices and mass divisions and schisms, either by private individuals or by government or its agencies, or its officials, or its opponents.

If people can be frightened out of their wits by mythical men from Mars, they can be frightened into fanaticism by the fear of Reds, or convinced that America is in the hands of sixty families, or aroused to revenge against any minority, or terrorized into subservience to leadership because of any imaginable menace.

The technique of modern mass politics calling itself democracy is to create a fear--a fear of economic royalists, or of Reds, or of Jews, or of starvation, or of an outside enemy--and exploit that fear into obtaining subservience in return for protection.

I wrote in this column a short time ago that the new warfare was waged by propaganda, the outcome depending on which side could first frighten the other to death.

The British people were frightened into obedience to a policy a few weeks ago by a radio speech and by digging a few trenches in Hyde Park, and afterward led to hysterical jubilation over a catastrophic defeat for their democracy.

But Mr. Welles went all the politicians one better. He made the scare to end scares, the menace to end menaces, the unreason to end unreason, the perfect demonstration that the danger is not from Mars but from the theatrical demagogue.

> --Dorothy Thompson in New York
> Herald Tribune (November 2,
> 1938).

- WHAT MAKES YOU TICK? (ABC, 1948-1949)

In the gaudy and discordant symphony of our life and times, a completely sour note is often struck by a disillusioned wife shooting her philandering mate in the back. Or in reversal of this role, erotic and slightly imperfect herself, she may succumb to the blandishments of, say, an itinerant optometrist. Gazing into her nearsighted eyes while fitting her new rhinestone harlequin reading glasses, he has given her an entirely revised outlook and she flies with him to Kansas City, where she hopes to live happily in sin forever after.

When this sort of thing crops up, professional viewers-with-alarm like to bundle up the whole mess and lay it at the door of radio's soap operas. Trying to keep up with things like John's Other Wife may breed in the heart of the little woman, stout homemaker that she is, restlessness and vague yearnings to live dangerously. As she listens and irons, irons and listens, to Gale Golightly, she works out adroit little plots patterned after Gale's adventures but with herself as heroine.

Soon she begins to think in terms of champagne suppers in strange men's apartments. Sometimes she pretends that she is really a Persian princess, stolen by gypsies and abandoned in Long Beach as an infant. Or she conjures up escapist dreams in which she drops a soupçon of cyanide in her dull husband's mustache cup, or gives a cold drink to an old tramp who bequeaths her four million dollars.

Naturally, this blurs for her the milder excitement of Saturday night bingo and the bucolic pleasures of an Odd Fellows' picnic. Prolonged exposure to the evil forebodings and high imagery of the daytime radio serial can, in the opinion of many experts, lead to dire neurotic consequences. In short, listening to these volcanic sagas of love and romantic villainy day in and day out, a person can go nuts.

Undoubtedly with this thought in mind, Procter & Gamble have added recently to their radio diet for housewives, the services of two trained psychiatrists in a brave new program provocatively called, What Makes You Tick?, heard Monday through Friday, at 10:15 a.m., PDT, over ABC network stations.

It is this kind of forward-thinking step that renews faith in Big Business. Faced with the accusation that they were slowly but surely undermining the mental structure of American womanhood, Procter & Gamble did something about it!

"Yes, indeed," they must have reasoned, "Joyce Jordan, Helen Trent, and The Second Mrs. Burton have sold an awful lot of soap, and if their memoirs are causing any mental irregularity, we're going to see that our listeners are educated in the care and feeding of neuroses."

Understandably conservative, the advocates of gentle Ivory Flakes usage on a world-wide basis are proceeding cautiously with this new public service. John K. M. McCaffery, master of ceremonies, hastens to point out that the program does not attempt clinical psychiatry--merely a sort of psychiatric "game." This is the same soothing principle of harmless deception which prompts the rigging up of children's barber shops in the merry-go-round motif, thereby disguising as a lark the grim business of getting a haircut. Unlike the youngsters who are never taken in by the carousel dodge, screaming just as vigorously on a pseudo charger as they would in a plain barber chair, contestants on What Makes You Tick? seem to enjoy their ordeal immensely and bare their failings.

The format of the show is based on the patient's ability at self-rating a specified trait or habit. "How much pride do you have?" Mr. McCaffery asked a Washington Heights, New York City, matron recently. "Would you rate yourself at 50 per cent? 75 per cent?"

Neuroses on a percentage basis must be a new development.
At least, I hadn't heard of it before. It may very well be an exclusive Procter & Gamble process, like the Camay "Come-closer complexion" which today has the scientific world on its ear. Anyway,
the lady from Washington Heights said she thought she was 60 per
cent proud. Whereupon Mr. McCaffrey proceeded with the set of
questions which would authentically determine her correct pride
rating.

Personally, I was able to decipher nothing of her inner workings from her replies, except that if her husband asked her to tuck
him in bed, she would do so willingly, and that she would probably
make up with him if he beat her over the head with a heavy cane.
Oh yes, and that she did not enjoy asking him for money, nor did
he enjoy giving it to her.

These answers, however, have special significance for accredited psychiatrists like the program's experts, Drs. Leon Arons
and Sidney Roslow. Concealed in the draperies or some place off
stage, they can tabulate such symptoms, and at the close of the program a grand prize is awarded to the patient coming closest to pre-
dicting her or his own rating.

Each guinea pig also gets a modest gift merely for climbing
up onto the table and letting the radio audience ogle through the
psychiatric microscope. This premium for exhibitionism is, of course,
unnecessary, as the rise of the audience-participation show has
proved indisputably that every studioful of people can produce vol-
unteers for any stunt, experiment, contest, or embarrassment conceivable to the human mind. It is a nice gesture, though, and since
many of the gifts are washable, like underwear and blankets, it also
affords a gentle plug for gentle Ivory Flakes.

The position of What Makes You Tick? in the daytime line-up
reflects strategic timing, since it precedes the catastrophic chain of
events through which the soap opera fan struggles daily, pausing
only long enough to change heroines and pick up a fresh sponsor.
Starting with a stimulating bracer of psychological chit-chat and a
few playful diagnoses of folks in the audience, our homemaker, busy
in her kitchen, is ready to cope with any ruthless cads, pregnant
lady internes, crippled widows with no money for crutches, local
Errol Flynns, or beautiful, misunderstood stepmothers.

Unfortunately, a contest format does not fit into a fifteen-
minute segment, especially a contest with psychological overtones.
Originally heard last summer on Sunday afternoons, What Makes You
Tick? was a half-hour show. Now cut to fifteen minutes and with
the added responsibility of a sponsor, proceedings are rather
cramped. Jammed into the quarter-hour session are three interviews,
interpretation of the three subjects' reactions, an explanation of the
program, two lengthy commercials, and awarding of the prizes.

Somehow you get the impression that the broadcast is being held in
a revolving door.

Frankly, I like to think that I am as neurotic as the next
one, so I am avidly looking forward to the day when Mr. McCaffery
finds himself facing a real, live psychopathic specimen across his
microphone. He may not necessarily recognize the symptoms. Perhaps only Drs. Arons and Roslow, peering from their peepholes in
the curtains, will deduce from her answers that here is a "case"!

Now the question is, what would they do? Would they tell
her that she had won the grand prize, thus luring her directly
into a strait-jacket camouflaged as a mink coat? Or, like a store
detective trailing a shoplifter, would they wait until she was safely
out of the studio? After all, she might turn out to be a Russian
schoolteacher.

But let Mr. McCaffery cross that bridge when he comes to it.
Meantime What Makes You Tick? has made a fine beginning. While
this pioneer effort does not do the complete job of rehabilitating the
soap opera addict, still it is a step in the right direction and a
courageous example for other sponsors.

Shoving Drew Pearson aside for a moment, I'd like to predict
that What Makes You Tick? will eventually abandon its present general approach for a more specific one. By simply sending in the
top of a pair of her husband's pajamas, which has been laundered
in Ivory Flakes, the listener will receive, in a plain wrapper, a live
psychiatrist. Deftly tossing her onto his portable couch, and plac-
ing a cool hand on her fevered brow, he will personally stroke her
subconscious, through the courtesy of Procter & Gamble. And with
the high cost of living in general, and psychiatrists in particular,
this will be quite a boon to the family's budget of ego.

Yes, as young Dr. Malone would say, this is only the beginning. I can see our beloved sponsor going on to bigger things.
I can see imposing, modern buildings, with fine, strong bars at the
windows and soft, padded walls.

And I can hear those two lovable old characters, "Ma"
Procter and "Big Sister" Gamble, with hearts full of joy and pockets
full of money, voice a beautiful promise for tomorrow, "Yes, we'll
build 'em, and if we keep right on with soap operas, we can fill
'em."

> --Mary McSkimming in Script
> (November 1948), pages 42-45.

● DON WILSON

There's much in a voice. It can be strong, vibrant,

confident; warm, persuasive, infectious. The voice of Wilson, currently heard on The Jack Benny Show (and other programs), has
these qualities. It has been termed: "America's finest selling
voice." Wilson made his radio debut in 1923 and has run the gamut
of announcing from grand opera to sports on hundreds of programs
making his one of the most familiar voices in the US. He is in his
18th year with Benny.

> --Fortnight (November 12, 1951),
> page 28.

● WALTER WINCHELL

Few people do the individual job turned in by Walter Winchell.
Each week I expect to learn he's in a hospital. He burns up words
so consumingly, smoke gets in my ears.

> --Dale Armstrong in Rob Wagner's
> Script (December 16, 1939),
> page 26.

● TONY WONS

This voice has a lush deepness which ideally agrees with the
collection of philosophical tags it expresses, most of which have been
borrowed from minds long dead.

> --Cyrus Fisher in The Forum and
> Century, Vol. 88, No. 2 (Au-
> gust 1932), page 127.

● ALEXANDER WOOLLCOTT

That darling old male squealer, Alexander Woollcott, is back
on the air, bursting with enthusiasms and flushed with his whims.
I welcome him back with open ears, because he's one of the few
talkers in radio who thinks more than an inch deep or who gives us
credit for more than 8-year-old intelligence.

I was delighted to have Mr. Woollcott recently hop hob-nailed
on one of my pet aversions ... art museums. He had a grand idea
for distributing the Mellon art collection around all over the country,
one picture to Detroit and one to Nashville, and so on, and then
keeping them moving around like Chautauqua bell-ringers.

> --Don Herold in Judge, Vol. 112,
> No. 2701 (April 1937), page 23.

● YOUR HIT PARADE (NBC, 1935-1959)

    At a cost of millions of dollars, a transcontinental survey, and an exhaustive analysis, compilation and recapitulation is made of the country's choice of the week's most popular songs. So what? Any college sophomore could give them an equally good list for $2.

--Don Herold in Judge, Vol. 113,
No. 2704 (July 1937), page 22.

PART II

•

TELEVISION CRITICISM

- TELEVISION (IN CASE YOU'RE INTERESTED)

When the sacred duty of reporting on radio for Life was intrusted to me, I made a solemn vow always to look on the beautiful and romantic side of broadcasting and never to annoy anyone with the sordid and indecent technicalities of the business. I resolved that such words as "hook-up" and "grid trouble" and "frequency" should not sully my lips--or rather my typewriter.

Now here I am smack up against Television and once more a Victorian inhibition will have to be swept away by the march of progress. Because you can't talk about television without getting technical; so far, it is nothing but a heap of mechanics. At present, it is in the state that radio was in along about 1908, or motion pictures in 1895; but that doesn't mean that we shall have to wait twenty or thirty years before ship launchings and monument unveilings can be seen in our own homes. No, things move faster these days and I know optimists who are looking forward to seeing this fall's football games right in their own living-rooms, without risking life and limb on the Boston Post Road.

There are three separate phases in the development of television. The first is sending photographs by radio. This is being done every day and is mere child's play. Try and do it. The second is transmitting motion pictures by radio, Heaven help us! The third is televising actual events. And that's the thing that makes sport magnates, movie kings and theater owners tremble in their little boots.

Until a few weeks ago it was impossible to send anything but highly illuminated scenes over the radio because the photoelectric cell, which is to light waves what the microphone is to sound waves, demands intense illumination. If you know anything about photography, you will see why when you realize that the photoelectric cell--the eye of the contrivance--is only exposed to the scene for one fifty-thousandth of a second. Thus it was impossible to televise any scene in natural sunlight or any scene with human actors--except for very short flashes--because of the intensity of the illumination.

The Bell Telephone Company has a new system of television whereby it is possible to transmit scenes taken in ordinary sunlight.

The necessary light at the receiving end is furnished by a series
of amplifying tubes.

Are you still with me, or have you gone home?

Another present defect of television is being rapidly overcome.
So far television has only been able to show stationary or slow-
moving objects without blurring the picture. Also it has only been
able to show its scene on a small screen two inches square. Most
of the machines in this country are limited to a capacity of 40,000
light impulses a second, which is just as though a motion picture
were projected at less than half the normal rate of speed.

Professor Karolus of Berlin has brought the speed up to
80,000 light impulses a second and thinks it is possible to speed
up his mechanism even more. To transmit a four inch square
picture would require 160,000 impulses. The Herr Professor is now
able to project his visions on a three and one-half inch screen.

We are getting along, but if I were you I'd put in my application for those football tickets now, just in case.

I wish I'd never got into this. I wish I had decided to write
about the Night in Paris Hour. But as long as I have gone this
far, I am going right ahead with C. Francis Jenkins and his radio
motion pictures. I like the story of Mr. Jenkins and his inventions.
It is a Greek drama.

Mr. Jenkins was one of the inventors of the motion picture
projector. For his part in perfecting the machine he received a
measly $2,500. All these years he has been waiting for his revenge.
He has been working nights to try to find something that would
give the movies a sock in the eye. And now he's hit it. Mr. Jenkins has demonstrated radio movies in his home in Washington, D.C.
As "Bugs" Baer once said, the big problem of the future will be
how to keep covered wagons out of the dining-room.

Incidentally, all the contrivances necessary for constructing
a television receiving set are now on the market. What you will
receive after the set is all made, I do not know. But I cheerfully
recommend this new form of indoor sport to anyone who wants
either to become famous or go insane.

> --Agnes Smith in Life, Vol. 92,
> No. 2390 (August 23, 1928),
> pages 7-8.

● HOLLYWOOD'S GREATEST ENIGMA--TELEVISION

Whenever people ask me whether television will take the place

of the movies, I blush, pant rapidly, stammer, and finally manage
to ask them whether they think the automobile will ever take the
place of the horse. To which they reply (if they bother to reply
at all, and some of them do not) that the motor car has already
taken the place of the horse, which is exactly what I want them to
say. Because, if you examine that statement carefully, it turns
out to be one of the silliest on record. For certain common purposes, the car has displaced the horse; but even that was a long
and tedious process. There were as many horses between the shafts
in 1912 as there were before Ford ever tinkered or Selden took out
a patent. What's more: if the motor car had merely taken the
place of the horse, it would be comparatively unimportant today.
Actually, millions of people own cars who never owned--because
they couldn't afford to own--horses.

Later, people said that the movies never would take the place
of the horse--I mean, of the theater. And there, too, the facts
are illuminating. To be sure there used to be eighty legitimate
theaters in New York City and now there are less; there used to
be shows with living actors in hundreds of small towns, and now
there are not, unless the Federal Theater comes around. But,
again, if the movies had merely taken the place of some other form
of entertainment, they wouldn't be important, Hollywood would lack
dazzle, and you would not be reading a magazine devoted to the
pictures. The movies are important, not for what they displaced,
but for the new things they did; for the new art they created;
above all, for the new millions to whom they brought entertainment--
millions who didn't know the theater at all.

The above ought to make clear my slant in this matter. Actually, I refuse to make short-range prophecies; for long-range,
anything is possible in fifty or a hundred years. We have speeded
up invention so much in the past two generations that in a century
all our present forms of entertainment may be outmoded and forgotten.

We have also speeded up economic confusion and military
preparation so much in the past ten years that within fifty years the
world may not have time or capacity for entertainment--by which I
mean that too many of us may be dead. Anything is possible in a
world so inventive, imaginative, enterprising, and stupid as ours.

But, for the immediate future, I do not think that television
is going to take the place of the movies (or of the radio) and I have
no concern in seeing that it does. Quite the contrary, I hope to
enjoy all three. If I saw no future for television except as a re-
placer, I would have little interest in it. Like radio and the movies,
television will have to create something of its own if it wants to become interesting and significant. I think it will.

When it does, will it have any effect on the movies? That's
a different and a better question. Let me say at once that for a
long time, whatever effect television may have will not touch the

essential parts of a movie program. I foresee--on the basis of current experiments in television--two reasonable effects on the movies,
one being only partial, the other, I sincerely hope, an improvement.
Before giving you the details, I propose to pause and bring the
readers of this magazine up to date in regard to recent television
equipment and uses.

As you probably know, television is a name given to several
methods for the instant transmission of visual effects--just as radio
is a method for the transmission of audible effects. When you talk
into a microphone, you set up certain disturbances which are trans-
formed and transmitted electrically and are changed back into sound
when they reach your radio receiver. When you move in front of a
television camera (or scanner) you create certain disturbances
which go through much the same process, and are turned back into
pictures on your television receiver. Because these pictures follow
one another at a certain speed, they seem to have motion, just as
the quickly changing pictures on your movie screen seem to have
motion. The scanners and receivers may be of various types, but
the end result is pretty much the same. You get what seems to be
a moving picture.

About a year ago, the average size of this screen was eight
by eleven inches, or seven by ten--about the size of an ordinary
business letterhead, turned sideways. This is still a common size,
but two experiments are being made: for a table-set in which the
picture is almost miniature, about half the regular size; and for a
screen about two feet by eighteen inches; and, in addition, television pictures have been projected, by an ingenious invention, on a
screen approximating the usual movie-house size. I know of no advantage claimed for the smaller size, except economy. The larger
sizes are important. The small screen of television distresses
people considerably at first; and, even after a year, the British
public has registered its opinion that a larger size would be agreeable. I have a hunch that something approaching the middle-
large size may become standard.

But size alone is not important. The picture that comes on
the screen has to be clear; the moving figures have to be sharply
defined; and those in the background must not blur (unless you
use blurring for a special effect). Remember any movie you have
seen lately and think of a long shot in a cabaret or on an athletic
field. You have seen quite clearly little figures in the far background; you knew what they were doing and why they were there.
Television is slowly working up to that same clarity and definition,
but it has some distance to go.

If you want close-ups in television, you can get them, at the
expense of the rest of the cast; if you use semicloseups, you may
get three characters comfortably into your picture, but a fourth
may not be clear, and you won't get any of them from head to foot.

For that, you have to move them a little farther into the background --or wait for new cameras which are being perfected regularly.

Already cameras are in use which are reported to be ten times as sensitive as those of a year ago; and a year ago the cameras were vastly better than those of 1936. So progress is made--and remains to be made. A "mob scene" of ten or fifteen has been televised, with reasonably good effect. But a lot remains to be done before the television director can handle a group of people as easily before his scanner as a movie director does before the camera.

I don't suppose the technical details about lights and tubes, upon which television scanning depends, are of great interest to the layman. But one thing has proved of overwhelming interest: the new use of the latest cameras. They are mounted on trucks, and, accompanied by an ultrashort-wave transmitter, roll to an appointed spot. Then one of the true miracles of modern days occurs. Because these mobile units can be set up near a grandstand and transmit to you a baseball game, pitch by pitch, hit by hit, errors and runs and put-outs--not a few hours later, but at the very moment they occur. Tennis matches, parades, inaugurations, boat races, horse races, prize fights, naval reviews, and any number of stunts are made instantly available, and the scanner gives you events completely, including accidental excitements.

Last year during the two-minute silence at the cenotaph in London, on Armistice Day, a man broke through the crowd and shouted out that the King and his ministers and all the notables assembled were hypocrites, planning another war--and he was seen and heard at that very moment, thirty miles or forty miles away. Familiar as I am with the workings of television, that still strikes me as miraculous--and exciting.

Now this portion of television (which the British call "outdoor broadcasts") obviously competes with the newsreel, and this is one of the two points at which the movies will be affected by television. Not that the newsreel becomes superfluous. Let us say that you are busy on Tuesday afternoon--and are interested in the World Series game played that day. You can't watch the game on your television receiver, so if you want to see what happened, you go that evening (or the next day) to the movies--and you want the newsreel just as much. Television, in short, loses by being immediate and instantaneous, just as it gains. But a rival for the newsreel it certainly is. In one theater, at least, in London, arrangements have been made for television spot news to be received on the picture screen. I have not yet had a report on the reactions of the audience.

I do know the effect of these spot events on the heads of British television, however, and on the people who receive the events at home, on regular size small screens.

A year ago my correspondents in England were pretty enthusiastic about television and cited to me such ambitious projects
as an act of Tristan and Isolde, a performance of Journey's End
or of the American comedy, Once in a Lifetime, all of which seem
to have given great pleasure. Today, these same correspondents
are even more enthusiastic, but out of ten highlights they mention,
seven or eight are sure to be spot events, not sketches or plays in
the studios.

And, to make it pretty official, take the case of Sir Stephen
Tallents. (He is, I understand, responsible for publicity for the
British Broadcasting Corporation which runs all the television experiments in England. As part of radio, television is an enterprise
under the government; every owner of a radio instrument pays a
tax, and part of this tax is devoted to television experiments. In
other words, experiments in television are conducted in England by
the government, in public, at the expense of the public. Here they
are conducted by private individuals or corporations, at private expense.)

Well, a few months ago a magazine announced in an ad that
its people had observed television in England where it has "failed
dismally." Sir Stephen wrote to complain, to object, and to give
proof. The magazine apologized. Of supreme interest, however,
was the proof which Sir Stephen gave. He said that the British
were enthusiastic about--a boat race, a prize fight, a tennis match,
and so on. Every single program he mentioned was an event, an
outdoor broadcast. Perhaps some people liked the studio stuff; they
were not sufficiently impressed on the mind of one of the chiefs of
television in England even to be mentioned.

If this direction of television were to continue, you can see
that no effect on the feature movie would ever occur. But television began with the effort to transmit a picture of someone in a
room, and there are a dozen reasons why studio work will continue
to be an important part of a television program.

One reason--a mighty good one--is that parades and proces-
sions can become deadly dull. Some of the things you remember
best of the newsreel are the accidental shots, the lucky breaks--
and you can't count on them.

Sporting events and beauty contests will always be good because you don't know what the outcome will be; but you do know
what the beginning and middle and end of most parades will be.
Moreover, a full program of news events would be hard to compose
(until television becomes a network, which is still in the future)
as there simply aren't enough in any one city to go round; and
finally, the observer will probably grow weary after the first few
hours. What is worse, the outdoor events, coming when a vast
majority of the population is either at work or at play (outside

the home), will be seen by only a tiny fraction of the television fans.

So television will have to provide, as every good form of entertainment does, a certain variety. Variety it may be in the old sense of vaudeville--as many acts which are essentially vaudeville go well on the television screen: I can see acrobats and magicians and solo dancers having a wonderful time and--more important-- giving the audience a wonderful time. I have a list of a dozen individuals who are "made for television." Solo performers on musical instruments need to be made interesting as things to see as well as to hear; but it can be done.

And the whole field of demonstration is available, from how to cook to how to learn jiujitsu, not to mention a lot of highbrow subjects which will become vastly entertaining when you can show what you are talking about.

Still, that leaves out the drama, and both on the air and the screen we are lovers of the dramatic moment. In England, a number of quick critics have reared up and said that the place to get drama is in the theater, so the mobile unit ought to be backed up to the stage door, the scanner inserted in the wings, and the play or musical show or circus taken right on the spot.

The reason they say this is that the dramatic programs have not been tremendously satisfying. Both the limitations of the equipment and, I suspect, the limitations of the actors, have troubled the enthusiasts. So they say: abandon the studio and go where good drama can be found.

This is exactly what the movies tried to do at the beginning. Luckily for the movies, the attempt was abandoned. In the silent days, the effect was pretty awful: there is the story (told in the recent History of Motion Pictures by Bardèche and Brasillach) of the famous French actor who refused to cut a line of a classic speech, when he was doing it for the camera, and stood there spouting unheard words for minutes at a time; in America the movies tried to repeat stage effects and stage situations until they learned better. Nowadays, movies are primarily movies, which is why they are good.

And, if television means to be good, it will have to use its material in the way best suited to the instruments of television. Merely to take a stage play or even a vaudeville bill or a circus will not make good television. It will appeal as novelty for a while; it may do as a stopgap; but in the end you have to roll your own--or create your own stuff--to succeed.

Here we come to the second place at which television may have an effect on the movies--the effect which, I said, may be an improvement. I suspect that one weakness of television drama so

far has been in the acting. Neither stage nor movie acting seems
to be exactly what's needed. This is the hardest thing to explain
about television--harder than all the technical details--because you
have to feel it yourself. And you do feel it: you feel that the
person on a television screen is more in the room with you than the
same person on the stage or on the screen.

One reason may be that you get this person while you are,
yourself, in your own room; it may have something to do with the
size and the sharpness of the picture--but, whatever the cause,
it is an undoubted effect. You know that the actor is a mile or forty
miles away--yet he seems to be there with you.

And most television acting has neglected this effect, so that
the actors still go on as if you were across footlights or sitting in
a movie house. They haven't allowed for the chief virtue of television itself, that immediacy--or you might call it "present"--which it
invariably gives.

When this is recognized, I believe that a new style of acting
will develop. Don't ask me now for details--I hope to work them out
in practice, by trial and error. I am convinced that the right kind
of acting will be found and then--this is my hope--if people like it,
when television grows common, that style of acting will have an influence on acting in the movies. I think it will be an easy, unforced,
warm and simple style; and it ought to correct some of the stiffness
and artificiality of movie-acting.

Television, like the movies, is a great "putter-over" of personality, and my guess may turn out wrong. We may develop such
tremendous television personalities that acting will be comparatively
rare, as it is rare among the great personalities of the pictures.
(In nine movies out of ten, you can be sure that the best acting is
done by the men and women who are not the most highly publicized;
these supporting people in the cast have to act to keep their jobs;
the stars keep theirs by their dazzling build-ups.) Yet I am hope-
ful. When we have added a third popular form of entertainment,
the movies and the radio will have another competitor; this competitor,
in a reasonable way, will learn from both during its first ten or
twenty years; after that, it ought to be able to pay back for its
borrowings by doing a little teaching on the side. Certainly a good
movie producer would look with eagerness to see what the new type
of art will develop.

There is no occasion for jealousy and none for alarm. And
the public will be the gainer. Because television will come gradually
into common acceptance--you can't rush a business, which is also an
art, so full of complexities--and, as it comes in, the movies will also
be making progress, and the radio, too. Maybe in a hundred years
all these arts will merge into one. We shan't be there to see--and

anyhow, if the best elements are, as the formula goes, combined, what do we care?

--Gilbert Seldes in Photoplay,
Vol. 52, No. 10 (October 1938),
pages 36 and 94-95.

● RCA-NBC INAUGURAL PROGRAM (NBC, May 10, 1939)*

Inaugurating regular television service, RCA-NBC presented a program Wednesday evening, including an especailly made news-reel, Fred Waring's Orchestra; Helen Lewis, emsee; Richard Rodgers, composer, and Marcy Westcott from the Boys From Syracuse; Bill Farren, the Three Swifts; a Donald Duck cartoon, Donald's Cousin Gus; Earle Larimore and Marjorie Clarke in an Aaron Hoffman sketch. Lowell Thomas and a New York Port Authority trailer.

The program was a complete technical success, especially in view of unfavorable reception conditions obtaining in Radio City, with its many steel buildings. It showed, too, that television has a long way to go to solve its programming, production and talent problems. It showed, too, that a $7\frac{1}{2}$ by 10-inch screen makes for poor watching. Altho there was no semblance of flicker, the 90 minutes resulted in eyestrain.

The punch of the program was probably the actual pick-up from the New York World's Fair. Bill Farren, regular staff NBC an-nouncer, interviewed fair visitors. These interviews showed where television's most important drawing power will come from. There was tremendous impact seeing and hearing Farren and his interviewees as they spoke. Oddly enough, the strong lights needed by tele cameras did not seem especially troublesome, altho they were of enor-mous power.

The small screen and the difficulty yet to be solved of how to get greater scope from the cameras handicapped practically all of the other acts, except Rodgers, the composer, and Miss Westcott. Camera moved from one to another, and since neither required con-siderable range the problem was easy to solve. But in handling the Waring troupe and the Three Swifts the tele camera showed that its directors and producers have far to go. The Swifts are a strong act in any theater, but in trying to show the three of them working simultaneously the punch of the act was lost. When just two or so of the Waring menage were working it was again okeh, but when the ensemble was on the screen the camera's weakness was appa-rent.

---

*The program was reviewed on RCA Television Receiver Style TRK 12, with a $7\frac{1}{2}$" by 10" screen, on station W2XBS.

Greatest sign that NBC is slow on television production came in The Unexpected, a playlet by Aaron Hoffman--an antique if ever there was one. There was no need for doing the piece, and the newness of television is no excuse. It was badly written, badly staged and badly played by Earle Larimore and Marjorie Clarke.

Miss Lewis made an agreeable emsee and successfully blended the various portions of the show. Lowell Thomas, doing his customary news talk, indicated he may not be television fodder. Somehow his bearing makes for good radio listening but bad television watching. Donald Duck, of course, was amusing. Produced in Technicolor, the color contrasts as seen on the tele screen were somewhat freakish.

Sound revolutionized Hollywood. Television may do the same for radio. Acts may no longer work from scripts, and vaudeville acts, used to the help of audiences, will not know how they are going over. Lack of laughter during the Waring and Swift routines showed that unless a method is worked out whereby acts know how they are faring the performers will feel as tho they are working in a vacuum. Should be easy to solve tho.

Tele is here technically, but it is still back in 1936 or 1937 insofar as talent and production are concerned.
                                    --[Jerry] Franken in The Billboard
                                    (May 13, 1939), pages 8-9.

• NBC SECOND REGULAR PROGRAM (NBC, May 12, 1939)*

Second of NBC's regular television programs had Mitzi Green, Ed Herlihy; Novello Brothers, whistling act; Roy Post and his lie detector, a newsreel; a play with Josephine Huston and seven girl emsees, each of whom introduced one act. Girls, who are being tried out for a permanent spot, were Muriel Fleit, Joan Allison, Mary McCormack, Louise Illingston, May Stuart, Evelyn Holt and Sandra Ramoy. Warren Wade, Burk Grotty and Eddie Padula shared the direction.

Eschewing actual comment on the performances, none of which were especially noteworthy, this second program solidified opinion that television's present production methods can be compared only to those of a kindergarten play. Obvious things such as moving out of focus and other roughness in performances seem to this reviewer to be unnecessary. Unnecessary because NBC has had time during the past year or so, at least, to improve methods. Experimentation on

---

*Reviewed on Dumont Television Receiver Style No. 183, with 8x10-inch screen, on station W2XBS.

television technically was done in the studios and laboratories, and the same thing should have been done insofar as production is concerned. A purchaser of a $400 television set is not going to feel any great love to television when the shows provided are about on a par with not very good amateur stuff.

While all television receivers have screens more or less the same size, the 8-by-10 or 7-by-10 screens do not make for much comfort when watched for more than very short times. An offhand opinion, then, is that unless the screens sizes are made larger only outstanding programs will attract audiences as matters now stand. Radio allows for casual listening, but television does not. An hour or more of poor programs will only backfire against television itself.

Dumont receiver model, which sells for $435, gave good reproduction. Altho the screen is a bit larger than the RCA screen on which Wednesday's program was reviewed, the slightly larger area made scant difference. Dumont does not use a mirror as the RCA sets do, and the direct method seems preferable.

But it is still a puzzle to this reviewer that television production methods are so unprofessional.

--[Jerry] Franken in <u>The Billboard</u>
(May 13, 1939), page 8.

• WHAT'S HAPPENED TO TELEVISION?

Television's first year of agony is in the past. It is now in the second year of "hell and growing pains." These were predicted for it when President Roosevelt, the first Chief Executive to be televised, faced the radio cameras at the '39 opening of the New York World's Fair. The presidential smile was the cue for the curtain-raiser of regularly scheduled television programs for public reception in the New York area. The event was heralded as the launching of a "billion-dollar industry." So far it has fallen far short. Hope survives. Scientifically, television is almost ready to go; economically, it is not so frisky.

Where does television stand today? Chiefly in the New York area, about where it was a year ago. There is still only one station, that of the National Broadcasting Company, atop the Empire State Building, fed by programs from Radio City, enlivened and embellished by outdoor events. Home tele-radios are counted at approximately 3,000, while 110 restaurants and taverns in the New York district are equipped to look in.

While the year has been one of travail for the telecasters, in many ways--financially, economically and artistically--it has not been

exactly that for televiewers. They have sat comfortably at home and
with remarkable clarity have been eye-witnesses to numerous television "firsts."

The radio sightseers have seen Columbia play Princeton in
baseball; the Dodgers beat the Giants in an opener; Canzoneri
knocked out in the ring at Madison Square Garden. They have seen
football, collegiate and professional, getting up close to the plays
through the binocular-like views tossed through space from the
sidelines by means of the telephoto lens on the eye of a magic orthi-
con camera. They have seen the bike races, basketball and hockey
at Madison Square Garden; track meets and Ringling Brothers,
Barnum and Bailey circus, wrestling-matches, the St. Patrick's
Day parade and Broadway plays. A bird's-eye view of Manhattan
Island was telecast from an airplane; Easter religious services, the
Easter parade on Fifth Avenue, and no end of vaudeville and films
have been televised. All came through the air true to radio tradition, gratis, in "the public interest, convenience and necessity."

But while the onlookers, scattered as far away as 130 miles,
have been enjoying the new art as a social novelty or otherwise, the
telecasters have been scratching their heads, chiefly to find the
answer to "Who is going to pay for all this?" Already the bill for
research has totaled $26,000,000.

Aware of television's rich relatives--the radio and the movies--
the telecasters have looked to them to find an answer to the riddle
of revenue. They can erect no box-office in the ethereal lobby in
Hollywood style; they have attempted to emulate broadcasting by
displaying cakes of soap and cereal between the innings at baseball
games. They have dared to "subtly" dovetail pictures of products
and banners of trade names with news pictures. For some reason
or other, the eye trained by the movies does not like it. So at the
end of No. 1 year the question mark is as big as ever after the
conundrum, "Who will pay for television?"

Despite the terrific costs, estimated to run from three to ten
times that of a broadcast program, some telecasters still adhere to
the idea that the commercial sponsor is to be the "angel" of their
shows. Others, confessing that the problem of television is no longer
scientific but economic, contend that the solution lies in adapting television to travel on telephone wires. Then, just as the telephone col-
lects for its use, so will television build its box-office in each home.

But the radio people say no. Television belongs to the air.
It's illustrated broadcasting. It is not a "wired wireless" proposition
any more than is broadcasting, which in the beginning was also seen
as being forced to resort to wires in order to operate on a pay-as-
you-listen basis.

Television, the radio promoters assert, will remain on the

wave-lengths; they foresee the nation dotted with automatic ultrashort-wave relay transmitters, each about thirty-five miles apart.
Atop poles about 350 feet high, these miniature stations will bounce
the shows over hill and dale from city to city and state to state.
Advocates of this scheme are so confident of success that they are
suggesting the name "television" should be changed to "radiovision"
as a more accurate description for a nation-wide system, which eventually, they believe, will serve the nation.   They are going ahead on
the theory that the commercial radio sponsor will come to the rescue
as soon as a "circulation" is built up.

The question is asked at this point, "What is holding television back?"

Actually, nothing.   Television today is like a baby learning
to walk.   One does not have to hold a baby very tightly to prevent
him, no matter how rambunctious, from toddling off on a cross-
country hike.   He will get there naturally some day.   So will television find its electrical legs and scamper off across the country,
probably by wire too, with each supplementing the other.

Television is progress, but a gigantic undertaking nurtured
far more scientifically than was broadcasting, which was permitted
to grow just like Topsy.   Nobody worried about the future of broadcasting until it got under way as a national "craze."   Everybody in
radio has been tinkering or worrying about television, even the
Federal Communications Commission.   Broadcasting had none of that
motherly or fatherly guidance or advice.   But television has been
tied to the apron strings.

Once television sets can be built on a mass production basis
and at prices the average pocketbooks can meet, coupled with the
fact that programs are improved to attract a crowd, nothing can
stop it.   Good programs are to television what good roads are to the
automobile.   Put on a Joe Louis championship fight and see the
crowds around every television set.   Immediately, however, that re-
verts to the old question hurled by the promoters, "Who's going to
pay for all those outside for whom the camera looks in?"   The same
goes for the world series or any other event.

Another pertinent question at this time: Do the present
television standards provide good service?   The answer from one
who has had a standard machine in the home for a year is "Yes."
The 441-line standard at thirty frames per second has been entirely
satisfactory on a 9x12-inch screen.   If the screen size is increased
it may become necessary to increase the number of lines, as some
engineers contend.   And if the pictures are projected on a theater-
size screen it may be necessary to build up the lines to 1,000 to
meet the Hollywood standards.   But the present standards for the
presents sets are satisfactory.

No doubt as television receivers are improved the technical standards also will keep pace. It is that way in radio and all other fields; so it will be in television. Nevertheless, there is no evidence that home-television receivers will become obsolete overnight. If for no other reason, the FCC as a watchdog seems determined to avert such a situation at the expense of the public. And the manufacturers report that looking ahead for two years, all possible improvements or changes in receivers now foreseen can be made in home sets for less than $40.

The layman inquires, "Is it necessary to have sponsored television in order that it may succeed and become 'big time'?" The answer is that some sort of a box-office or pay-as-you-look system must be found. It will cost much more than $10,000 a week to keep the television show running even a few hours a day, and there are no indications now that it will run much more than three or four hours daily for many a moon. The cameras cannot grind out interesting pictures at the rate the "mike" consumes sound.

Based on comment of televiewers in the New York area who have had radio sets in their homes for a year, the radio sponsorship idea is not the right answer for television's economic problems. It all may be solved naturally and simply as was the same riddle of broadcasting in 1922, when the pioneers, suddenly gripped by the mounting costs, saw themselves becoming philanthropists, and they began to hunt for means of revenue. One day a New York broadcaster suggested that a real-estate man rent existing facilities and become a program sponsor instead of building a station. He followed that advice. Overnight on thin air the problem was solved. Broadcasting became big business. Too many may be hunting for the television answer; it, too, may pop up unexpectedly when the time comes.

The performer, of course, has a stake in this thing called television, too. Will the new field offer jobs to new talent and to technicians or will they be drawn from the existing ranks of radio, the films, concert, opera and vaudeville?

Television is a free-for-all. It demands, however, telegenic personalities. It's an intimate show in the home; far more intimate than the theater or movies. One can only realize this by having a machine in the living-room. The artists step into the family circle; professionalism counts, but it must be softened by a natural, friendly personality. Television offers new opportunities to established artists; it promises opportunities to newcomers, for as a medium of entertainment it will discover and build up stars of its own. But in all cases a pleasant photogenic face is paramount. Amateurishness is quickly detected; poor acting cannot be glossed over. And another point: Memory comes back as a vital factor in this new theater of the air. Reading of scripts as in broadcasting is taboo; that's suicide for a television actor, and it will be also for newscasters and commentators. They lose the intimate touch when they duck their heads, close their eyes to the audience and read. The telecaster must look the audience in the face, and that goes for clown or commentator, singer or actor.

The radio listener outside of New York is heard to ask, "When will we have television? Will networks be a reality soon, and if so, how will it be accomplished?"

No one knows how soon. Seven years passed from 1920 to 1927 before the first Coast-to-Coast radio network was spun. It may be less, it may be more before television wings its way east with the Rose Bowl football scenes, or before Californians see the sunset against the skyline of New York three hours before it dips into the Pacific beyond the Golden Gate. The hope rests in adapting television to the telephone wires, in automatic radio relays or in the coaxial cable, which definitely will do the trick of carrying motion pictures. But it is a long, laborious and expensive task to string such a television "pipe" across the continent.

While all this development is going on and pictures become clearer and clearer in space, as television adds to its flexibility and all-seeing qualities, the theater man is perking up his ears and opening his eyes. He wonders, "Will theaters become television centers or will there be special television playhouses just as there are newsreel theaters?"

The theater and the movie became interested because a new amusement threatens competition. Shall they fight it or pick it up as a new tool and use it in the modern way to help the theater?

"What is your interest in television?" a motion-picture executive was asked.

"It is economic," he replied. "We are interested in any competition that might empty the theaters. But we do not intend that shall happen. We shall use television ourselves to build up business; to pack the theaters. Let me illustrate this point: We have learned valuable lessons from radio. People stay at home when there is a big championship fight on the air. They stayed at home from Coast to Coast when President Roosevelt delivered his first two 'fireside chats.' Theater attendance was a good index of the public interest in those broadcasts.

"Now, we do not propose that television of such events of public interest shall empty the seats. We will pick up telecasts of these events and project them on the large theater screen. The audience need not stay home. They will see and hear the public event and see the regular show at probably the same price. In that way we shall capitalize on television."

At this time it takes a long stretch of the imagination to

envisage special tele-theaters. It is difficult enough to comb the
world for interesting newsreels to put on a weekly show. Any such
attempt locally by television cameramen would be dull, because there
will be days on end when no interesting pictures are found to shoot
into the theater. The home itself will, for a long, long time, have
to serve as "the newsreel theater" of television.

      Such is the situation as the second year of agony begins!
By the autumn of 1941, television will have "steam up." Those in
the "game" are paying the price of pioneering in the greatest "Hall
of Mirrors" ever built.

                                        --Orrin E. Dunlap, Jr. In Movie
                                        and Radio Guide, Vol. 9, No.
                                        34 (June 1, 1940), pages 14-15.

• TV IN 'FIFTY-THREE

      What lies ahead for television? What electronic developments
will influence its future? What events, in the months ahead, will
tend to heighten or lower the quality of network video offerings?
Prophesying may be a fruitless game; but a brief consideration of
TV's present state and recent past may furnish the basis for an
estimate of days to come. If such an objective appraisal fails to
indicate definitely where television is heading, it may at least suggest what could be done to make the new sight-and-sound medium
better and who, exactly, should help accomplish that worth-while
end.

      In this year of our Lord 1953, television is, like Rabelais'
Gargantua, a stripling giant, growing so rapidly that it cannot be
ignored or overlooked by businessman, educator or homemaker. A
johnny-come-lately among the media of communication, TV attracts
more attention and has brought with it more problems than any
other channel of education, entertainment and persuasion.

      During 1952, television made its greatest impact in the field
of news and special events. The atom-bomb explosion at Yucca
Flats, the national conventions, campaigns and elections, for instance, brought home to millions of viewers the reality and the significance of current events affecting their lives. Without question, the
future pattern of politics in the United States has been and will be
changed by TV. CBS Board Chairman William S. Paley believes that
because video speeches can effectively replace long, arduous speaking tours, the period of Presidential campaigning in the future may
be shortened to a seven-week period, with national conventions
scheduled for early September.

      Television has the ability to bring the vast canvas of national

politics within human compass by reducing its scale to the dimen-
sions of the home. The character and personality of the candidate
for office are more clearly revealed when he is seen life-size on the
livingroom screen in close-up, discussing the issues and thinking as
he talks. The drama of Vice-Presidential Candidate Nixon defending
his financial status and his sources of income before election held
high human interest for the voter-viewers. The incident may well
have its counterpart in future campaigns, with history altered as a
result.

Last year's technical improvements will surely be matched or
surpassed in the twelve months to come. Additional electronic de-
vices will widen the scope of television both in the studio and in the
field. Industrial and medical application of TV will be increased
with the development of smaller, more efficient and remote-controlled
video cameras. I confidently expect that when the "Bing Crosby
Show" opens on television this June, it will inaugurate the use of a
Crosby-developed electronic tape recorder as a more effective sub-
stitute for TV film.

At the same time, it seems logical to assume that the swing
to the use of film which occurred in television circles this past year
will have reached full arc soon, and a reaction to the poor cinematic
quality and unimaginative content of the bulk of TV film will set in
by the middle of this year. The autumn of 1953 should see "live"
video programs on the increase again. Three-dimensional television,
like subscription video and general color TV, is still a couple of
years away. But all of these developments will eventually have their
effect not only on the broadcasting industry but on the lives of all
of us.

Like the little girl of the nursery rhyme, television can be
either very, very good or it can be horrid. The worst things in
TV tend to accentuate the areas where improvement is needed.
There has been a constant decrease in the number of worth-while
children's programs, while crime shows continue to increase by five
per cent annually. Scenes of violence, although taboo in every
network's policy book, are a regular attraction on the suspense and
mystery programs. There are few shows on television designed to
stimulate interest in reading and in the classics. The TV soap-opera,
with its heavy quota of neurotic, psychotic and trouble-laden characters inherited from radio, has found a foothold in daytime programming. Very old moving pictures, produced long before Will
Hayes had an office, combine with imported foreign movies which do
not come under any Hollywood production code to form a large segment of TV's cinema fare. And through all the video schedules run
multiple "plugs," clusters of commercials that often seem to assume
the proportions of a program in themselves.

In order to encourage viewer comment and criticism, the
National Association of Radio and Television Broadcasters has decided

to add to the TV "Seal of Approval," which member stations and
networks display on the air, the address of the NARTB Code Committee in Washington, D.C. This seems a sincere move and should
help the radio-television industry improve its voluntary task of self-
censorship. It seems to me that the Federal Communications Commission might follow this lead and require all stations at certain times
to carry on the air the address of the FCC as the Government
agency to which viewers should write. The commission, after all,
does renew and revoke licenses and is charged with the ultimate
responsibility of deciding whether a station has been operated in
"the public interest, convenience or necessity."

If television has its faults, it also has its virtues. Several
hour-long dramatic shows maintain a high level of production. The
NBC television network has done outstanding work in the area of
TV opera, notably in the first such work commissioned specifically
for the medium, Amahl and the Night Visitors. The Ford Foundation's Omnibus on CBS-TV has demonstrated that a ninety-minute
show, designed for experimental and educational TV productions,
can be made to pay for itself on a commercial basis. Dumont's
Life Is Worth Living (Bishop Sheen that is), and ABC-TV's See It
Now are among the series that indicate the possibilities inherent in
television.

Hugh M. Beville Jr., NBC's director of research and planning,
estimates that as of January 1, 1953, television sets in the United
States totaled 21.2 million, which meant an increase of 5.5 million
during the preceding twelve months. It is predicted that during the
current year some 6 million more TV sets will be produced.

With the lifting of the FCC "freeze" nine months ago, the
number of video stations began to increase steadily. As against 107
commercial TV transmitters in June, 1952, there are now (as of
February 11) 136 licensed commercial TV stations on the air in 85
cities. Eventually the United States may be blanketed by slightly
more than 2,000 TV outlets, the approximate maximum possible under
the FCC's order allocating channels for all types of Very High and
Ultra High Frequency television.

Until that saturation point is reached, the complexion of TV
will change from month to month and from year to year. It will
change for the better only if the viewer accepts his responsibility
of providing a demand for good programs, and if the men coming up
to key positions in the networks have the proper ethical training
and adequate norms of value.

Bishop Sheen said recently: "Television shows are born
either from directors giving the people what the directors think is
good for them, or from the public letting the directors know what
they want. Both methods are necessary."

This places a responsibility, in the former case, on colleges
and universities to prepare men and women of moral and esthetic dis-
cernment for policy-making positions in television. In the latter case,
it devolves on every member of the TV audience to look and listen
critically, to commend the good and to condemn the bad. But, in
particular, the intelligent or educated person, the intellectual who
views many programs but who writes few letters about them one way
or the other--on this lethargic literate, it seems to me, rests the
greatest responsibility to register his opinions and to make his tastes
felt.

In the phrase of Bishop Sheen, television can be "one of God's
greatest blessings to men." It will reach that high point of maturity
much more quickly if it has the interested attention and assistance of
higher education and you.

> --William A. Coleman in America,
> Vol. 88, No. 23 (March 7, 1953),
> pages 624-625.

• FRED ALLEN

Had lunch with Fred Allen the other day to find out how it
feels to be an unemployed actor. "I feel like God on the seventh
day." He was chomping his customary lettuce leaf at his customary
table at the Plaza. Allen has just had a bout of illness which has
left him twenty pounds lighter. On him it looks good. (I ought to
point out that this unemployment is voluntary. Fred, at the insistence of his doctors, is taking a year off.)

"It's wonderful, this freedom. You can live on the money you
save on aspirin," he remarked cheerfully. "The only trouble is I
keep thinking of jokes and I don't know what to do with them. I
thought of one the other day. 'These days the price of coffee will
keep you awake.' Well, that joke has been keeping me awake. I
don't know what to do with it. I wish you'd take it off my hands."

He nodded pleasantly to a lady who had smiled at him from
across the room. "I have to be very careful. My public has shrunk
to such an extent that I have to be polite to all of them. I say
hello to people in sewers. You know, I went off the air once before
--back in 1944. We got three letters, deploring it. This time we're
way ahead of that. I think we got fifteen. Man spends seventeen
years in this business, trying to build it up, and he goes off the
air and who cares? People still write me for tickets. They think
I'm still on the air. I think they have me confused with Red Skelton.
It makes a man bitter."

He chomped some more lettuce reflectively. "I had seventeen years. You don't even do that to land. You wouldn't plow the same land for seventeen years without giving it a rest. But radio does it to comedians.

"Anyhow, I'll be ready for the welfare state when it arrives-- not working. Most of you working people will be terribly ill at ease for awhile, but I'll be used to it."

In spite of all this talk about retirement, Allen has a contract with N.B.C. which will restore him either to radio or put him on television next fall. He doesn't know which yet, but he thinks there's no point in thinking about radio any more. "They're cutting the budgets way down. With a small budget you can't put a show like mine on the air without reducing the standards you set for yourself."

Allen is one of the most rabid as well as one of the most critical of television fans. We turned to that. "You can make more money in bed than you can in television. They ought to turn the cameras on the stagehands. They make more money than the actors.

"When you see Kukla, Fran and Ollie come alive on that little screen, you realize you don't need great big things as we had in radio. They ought to get one of these African fellows over here to shrink all the actors. We're all too big for this medium.

"What gets me is why they haven't sold the Dave Garroway show. Whoever does that show is turning out real television; he's creating something for television. Berle isn't doing anything for television. He's photographing a vaudeville act. That's what they're all doing.

"Even The Goldbergs, which has been so well received, gets tiresome after you see it four or five times. You know what the uncle is going to do and you know what the kids are going to do.

"The trouble with television is, it's too graphic. In radio, even a moron could visualize things his way; an intelligent man, his way. It was a custom-made suit. Television is a ready-made suit. Every one has to wear the same one.

"Everything is for the eye these days--Life, Look, the picture business. Nothing is for the mind. The next generation will have eyeballs as big as cantaloupes and no brain at all."

Allen has been trotting around sampling opinion on television in some effort to find out what people like. "I talked to the oyster-man at Grand Central the other day," he remarked morosely. "He likes everything on television. Even Morey Amsterdam looks good after staring at oysters all day long.

"That's one of the reasons you don't have color television.
You'd catch all the actors blushing at the things they have to say.
One thing I can't understand--all this advertising of television sets
on television. If you see the ad, you already own a television set.

"We all have a great problem--Benny, Hope, all of us. We
don't know how to duplicate our success in radio. We found out how
to cope with radio and, after seventeen years, you know pretty well
what effect you're achieving. But those things won't work in television. Jack Benny's sound effects, Fibber's closet--they won't be
funny in television. We don't know what will be funny or even
whether our looks are acceptable."

He nodded to another fan across the room. "Middle-aged,"
he commented. "I notice all the people who come up to me are middle-
aged. No kids. I've played to three generations on radio and in
show business. Now I've got to grapple with a fourth."
                                        --John Crosby in New York Herald
                                        Tribune (December 5, 1949).

• AMAHL AND THE NIGHT VISITORS (NBC, December 24, 1951)

    The first opera ever written for television, Gian-Carlo Menotti's
Amahl and the Night Visitors, is one of the most basic of Christmas
Eve stories, the story of a miracle of faith and of hope and of char-
ity--all three of the most elemental Christian virtues. Mr. Menotti,
as a matter of fact, was gravely concerned about it, feeling that he
hadn't any new ideas.

    He needn't have worried. Menotti simply can't do anything
badly and, while Amahl and the Night Visitors is hardly his best
work, it was a deeply moving and extraordinarily powerful piece
of musical drama. Menotti's great virtue, one that has shown up
in The Consul and The Medium and all his work, is a simplicity
and integrity of purpose which leads him straight to the heart of
the matter; he deals in the fundamental emotions, fundamental human
needs, and he writes about them with a terrifying directness.

    Amahl and the Night Visitors is, briefly, the tale of a crip-
pled boy who sees the Star of Bethlehem and hobbles home to tell
his mother about the wonder he has seen. "A star--this long.
Well, maybe only this long." She's much too obsessed with their
poverty--there's not a bite to eat nor a stick of wood in their hut--
to pay much heed. Presently the three Kings visit the hut and
mother and son learn of the birth of the Saviour. They have no
gifts to offer the new-born Christ except the boy's crutches. He
offers these and suddenly, the miracle, he can walk.

It's the sort of story that could have been drenched in sentimentality, and Menotti, because he is unabashed by the outer trap-
pings of sentiment, because he writes directly about mother love,
about poverty, about crutches, about miracles, somehow purifies
them and transforms them into genuine and profound emotion. This
is a very great gift indeed, the quality of candor, and one which
Menotti, almost alone, seems to possess these days.

But Menotti, of course, is much more than candid. He is an
enormously skilled and subtle dramatist as well as a magnificent composer, and the two arts, music and drama, go hand in hand with
him. He can hardly write a line of music which doesn't seem exactly
suited to the particular moment of the drama, inflaming the mind and
the heart simultaneously and intensifying the dramatic effect to an
almost unbearable degree.

The opera opened, quietly and simply, with the crippled boy--
played by twelve-year-old Chet Allen, whose singing is a miracle of
sweetness--playing his pipe in the marketplace, all alone, a scene of
wondrous freshness like the bouquet of a newly opened wine. There
are many other wonderful scenes. Three times the boy peeps out
the door at the newly arrived Kings. "Mother, mother, come see
what I see!" Three times his mother refused to believe anyone was
there, charging the atmosphere with a rising and terrible excitment.

Then there was the procession of the Kings into the hut,
reflected like silver balls in the shining eyes of the boy. They were
very human Kings, even a little stupid, but very kindly. "Have you
royal blood?" whispered the boy. "Yes." "Can I see it?" "It's no
different from yours." "What good is it?" Has ever a small boy's
heart and mind been so tenderly exposed?

Menotti drew his inspiration from the fifteenth-century Flemish painting, "The Adoration of the Magi," by Bosch, and much of
the staging and especially the lighting, which was altogether superb,
captured the quality of Flemish art--its composition, its opulence,
its rather earthy reverence.

Menotti's music, so powerful in The Consul, was marked here,
I thought, by a rare melodic sweetness completely in harmony with
the breathless sweetness of the tale he unfolded. Beside the boy, a
low bow is due also to Rosemary Kuhlmann for her performance and
singing as the mother, to Samuel Chotzinoff, who produced it, to
N.B.C., who commissioned it and who, I hope, will revive it many
times.

As for Mr. Menotti, I can think of no higher praise than to
say that everyone who saw it was a little better as a person and as
a Christian than he was an hour earlier.

                              --John Crosby in New York Herald
                                Tribune (December 2, 1951).

• THE AMERICAN ROAD (NBC and CBS, June 15, 1953)

    When your company has been around for five decades and has
been growing bigger and bigger with each generation, it's only
natural to celebrate that 50th anniversary with an all-out splurge.
The Ford boys chose the most modern medium of public relations
and communication for their purpose and, to do it right, they spread
themselves over two video networks on Monday, June 15, with a
two-hour history of the past half-century titled, The American Road.

    The lavish presentation was notable for many things, not the
least of which was the omission of commercials, as such, for the run
of 120 minutes. To be sure, there was a song about the Model T,
brief opening and closing identifications of the sponsor and a few
words anent the show from Henry Ford II before the final curtain,
but otherwise the period was refreshingly free of intrusive plugs
and "hard" selling. This is a thing that should happen more often
on TV shows; it is an effective way of impressing viewers with the
stature, the good taste of the national advertiser.

    The American Road, according to producer Leland Hayward,
was more costly than the most extravagant legitimate production in
the history of Broadway. Planned as a cavalcade of drama, music,
song, dance, comedy and historic newsreels, the show turned out to
be, for the most part, a gigantic showcase for the talents of Ethel
Merman and Mary Martin.

    The two girls did an old-time vaudeville routine to the sound
of a nostalgic Happiness Boys record. Together, they sang a clever
medley, partly duets, of portions of songs popular through the years.
Singly, they starred in scenes and sketches. Miss Merman, backed
by Teddy Wilson's jazz combination, sang "Alexander's Ragtime Band"
and, with a line of chorus boys, made a comic delight of the World
War I Number "Mademoiselle from Armentieres." Miss Martin was hilarious in a one-woman skit which traced the decade-by-decade
changes wrought by fashion in the feminine silhouette. She was
seriously and effectively ingenuous in a scene from Our Town for
which Oscar Hammerstein II served as the commenting stage manager.
All in all, Ethel and Mary dominated the program and had themselves
quite a time.

    Howard Lindsay and Dorothy Stickney presented a scene from
Life with Father, which was well done and which was about the only
segment for which a realistic set was provided. The remainder of
the program was put on in a "space-staging" manner which more often
than not had the stage in complete blackness with spotlights picking
out the principals. Most viewers, I think, would have liked a little
more relief from this severe bareness of the studio playing area.

    The "sour notes" that occurred during the two-hour offering

were few: an embarrassed silence during an old newsreel clip showing the Ku Klux Klan parading down Pennsylvania Avenue, a weak
joke regarding the Klan's role in a sequence from The Birth of a
Nation, and an inept attempt at humor at the expense of former
Presidents Coolidge and Hoover. This latter visual trick, the would-
be-funny repetition of some newsreel footage in which the ex-Presi-
dents together remove and replace their hats, backfired explosively
when the studio audience, at the first sign of the two statesmen, took
it seriously and burst into spontaneous, respectful applause.

Bing Crosby and Frank Sinatra were seen and heard on film
flown from Paris and London respectively. In both cases, the quality
was poor and the show gained nothing. Rudy Vallee and Eddie
Fisher were seen and heard "live" from the Center Theatre and, although they were in good voice, they sounded sad, perhaps even un-
comfortable. Wally (Mr. Peepers) Cox appeared from time to time
with impressions of off-beat types of the past half-century. In
spite of their brevity, he made them entertaining.

Before The American Road went on, Broadway producer Leland Hayward, who made his debut in TV with this program, was
quoted as saying that in readying the two-network extravaganza,
he had to "chop an eight-hour show to two" for the telecast. Unfortunately he sliced it a little too thin, and the last fifteen minutes
of his masterpiece ended up as a fumbling, dull and disjointed lack
of finale. The Road struck a detour.

Burr Tilstrom's boys, Kukla and Ollie, did yeoman service
throughout the program and could have closed it gracefully. Their
eloquent good-bye came long before the final sign-off, however.
Oscar Hammerstein II, who was (perhaps) adequate as a narrator
through much of the program, at this point was joined by Ed Murrow and the two of them spent five minutes or more mouthing banal-
ities about the past and the future. Part of this time, Murrow,
spouting pompously, blocked the background picture of the atom-
bomb explosion on a projection screen.

Eventually these two got around to bringing on Henry Ford
II. Mr. Ford had the good sense to say only a few well-chosen
words. The producer, Leland Hayward, then walked on to take a
place in the line-up. With brilliant aplomb he lingered haltingly
down-stage and blocked Mr. Ford. There was still a good chunk of
time to be filled, so Marion Anderson, who had thrilled with her
singing earlier in the show, was announced for another number.
She rendered a glorious "Battle Hymn of the Republic," but only
after the four men on stage had straggled off uncertainly.

The end was not yet. Curtain calls were in order but obviously they hadn't been prepared for, or rehearsed. Mary Martin
struggled nobly to oblige, bringing Miss Anderson along with her
for a bow. An unidentified man and woman from the show followed

them out, but the rest of the large cast stayed in the wings in
droves. An experienced video producer would have known that
every long TV show needs a certain amount of "fill" or "cushion."
Ed Sullivan, a noted Ford Co. salesman, meets this problem every
Sunday evening on his Toast of the Town program. A two-hour
single-shot of this kind should have been amply supplied with pro-
visional insert material. This one floundered badly while reaching
for the life-preserver.

After an eternity, the cylindrical drum bearing the program's
closing credits took over the suffering screen. The slowness with
which it moved indicated the reason why the gadget is called, in the
trade, a "crawl." Seldom has it ever been required to crawl so
slowly. We had reached the end of fifty years on The American
Road.

> --William A. Coleman in America,
> Vol. 89, No. 13 (June 27, 1953),
> pages 346-347.

* THE AMERICAN WEEK (CBS, 1954)

Eric Sevareid, who would be an asset to any journalistic enterprise, is indeed a bright jewel in the field of television news.
He is a great many things that a great many other newscasters and
commentators are not. For one, he is quite evidently a quiet, intelligent, and thoughtful man, perceptive, self-controlled, and independent. For another, he just as evidently thinks a situation or a problem through before he stands up in front of the cameras and sounds
off about it. For a third, he is a man who has a sense of history.
I do not for a moment mean to imply that he is the only member of
his craft with these attributes, but he is certainly a leading expo-
nent of the sane school of newscasting. Newscasters on television
are an odd and assorted lot, and the viewer must be on his guard
when watching them. Some are nothing worse than cute; impeccably
groomed, they just sit around grimacing and grinning and modulating
their voices to fit the temper of the item they are reading aloud.
An unwary viewer might fall into the trap of thinking that he is
watching a keen analyst of the dire events of the day when in reality
all he is watching is a male lead in summer stock. Some commit more
active crimes against the public, either by becoming hysterical in
front of the cameras and frantically and violently shouting out the
news, or by distorting events to fit a preconceived notion of what
they think should have happened, and some commit both crimes
at the same time.

All this is by way of a preamble to noting the fact that
Sevareid turns up each Sunday afternoon from six to six-thirty, over
C.B.S., on an excellent program called The American Week. I have

been watching it for a good many Sundays now, and while I felt
that several of his earlier programs had a cumbersome, self-conscious quality about them, it seems to me that he has lately hit his
stride. As a result, The American Week is an adult and instructive
half hour, during which Severeid--supplementing his own comment
with film shots and interviews--tries to put events of the past week
into some sort of intelligible context. Two Sundays ago, for example, he devoted his attention to the problem of Anglo-American relations. President Eisenhower, Sir Winston, Secretaries Dulles and
Eden were engaged at the time in their conferences. Severeid
started out by saying quietly, "Sir Winston Churchill walks again
upon American soil. A kind of presence is in our midst. It may be
that we shall not see this man again; it is almost certain that we
shall not see his likes again...." He then flashed on the screen a
shot of Churchill speaking at Margate last autumn, when he said,
"Had the United States taken before the First World War, or between
the wars, the same interest and made the same exertions and sacri-
fices and run the same risks to preserve peace and uphold freedom
which, I thank God, she is doing now, there might never have been
a second. With their mighty aid, I have a sure hope there will not
be a third." Severeid returned to discuss current differences between the two countries--how Churchill and his Government fear
that "the American exertions may be too great, too hasty," and how
"Churchill's old comrade-in-arms Dwight Eisenhower thinks that British caution today is more dangerous to peace than American haste."
Once again, we saw newsreels, this time of Churchill's arrival at
Washington Airport, his drive to the White House, and his welcome
there by the President and Mrs. Eisenhower. We also saw some
stirring wartime shots of Churchill touring installations in North
Africa, conferring with Marshall, Montgomery, and Eisenhower, and
crossing the Rhine.

Severeid meant business that Sunday, and he was intent upon exploring Anglo-American differences to the full. He proceeded
to show a filmed interview with Selwyn Lloyd, Minister of State for
Foreign Affairs, who was in London. The questions were frank,
and the answers were frank, too. "Mr. Lloyd," Severeid asked,
"how do you think we can resolve our deep-rooted quarrel over the
recognition of Red China?" Mr. Lloyd, looking cool and spruce,
replied briskly, "For us, recognition does not mean approval, it
means the recognition of a fact, recognition of the effective government.... And also we feel that the worse your relations with a
country, the more necessary it is to have the normal diplomatic methods of communication with it." Severeid next said, "Many Americans
feel Britain is not getting as tough with Communism as is necessary.
What about that?" And Lloyd replied, "I don't know what you mean
by getting tough. We in the United Kingdom are getting tough to
the extent of spending to the limit of our resources upon our defense program, and we believe in collective defense.... And I repeat again that negotiation, in our view, is not the same thing as
surrender or appeasement." The American Week went on to interview

London dock workers, who, in rich Cockney phrases, denied that
they were loading any strategic goods for China and insisted that
they could get along without aid but not without trade. Sevareid
then showed us some soapbox orators in the park beside the Tower
of London. The most notable orator was a magnificently bearded
gentleman, and we saw him at a moment when his speech was in full
flower. He was strident, arrogant, self-possessed, and obviously
under the glorious impression that nature had blessed him, and him
alone, with the answers to all questions. He had a word to say
about practically everybody. "I should have mentioned our wonderful Winnie, Sir Winston Churchill," he intoned, "for whom I've got
very little time, incidentally. I think he's a great man, but not
when it comes to greatness." The program ended with a reading
from some recent British editorials on the subject of Anglo-American
relations. Within the half hour, Sevareid had neatly discussed the
problem, had given us a vivid realization of our bonds with the
British, and had accomplished it all with grace and wisdom.

--Philip Hamburger in The New
Yorker (July 10, 1954), pages
39-40.

• MILTON BERLE

    When the history of the early days of commercial television
is eventually written, several chapters will no doubt be devoted to
the strange art of Milton Berle. In my book, they will be dark and
bloodcurdling pages. According to reliable authorities (assuming
for a moment that there are reliable authorities in the television
world), Mr. Berle, known along video row as Mr. Television, is a
phenomenon of massive proportions. His programs are said to have
so powerful a hold upon the television public that shopkeepers who
would ordinarily be open for business between eight and nine on
Tuesday evenings now close down their stores for lack of customers.
Where are the customers? They are watching Mr. Berle. Where are
the shopkeepers? They are doing likewise. All over town during
the Berle program, in taverns equipped with what the industry refers to as "the magic, kaleidoscopic eye of TV," people are reported
to be standing four deep at the bar, laughing, nudging one another,
and neglecting their warm beers. A traffic problem of sorts has
been created in front of television stores, where crowds gather to
watch Berle as people once clustered at the doorways of radio stores,
a generation ago, when Amos 'n' Andy were getting under way.

    What is Mr. Berle doing to produce so favorable a climate for
his antics? It's possible that he is doing nothing that is not being
done in third-rate night clubs and second-class hotels. One of Mr.
Berle's most recent variety programs is a case in point. He made
his first appearance as an acutely repulsive cupid, clad in long white

bunny-type drawers. In one hand was, of course, a cupid's arrow.
He jumped up and down, delivered a few fast "jokes," declared that
his entire program "depends upon safety pins" (a sensible remark),
and, trying to recapture some of the faded glory of vaudeville, kid-
ded with the orchestra leader and jumped over the footlights (his
program looks as if it's televised from what used to be known as a
"theatre") to snip off the necktie of an unsuspecting member of the
audience. "I'll buy you a new tie!" cried the funny man. "You
should live so long!" In his capacity of master of ceremonies, Mr.
Berle briefly and glowingly introduced the next act, then disappeared,
and the curtains parted to reveal a papier-mâché forest. Unicyclists
appeared. When all is said and done, unicyclists are unicyclists,
and they can go just so far on their unicycles and no farther. Generally, when unicyclists finish going around and around, all but one
discard their machines and climb up on the shoulders of the mounted
unicyclist. This is precisely what happened the other evening, and
it was at this juncture that the program ran into camera trouble.
The cameraman photographing the act had difficulty capturing the
full scope of the unicyclists' talents. One would be high on the
shoulders of another before the camera seemed to be aware that he
had left the ground. This sort of thing is unfair to unicyclists.

The unicyclists finally descended and departed, and, after a
brief and glowing introduction by Mr. Berle, two comedians, the
Messrs. Dean Martin and Jerry Lewis, came on. It is just possible
that they represent a trend in television, so they are worth consideration. At any rate, they represent something in television, since
obviously somebody has told them that their audience is not a radio
audience--that they are being observed as well as being listened to.
For the most part, their humor consisted of behaving like delinquent
children: poking their fingers in each other's eyes, putting their
hands in each other's mouths, and, in the classic tradition, insult-
ing each other. Basically, they were a watered-down and devitamin-
ized version of Ted Healy's memorable stooges, lacking both their
physical strength and their total abandon. Mr. Berle joined them,
and by his presence made them look like genuine comics. Berle was
at his best--or worst--with Martin and Lewis. He demonstrated a
few sorry tricks that may conceivably be the real reason for his
television success. No. 1, he puts his hand in somebody's mouth.
No. 2, he crooks his elbow and simultaneously bends his fingers in
a clawlike gesture that gives him the air of a singularly distressed
primate. No. 3, he twists his mouth and reveals his teeth in an
exertion that, at least to me, signifies nothing. Mr. Berle and his
two accomplices pretended to be symphonic conductors, and, inevitably
wearing outrageous wigs (as music-lovers well know, no local symphonic conductor, with the possible exception of Leopold Stokowski,
wears a wig), they leaped into the orchestra pit and had a squalid
time conducting the orchestra. Once again, not only the comedy but
the camera work was faulty. There were shrieks of laughter from
the studio audience, who presumably witnessed everything, but the
all-electronic audience was treated only to glimpses of the principal

parties--a flying wig here, a broken baton there, a mad figure
zooming across the screen.

Well, Berle's program went on and on. A woman dressed in
a leopard-skin ensemble danced one of those tortured dances with a
man wearing shorts. There was a skit involving people dressed up
as Buck Rogers, Flash Gordon, and Superman, and there was Miss
Ethel Merman, who seemed so discouraged by the prevailing humidity
that she didn't halfway achieve her customary glorious form. I must
confess that the arrival of Miss Merman brought me up with a start.
Here, I said to myself, is a lady of the theatre who can surmount any
obstacle. She sang a couple of songs, the titles of which all cleverly
contained the word "smile"--"Smile, Darn Ya, Smile," "Smiles,"
"When You're Smiling"--but her heart clearly was not in her work.
I think we can put it down as a rule that when Ethel Merman is defeated by a program, something is wrong with the program. Perhaps
it should have come as no surprise to me that as Mr. Berle's drew
to a close he appeared as a cowpuncher riding an electronic horse
and, as a clincher, a manful and bewildered little group of American
Indians performed a ceremonial dance.

Goodbye, Mr. Television.

> --Philip Hamburger in The New
> Yorker (October 29, 1949),
> pages 91-92.

*   *   *

*One night this week in New York, 1,000 people were to sit
down to a black-tie dinner at the Waldorf-Astoria Hotel, having paid
$50 a plate for the privilege. For their money they could see a tall,
raucous comedian named Milton Berle receive Interfaith in Action's
fourth annual award for furthering the cause of racial understanding.
Specifically, the comedian was awarded this recognition for more than
150 benefit performances he has played in the past year, notably
including the half-million dollars he raised during his celebrated 16-
hour marathon for the Damon Runyon Cancer Fund.

But the $50 guests, whose money went toward building an
Interfaith Center in New York, were on hand no less to see Berle
honored than to watch him perform. For a view of Milton Berle
performing (and he rarely misses a chance to do his stuff) is a
view of a radio-stage-screen comic who has become not only the
country's top-salaried night-club entertainer, but the first and biggest star in the newest and most difficult of all entertainment
mediums--television.

In his doggedly chosen profession, one significant measure of
success is the relative bitterness of what your competitors say about

---

you. The best-known professional appraisal of Berle's present work
is that nobody likes it except his mother and the public. There is
therefore little doubt that he is magnificently in.

Body and Face: It was not always so. Until less than a
year ago, the taste of rue was monotonously familiar to Berle's
tongue. All but the first five of his 40 years were spent in show
business. Nevertheless, he was a flop in radio and a poor bet in
the movies. He became a real vaudeville success--just as vaudeville
died. His night-club dates, for which he lately turned down offers
of $20,000 a week, offered him only a limited audience.

Berle felt that he failed in pictures and was never a resound-
ing Broadway hit because directors wouldn't let "Berle be Berle."
His trouble on radio, a lot of show people said, was that Berle was
a "body-and-face man." To be amusing he had to be seen. Whatever the difficulties were, they have now been resoundingly resolved
on the Texaco Star Theater (NBC-TV, Tuesday, 8-9 p.m., EDT).

In New York City the Theater currently has an 80 Hooperat-
ing, which means that of all the sets tuned at that period, 80 per
cent are tuned to Berle. The estimate, based on 535,000 present
sets, is that more than 1,800,000 people see him in the nation's
largest city. In the 23 other cities where his program is viewed,
his popularity, with very minor deviations, is proportionate. The
total audience may reach 5,000,000. His sponsor and its advertising agency claim that no other comedian has ever been simultaneously seen by so many people.

Movie exhibitors and even Broadway producers have said that
Berle has made Tuesday night poisonous at the box office. Homes
that own both radio and TV sets almost black out radio at that
period (although Berle's own Wednesday-evening Texaco radio show
undoubtedly gets a stimulant from his television operation).

The Show: There remain, of course, quite a few millions of
his fellow citizens who have never seen Milton Berle in action. If
and when they do, his offering may impress them as a combination
of medicine showmanship and the delivery of the text of a joke book
by an Anglicized whirling dervish.

Berle begins by warming up the audience of his variety show
before it goes on the air with a few minutes of machine-gunned gags,
some very old, some very bad, but all coming in such profusion as
to wake up even the dullest customer. He then brings on the rest
of the show. He has clowned with such eminent performers as
Lauritz Melchior, Gracie Fields, Basil Rathbone, and Walter Huston,
and with an endless series of acrobats, unicyclists, dog acts--and
even other comedians. His wealth of ad libs, his quick improvisa-
tion, and above all his seeming urge to work himself to death are
qualities now regarded as the ultimate in good video.

The Show-Off: But the audience is the basic element. For almost as long as he has been alive, a crowd of people watching him has had about the same effect on Berle as catnip to a febrile tom. As a little boy he was so fond of mugging into a mirror that his father complained that the habit was ruining the child. Milton's mother, however, demurred, and Milton went right on mugging. Her espousal of Milton in this respect was the beginning of one of the American theater's firmest and most famous mother-son relationships.

Moses Berlinger was a paint salesman when he married Sarah Glantz (who then changed her name to Berlin, in honor of Irving Berlin, and then to Berle). She had been a successful department-store detective. Milton was their fourth son, brother to Philip, Francis, and Jack. Shortly after Milton's baby sister Rosalind was born, his father's health failed. The burden of keeping the family together in a railroad flat on West 118th Street in New York fell on the resolute wife. Mrs. Berlinger had to take part-time work, again as a store detective.

Psychiatrists probing into Milton's motivations might well find in these harsh early days explanation for the star's later behavior. Despite the fact that he is now a millionaire, a celebrity, an actor who has the profound, if sometimes grudging, respect of his colleagues, Berle is often loud, demands attention, yells to make his point, is easily hurt, and insists that things be done his way--all characteristics indicative of a basic insecurity, a sublimation of long-buried frustrations. For whatever he has gotten has been gotten the hard way.

Perhaps the test of a great comedian is whether or not the audience receives the impression that his personality is consciously superior to his material. Into the superiority group fall those great men of the classic mettle of W. C. Fields, Joe Frisco, Julius Tannen, Joe E. Lewis, Fred Allen, and Groucho Marx. This is not the group to which Milton Berle is usually nominated by his peers. By contrast, he is regarded by the profession as a sort of common man's common comedian, a gag artist, a feverish user of props and costumes, a mimic--but one of the first order. Humor being the rare commodity that it is, both types of comedians are forever welcome.

The Imitator: Berle's first job, to which his mother naturally accompanied him, was the performance of an imitation of Charles Chaplin. It was offered by him on an amateur show in White Plains, N.Y., and won him the $5 prize. To this day he is never happier than when he can put on an outlandish costume and corn up a role. The television audience has been him as a French cancan dancer, Carmen Miranda's "sister", a Sherlock Holmes detective, an acrobat, a Mexican bandit.

His enormous versatility was learned the hard way too.

After the victory at White Plains, Mrs. Berlinger took her young son to other amateur competitions and church socials, then into vaudeville. Milton loved it. Before he was 10, he was playing child roles in such movies as The Perils of Pauline with Pearl White. From early movies Milton picked up plenty of tricks from his elders and betters, but shows where he could see the audience and they could see him were more his meat.

The Know-It-All: In 1920, when Berle was 11, he was cast in a children's sextet in the Shuberts' revival of Florodora. Confidently, he suggested to Lee Shubert that he be allowed to execute a planned "ad lib," Shubert concurred. But, as Mrs. Berle recalls it: "I used to have to square him all the time with directors who didn't like to be told what to do."

The life the youngster led was a tough one. Home often was a cheap hotel room on the road. Dinner was cooked over a portable gas burner Mrs. Berle carried. The family was generally limited to his mother and sister Rosalind, who as the baby usually went along with Mom. The three of them trouped up and down the country. Their life left a lot to be desired. "I played toilets," Berle recalls in disgust.

And yet, wherever he could find an audience there was Milton. Benefits always appealed to him ("It was good experience," says Mom Berle) and by 16 he was an M.C. And all along the line he picked up other people's ideas and gags. This propensity for gag thievery is unparalleled and is now morosely taken for granted by the profession at large.

And Now TV: Until 1936 Mrs. Berle was her son's combination valet, manager, and stooge. For years her booming, infectious laugh cued audiences. But at 71 the boom is a little low, and while Mrs. Berle still attends as many of Milton's television performances as she can, her daughter Rosalind, now married to a physician and the mother of two children, stands by to give the loudest yocks.

Milton's (and the family's) big switch to television came about this way. Last year the Texas Co. decided to go into video and the Kudner ad agency sold it on a vaudeville show. The idea was to use a different M.C. every four weeks, with Berle as the starter. By the time the comedian had completed three shows he had learned the medium well enough to tell technicians how to work. After Texaco had used seven other M.C.'s including Georgie Price and William Gaxton, it was evident that the job was a permanent one--and Berle's. As the deal worked out, Texaco also bought his radio show. This gave Berle an over-all net of between $5,000 and $6,000. In the trade it is regarded as peanuts, considering all the work involved. But Berle got a viewing audience and thereupon proceeded to make himself the biggest talent news in the infant television industry.

In T-shirt and slacks, Berle runs the rehearsals of his show
--cast, band, and guests--with an iron hand, and indeed of so rough
a grade of iron that there are some performers who will not repeat
their visits on the program. How much of this pressure is caused
by his own personality and how much by the frantic demands of a
wild and unexplored new medium would be hard to say.

The Satisfactions: There are still those to whom television
itself, with its fledgling productions and unsure reception, is something like the Zeppelin: a great modern invention that doesn't
quite work. Nevertheless, some $9,000,000 was spent by advertisers
on time charges alone last year. That is not a great deal compared
with radio time charges of $398,000,000, but it is not the worst qual-
ity of hay. Obviously, the great problem is to attract audiences that
will buy enough of the products of the advertiser to pay for the
shows. Milton Berle is the best audience getter the medium has yet
turned up.

Even so, Berle is not a particularly happy man. He has
never learned to relax. He "unwinds" by sitting in night clubs
clowning with anybody who will listen--but never touching whisky
because he doesn't like it. In 1941 he married a beautiful show girl
named Joyce Matthews, and they adopted Victoria Melanie Berle in
1945. When the Berles were divorced in 1947, he asked and got
joint custody of the child and does his best to see her every day.

He is scourged by an urgent restlessness. In June he will
begin a daily newspaper column, full of Berlisms, for the McNaught
Syndicate. Next fall he intends to start Milton Berle Television
Productions, Inc., to package video shows for other actors. During
his summer vacation he may try the movies again, this time as his
own producer.

And there will always be the benefits. No one can tell how
much Berle has raised for charity, any more than anyone can say
what the intoxication of people watching him work means to him.
But nobody gives more of his time to that particular kind of good
works than Berle. In the language of show business, can that be
wrong? In anybody's language, have his struggles been worth his
pains?

On the eve of the Interfaith affair this week his mother
thought back upon the rewards that have now come after so many
bad years and gave an answer. Just a bit grimly, she said: "It's
those little satisfactions that are so nice."
--Newsweek (May 16, 1949), pages
56-58.

*   *   *

There was a scurrilous rumor going around the corridors that

Milton Berle has become sufferable.   This was belatedly investigated
and can now be pronounced a base canard.   Uncle Miltie--the man,
not the horse--has made spirited attempts the last year or so to become lovable, which would involve a personality change almost as
profound as that of Dr. Jekyll.   He hasn't quite made it, though
beads of perspiration stand out all over him in the attempt.

This essay at lovableness has been made in various ways.
For one thing, Mr. Berle has even gone so far as to keep himself
out of other people's acts from time to time, something I never
thought I'd live to see.   Don't pay any attention to the gossip that
four men have to thrust him into a straitjacket to keep him off the
stage.   I understand it only takes two men.   More importantly,
though, Uncle Miltie has adopted the children of America as his
special province.   What the G.I. is to Bob Hope, what charity
drives are to Eddie Cantor, childhood is to Uncle Miltie.

That makes Uncle Miltie a target almost as difficult to hit as
the Germans around Cassino.   Artillerymen couldn't hit the Germans
without hitting the monastery.   Children, charity and G.I.'s are
all sacred subjects.   By wrapping themselves in these sacrosanct
vestments, the comedians become almost immune to criticism.   Criti-
cize Berle and you're against childhood.   One word about Hope and
you're hindering the war effort.

In the cases of Mr. Berle, Mr. Hope, and Mr. Cantor, I
hasten to say they are all very likely dominated only by the highest motives.   However, the public ought to be warned that some
comedians have been pushed into embracing lofty causes of one sort
or another by agents whose concern with, say, the suppression of
snakebite is entirely a matter of money.   Most agents are privately
very much in sympathy with snakebite, being more or less in that
profession themselves.   Publicly, though, they're against it, knowing by instinct that this is a popular stand.

When one of their properties, as comedians are known in the
trade, faces starvation through lack of employment, a livewire agent
may take the property aside and say: "Look, stupid, we must em-
brace a cause.   We must be against something.   Or we must be for
something."   He then explains as delicately as possible what a snake
is, most comedians thinking that a snake has two feet and inhabits
the upper floors of the R.C.A. Building.

Presently you'll find the comedian ending his program with a
one-minute attack on snakehood.   And send the two dollars to the
Anti-Snake League, a new organization of which the comedian is
honorary chairman.   The public instantly perceives that Joe Schmaltz
is not only very skillful at pratfalls but is also a civic-minded individual whose pratfalls it is now a public duty to witness.   It is not
only a public duty to witness these pratfalls but all right-minded
citizens should laugh at them or they will be suspected of being
secretly in sympathy with snakebite.

Well, it's a fairly harmless, though hardly disinterested,
game and it raises a couple of bucks to combat snakes. The trouble
is that there are only so many causes and most of them have been
gobbled up long ago by other comedians. Motherhood was pretty
well retired from the lists by Al Jolson. Bob Hope owns the G.I.'s.
Cancer, heart disease, Communism have all been spoken for.

That left little except childhood for Mr. Berle, who came to
the feast late. It wasn't the happiest choice but it was just about
the only one. Emotionally, psychologically, every way, Berle and
childhood seem antipathetic. Even on my ten-inch screen, Berle
regards the children and the children regard Berle with what appears to be ill-concealed distrust. Both, I think, have good reason.
In our family, we use Uncle Miltie as a threat. If the little so-and-
so doesn't go to bed this minute, we'll make him look at Milton Berle.
That sends him, scampering.

But after Berle, what? There aren't any four-square causes
left. A comedian can't take on any controversial causes. He couldn't
take sides on, say, the Brannan plan, even if he could understand
it, which is doubtful. It's got to be as incontestable as the Bible.
And there isn't much left. No, you can't take over fatherhood,
either. That belongs to Bing Crosby.

> --John Crosby in New York Herald
> Tribune (December 18, 1950).

● BOB AND RAY (NBC, 1951-1953)

A pair of extremely agreeable comedians named Bob Elliott and
Ray Goulding, who bill themselves as "Bob and Ray," turn up each
Tuesday evening (N.B.C., 7:15-7:30) and poke some wonderful fun
at certain folkways of television. One aspect of the great new cultural medium that they take an especially hard whack at is, not unexpectedly, the commercials. Their program opens with a few words
from a substantial-looking, somewhat elderly announcer, a man whose
face can probably best be described as being as honest as the day
is long. He is clearly a fellow who believes in the product he is
pushing; you feel, just from looking at him, that he is sincere. It
is unthinkable that he would have anything good to say about a
product that he had not himself tested a hundred times. He speaks
slowly, warmly, convincingly of "the old established firm of Bob and
Ray." He calls attention to their Special Burglar's Kit and their
Busy Executive's Kit, and he asks, his voice ringing with sympathy,
"Do you feel well? Wouldn't you like to feel sick?" Bob and Ray
then take over. One of them is tall and one of them is short; one
has a mustache and one has not; both are eager and earnest and
dedicated. They may have on hand a supply of trapezes, which
they offer at ridiculously low prices and which they guarantee for

comfortable home use. Their "overstocked surplus warehouse" may
be bursting its walls with sheets manufactured by "a famous-name
sheet manufacturer," but they cannot reveal the name of the maker--
they simply can't--because the sheets are to be sold at "a laughably
low price." When Bob and Ray sell a famous-name sheet at a laughably low price, they laugh so hard that they can't speak, and although it is entirely possible that I am becoming softheaded, I laugh,
too.

One night recently, Bob and Ray parodied a well-known program that originates in a well-known midtown saloon. They hopped
from table to table, introduced the "socially acceptable" guests (a
number of them were exceedingly unpleasant waxworks), and finally
sat down to interview a husband-and-wife actor team, neither member of which would let the other say three words in a row. From
time to time, the camera showed us the trademarks of the saloon
(it was called the Sandpiper Club)--half-empty champagne glasses
and ashtrays piled high with butts. Once again, softheaded or not,
I liked it.

On each of their programs, Bob and Ray take a few minutes
to relate the continuing story of "Hartford Harry, Private Eye."
Hartford Harry (Ray) is referred to as "a two-fisted defender of the
law." His main interest in life is the ceaseless pursuit of the Barracuda (Bob), a master criminal who speaks in the sly accents of
the East and wears a kimono and a turban with a feather on top.
Hartford Harry is on a par with most of the private eyes of television; that is to say, he is an unmitigated boob and all-round incompetent, arrives on the scene of a crime several minutes too late
or, if he arrives before the criminal gets away, is outwitted by the
lawbreaker. The Barracuda delights in knocking Hartford Harry
over the head whenever they have an encounter; he precedes the
blow by orally dressing down the eye. Harry has, of course, a
secretary, whose sole occupation seems to be answering desperately
ringing telephones in the eye's office. She mumbles a few words
about getting something or somebody over to "the warehouse" on
the double. The secretary is played by Audrey Meadows, and Miss
Meadows is, as far as I am concerned, a truly engaging young woman,
with a deadly, comic approach.

Bob and Ray generally finish up their programs with a plug
for one of their seemingly endless supply of products. The other
night it was Woodlo, a product "all America is talking about."
Speaking rapidly, Bob and Ray said that Woodlo was the sort of
product "that appeals to people who." Moreover, it was "immunized."
"You can buy Woodlo loose!" one of them cried. "Yes, mothers and
dads!" cried the other. "Available at your neighborhood!" cried
Bob. "Drop in on your neighborhood!" cried Ray. Well, that's how
it goes.

--Philip Hamburger in The New
Yorker (March 8, 1952), page 54.

• RED BUTTONS

First time we'd had a long talk with Red Buttons, it was just
after the sensational debut of his own TV show in the fall of 1952.
No comedian, either before or since then, had ever captured the
fancy of the American televiewing public so instantaneously. But
Red, with 16 years of rough-and-tumble experience in show business
behind him, was taking nothing for granted. "Friends have been
asking me what my future plans are, with the TV show going so
well," he said then. "You know what? I don't have any other
plans. I'll be happy just to see this thing last."

His sobriety was prophetic. This past season (his second)
the Buttons tornado subsided almost without notice. His sponsors
announced they would not be renewing him for next season, and
CBS did not bother to pick up his options. It was the most bizarre
form reversal since Christine Jorgensen. Buttons' luck has swung
full circle again, with NBC signing him for a new show, sponsored
by Pontiac, which will be seen Friday nights at 8, at which time
CBS will be presenting Mama, sponsored by General Foods, the outfit which dropped him.

But at the time we were talking, a month or two ago, the
good news hadn't come in. The boom had just been dropped. There
was really only one question to ask: "What happened?"

Buttons got to his feet, began pacing slowly back and forth
across the rich carpeting of his Sutton Place apartment. He narrowed
his eyes the way he does in his comic portrayal of a tough Hollywood
cowboy. "The writing," he said. "I just didn't have enough good
writing. A guy who's already made a big rep in another medium--
he can come into TV and manage to get away with doing a certain
amount of junk. But I had no such rep to fall back on. My material had to be terrific--and it wasn't."

Buttons finds comfort in the belief that he didn't finish the
season as a flop. "My last eight or nine shows were darned good,
I thought, and at the very end I was in the first ten or 12 of just
about every rating service there is. It was in the middle of the
season that I was going real bad. Slipped to about 33rd place.

"I don't care what anyone says, ratings are important in this
racket. Sometimes they don't make sense, but they're important.
In one month I was number three, according to Videodex--right after
Lucy and Dragnet--but according to Nielsen I was 24th. You figure
it out."

In his frantic desire to thwart the sophomore jinx--if there is
such a hex--Buttons changed formats a number of times, but it was
as futile as switching seats at a poker game. One week, he holed

himself up in his apartment and ran off kinescopes of every TV show
he'd ever done, desperately looking for clues.

"Some of them were pretty awful," reflected Red. "One of the
regular characters I played--the sappy high school kid--never got
off the ground. He was the kind of ninny who opens a door and
falls into a puddle of water. He was ridiculous. But I'll take the
blame for that mistake. I thought he'd go over. Now I realize he
never could. He was an out-and-out stoop. There was nothing
about him to like or to sympathize with."

Other, and more firmly established, characters in Buttons'
repertoire--the "kupke" kid, the punch drunk pug and the German
submarine commander--held up better. But Buttons thinks the
finest thing he's ever done was the eight or nine-minute Charlie
Chaplin bit he did on one evening last winter.

"The fan mail was phenomenal after that one," he reported.
"One man who used to work with Chaplin in the movies many years
ago, wrote to tell me that he was sure he'd been watching an old
Chaplin film. Of that I'm proud."

Some months ago several Broadway and television columnists
ran blind items about a certain big-time TV comic who was no longer
responsible for his actions and whose cast was physically afraid of
him. "Sure, I saw the items," said Red, when we reminded him
about them, "and they bothered me. Not that I felt they applied to
me, but when everything else is going against you, you get to be
sensitive about that sort of stuff. I knew there'd be a certain number of readers who'd guess they meant Buttons, and I wasn't in any
mood to take that kind of injustice in my stride."

Before his final show of the past season, his camera crew
presented him with a swim outfit for the summer, and immediately
after that same performance, he was given a party in a midtown
restaurant by his director Don Appell and the four writers who were
with the series at the finish--Buddy Arnold, Woody Kling, and Danny and Doc Simon. "Does all that," asks Red, "make me sound like
a guy who's tough to work with?"

With justifiable pride, Buttons feels he's at least partially
responsible for the fact that sales of Maxwell House Instant Coffee
(his old sponsor) now exceed sales of the firm's regular coffee.
Why, then, did they decide to drop him? "Maybe they didn't know
where I was going," Buttons suggested. "I guess they just didn't
want to take any more chances. One thing I'll tell you. They had
an honest jockey. I was trying all the way."

Buttons has never been the kind of man who spends everything he earns. As a youngster working in burlesque, he saw too
many broken-down performers hanging around the stage door waiting

for handouts. He's determined that no one will ever have to run a benefit for him. Over the past two seasons he's had a handsome income from TV. And his first recording ("The Ho-Ho Song" and "Strange Things Are Happening") sold well over half a million discs. A more recent disc ("The Buttons Bounce" and "Oh, My Mother-in-Law") is not meeting with that kind of success.

Actually, Buttons' position--even before NBC signed him up-- was hardly calamitous. Early in September he begins a two-week engagement at The Sands, in Las Vegas, for $15,000 per week. Yet, as we left his Sutton Place apartment (the kind of layout you don't even see on Studio One) we felt a trifle sorry for the guy. Within the short space of two TV seasons, he'd known unqualified victory and unforeseeable defeat. And that, perhaps, is the unkindest gamut of all. Maybe the new show will shoot him back on top. He's too young--and too talented--to be a has-been.

> --Philip Minoff in Cue (August 7, 1954), pages 12 and 34.

● SID CAESAR

When Sid Caesar was just a little Caesar, he and his father journeyed from their home in Yonkers to downtown Manhattan at least once a week for an evening at the Turkish baths. Caesar senior liked to brag about his youngster's ability to withstand the heat of the steam room, and his proudest day came when Sid, just turned thirteen, joined the veterans of the "top shelf," the bench closest to the pipes. "That was the moment," Sid recalls now, "that I felt like shouting, 'Today I am a man.' I had arrived."

During the past couple of months, the six-foot, 190-pound Caesar has graduated to another kind of "top shelf," where the pressure is equally great. As the star of the New York portion of WNBT's Saturday Night Revue, he carries a $50,000-a-week television show on his expansive shoulders. True, he's surrounded by other top-grade talent. He couldn't have found a better comedy cohort than protean Imogene Coca, and the guiding hand of production chief Max Liebman is always evident, but the final judgment of the tele- viewer each week depends on how funny Caesar has been. A pret- ty pivotal spot for a lad who won't be twenty-eight until October.

Caesar's genius for capturing the universality, humor and pathos of everyday situations has led observers to compare him with Chaplin, W. C. Fields and the late Raimu. He is a comedian who cannot tell a joke, and doesn't try. In a duel of wits with a rapid- fire comic like Milton Berle or a verbal satirist like Fred Allen, he would be mangled. But when he's doing the waiting-room monologue of an expectant father, a parody on Hollywood prize-fight films, or

the "autobiography" of a penny-chewing gum machine, there isn't
a performer around who can hold his coat.

"The things I do," he explains, "are stories--stories that
have to be seen and heard from beginning to end, or not at all."
It is for this reason that he detests working before night club audiences. "They're too busy entertaining each other to watch or listen
to a paid entertainer."

Nine years ago, when Sid was thinking of becoming a serious
musician (he subsequently played the saxophone in several name
bands) he got a job as an usher at the Capitol Theatre to help pay
for his studies at Juilliard. "When the cold weather came along,"
he says, "they promoted me to doorman. A wonderful break, eh?
I had a clear view of the crowds going into Lindy's but my own
lunches were brought to me by my mother, who carried hot soup
and sandwiches all the way from Yonkers."

Caesar joined the Coast Guard in 1942 and made a king-sized
splash as the comedian in the service show, Tars and Spars. No
one who saw the movie version of that musical will ever forget his
one-man takeoff on a typical Hollywood aerial-combat scenario, in
which the enemy flying ace looks so mean, but the American pilot
is "always smiling."

Following the war, Sid continued his ascent to the "top shelf"
with successes in Make Mine Manhattan and television's Broadway
Revue. In his current assignment, he is not only making three times
as much money as he did on TV last year, but is being hailed as the
most original comedian in the medium. Unlike most professional buf-
foons, he creates a healthy portion of his material, drawing ideas
from personal observations of people and situations. He works as
hard as any of his writers (Mel Tolkin, Lucille Kallen, Liebman and
Mel Brooks) in tailoring each week's script.

Caesar, his wife, Florence (a Hunter College graduate), and
their daughter, Michele, who'll be three years old this summer, live
in a four-and-a-half room apartment in Forest Hills. His father
died five years ago, but his mother visits them regularly, weighed
down with jars of home-made pickled herring and borscht. His
brothers, Abe and Dave, run a Yonkers stationery store, whose walls
are lined with photographs of Sid. "My brothers are not only much
taller and heavier than I am," says Caesar, "but about four times
as funny." Television scouts, please note.

For all his whirlwind progress, Caesar (a self-punishing
perfectionist) is never entirely satisfied with his performances and is
sharply aware of his limitations. At a party a couple of months ago,
Frank Loesser approached him with, "You're just what I need for
my new Broadway show--a big, good-looking guy, just like Clark
Gable, who can sing, dance, act and get laughs!" Caesar's reaction

was as immediate as it was honest. "I live in Forest Hills," he
said. "If I ever come across a guy like that, I'll tell you about
him."

> --Philip Minoff in Cue (April 22,
> 1950), page 16.

• JOHN DALY AND OTHER MODERATORS

There is an unfounded rumor that John Daly, one of the
busiest of the many Masters of Ceremonies in TV, is considering
adopting as his motto, "Moderation in All Things."

Whatever the phrase that graces his escutcheon, it is generally agreed that Mr. Daly possesses the proper combination of attributes that make for success as a video moderator. He does well all
the things a moderator should do. He can handle either light or
serious programs. He puts both guests and panelists at ease. He
is always properly prepared with information about his guests and
subjects. He keeps a show moving and handles its timing well.
And he is never at a loss for words.

All of these things we may expect from a professional TV
moderator; but usually we have to be satisfied with a less-than-
perfect performance. If you ask Mr. Daly what a moderator's principal job is, he'll tell you: "It's to get as much good talk as you
can out of the people on the show." This is basic, of course, and
underlies the popularity of the panel program. Almost without exception, viewers enjoy "good talk." But evidently the moderators
on TV equipped to stimulate interesting conversations and to keep
it within designated channels are few and far between.

In the "light" category of panel programs, it is common practice to cast a comedian in the role of moderator. If the format of
the program allows the comedian opportunity to display his own brand
of wit, this may prove successful; in such cases he is performing
rather than moderating. Thus a Groucho Marx may "shine" when
his contestants' backgrounds are known to him beforehand. A Herb
Shriner may take time to spin tales of the Hoosier State which have
little or nothing to do with the questions to be asked participants.
Among the few top entertainers who can fit easily into a quiz or
panel show as moderator and bring to it easy wit, proper pacing and
control are Robert Q. Lewis, Steve Allen, Garry Moore and Walter
Kiernan.

Comedian Jack Paar has recently appeared on the air as emcee
of a program titled Bank on the Stars, in which contestants watch
brief scenes from recent movies and then are required to answer
questions about the sequence shown. In his interviews with guests

and in his questioning of them, it seems to me, Mr. Paar demonstrates that he is unsuited to this type of program. As a stand-
up "single" monologist he has been and, I am sure, will continue to
be, highly amusing. As a moderator he is unsure, unfunny and
unentertaining.

On another program, this one a returning panel show titled
Masquerade Party, newscaster Douglas Edwards tries his hand as a
moderator with just as undistinguished results. He isn't bad, you
understand, and he isn't good. He's just mediocre. The mediocrity
is emphasized by the fact that the program's panel includes Peter
Donald, an experienced comic-actor-dialectician who has in his time
displayed outstanding talent as a moderator.

When a panel program deals with a serious topic, there is
always a danger that the moderator may be either so ponderous in
manner as to drag down and smother any possible interest in the
show or so subjective in his approach as to make the discussion un-
balanced and prejudicial. Whether the material under consideration
is a book, politics, civic improvement or social conditions, fairness
dictates that proponents of conflicting views be given equal voice.
If the moderator enters the argument definitely on one side in opposition to the other, or if he makes unfair use of his authority to
curb unduly the utterances of the side with which he disagrees, the
result is a slanted program which loses its value as a public service.

Although male television moderators occasionally may be guilty
of a lack of objectivity, the failing is more often apparent, for some
reason, in the female of the species. A notable exception to this
generalization is Martha Rountree, moderator and co-producer (with
Lawrence Spivak) of Meet the Press. You may or may not cotton to
her Southern accent, but you must admit that her own opinions are
usually shelved as she presides. It is obvious that Miss Rountree
is careful not to become personally involved. She is on hand to put
on a good show, to help the newspaper men who participate ferret
out the information they want from the guest of the week. When
the queries and answers are interesting and the show is moving
along rapidly, she often remains in the background.

By way of contrast, I would cite the Author Meets the Critics
program. John K. M. McCaffery, I believe, was the last moderator
who honestly can be said to have "moderated" this telecast war of
words. He brought intelligence, good manners and authority to the
middle seat.

Following Mr. McCaffery, Miss Faye Emerson was left wringing
her hands in the moderator's chair while critics and authors tore
each other apart. Viewers got the impression that she would have
liked to have pitched in and taken sides, but unfortunately she
seldom could succeed in making herself heard in the Donnybrook
Fairs that ensued.

Virgilia Peterson, the program's most recent interlocutor, is entirely different but hardly better. Reportedly, she was named after the wife in Shakespeare's Coriolanus whose husband refers to her as "my gracious silence." The resemblance ends with the name, for Miss Peterson is seldom silent and often loses her gracious manner when a panel member attempts to propound views with which she disagrees. In such a case, she has been known to cut off the panelist in question and to summarize with a few slanted comments of her own. The producers of Author Meets the Critics should have known in advance of Miss Peterson's penchant for partiality; she displayed it nightly when she presided over a previous discussion show on the Dumont network.

Unfortunately for TV, precious few of its moderators are in the same class as John Daly.

--William A. Coleman in America,
Vol. 89, No. 15, July 11, 1953,
pages 386-387.

• JIMMY DURANTE

Jimmy Durante appears every fourth Wednesday evening over N.B.C. in a full hour of comedy, starting at eight o'clock, and the results so far have been nothing short of spectacular. Along with many other people, I have known for years that Durante is a great man, but it has taken his television appearances to make me aware of the extent of his greatness. He seems to have an uncanny instinct for this new and baffling medium. He knows, for example, that the television camera picks up the slightest gesture and the faintest expression, and gives each gesture and expression a strange, special emphasis by reducing it, on the tiny screen, to something bigger than life. Durante has caught on to the fact that when a television performer blinks, that blink is the equivalent of a toss of the head on the orthodox stage. He not only makes every motion count but he is in constant motion. He glides, crouches, turns, whips his head back, leans forward, takes off his hat, scratches his head, puts his hat back on, wiggles his mighty nose, sits down at a piano, bangs out a few notes, slams his hand down on top of the piano, crouches, glides, wiggles his nose some more, and so on. Through some magic, each motion is kept within range of the camera, and no motion is out of proportion to any other. As a result, Durante's personality emerges in all its barbarous and frenzied glory.

In addition to keeping active physically, Durante rarely stops talking. He is onstage almost continuously, and I cannot recall more than a moment or two during which he was not huskily making some remark or other. ("I'm going to play one of Choppin's études," "I've created a Frankenfurter monster," "I must have an inferiority

duplex," "Look at the Leaning Tower of Pizza" are representative.)
Durante performs solo a good deal of the time, but his hour also
contains sketches. Most of those I have seen are of a pretty high
order, as television sketches go. I remember with particular delight one in which Durante, sitting up in bed and mortally ill, was
visited by a doctor, who put on his stethoscope. He was inter-
rupted by a coarse yell from the patient. "Just my luck to get a
doctor who's hard of hearing!" shouted Durante. This episode
followed a mad search through the bed for a hot-water bottle.
"Where's the top?" his valet asked. "Never mind the top," said
Durante, extracting the bottle from beneath the sheets. "Where's
the water?"

From time to time, a guest star turns up and tries to slip in
a word or two. Of all the guests so far, I should say that Helen
Traubel was not only the most unexpected but by far the most winning. She more than held her own with Durante--a formidable task,
even for a diva. Miss Traubel arrived in the armor of Brünnhilde,
complete with metal breastplate and spear. "Holy smoke! She's
been drafted!" cried Durante. Toward the close of the program,
Durante brings on his old partner, Eddie Jackson, who, as in the
past, wears his high hat, swings his cane, and dances and sings
with uncommon skill. To watch Jackson and Durante clowning together in their wonderful old style is a heart-warming sight and provides
just about the perfect ending to an astonishing hour of fun.

> --Philip Hamburger in The New
> Yorker (January 6, 1951), page
> 64.

• FAYE EMERSON

Today I'd like to take up Faye Emerson, a pioneer in the
art and one of the most indefatigable guests on everyone else's
program in the business.

Miss Emerson now has her own program on WCBS-TV in New
York, a chatter-gossip-interview program, at 11 p.m. E.S.T.,
Mondays. In other words, safely out of reach of the children,
which is just as well. (They couldn't understand Miss Emerson's
peculiar gifts.) Television Guide, a smallish magazine, referred to
Miss Emerson recently as "the plunging neckline Woollcott," a tart
though not entirely accurate description.

Miss Emerson, I'd be the first to admit, fills a ten-inch
screen very adequately. Very adequately. The gowns are impressive. (One of the qualifications for this line of work is a wardrobe
that stretches from here to there.) Besides clothes, Miss Emerson
possesses a generous and mobile mouth, a brow of noble proportions
and conceivably the most eloquent eyebrows in all television.

She is no Alexander Woollcott, though, and appears to have no pretentions in that direction. Her fifteen-minute show opens, as do all the feminine TV shows, with a gush of volubility, much of it the smallest of small talk. "Hello," she says, "I have a little bit of gossip."

She had a wonderful dinner, she'll tell you, at someone-or-other's house and they discussed Tim Costello's "Where all the newspaper men hang out." (Not all of them, dear. A great many of them hang out at Bleeck's. Some of the richer ones hang out at Twenty-One. And then there's that small, conservative minority which hangs out, of all places, in its own homes.)

She saw the Katharine Cornell play and thought the critics were very unkind. Poor Kit. She's such a wonderful person. She saw the opening of Milton Berle's movie. Mr. Berle was terribly nervous. (That, I refuse to believe.) Miss E. had also been to a party at Mrs. Martin Beck's and thought we'd be interested in how the apartment looked. Description of apartment. "She was wearing just simple chamois--just simply chamois, that's all." (That can't be right. Looks like chamois on my notes but I refuse to credit my own eyes.)

After about five minutes of this, the first guest--there are two on each show--appears and there is a display of profound surprise on the part of both parties that they ran into each other in this unlikely way. "Why Denise Darcel, of all people!" One of these days Faye Emerson is going to catch sight of herself in a mirror and exclaim: "Why, Faye Emerson, whatever brought you here?"

The interviews follow the usual line. How did the guest get into show business or novel writing or interior decoration or whatever? There is conspicuous mention of the guest's latest book, play, movie or recipe. If the guest happens to sing or play the saxophone, he is asked to perform and does. If he knew any card tricks I expect he'd be asked to do those too. Among the guests so far have been Joey Adams, George Jessel, Abe Burrows, Irene Rich, Earl Wrightson, Robert Q. Lewis and Mercedes McCambridge.

After grappling with the guests, Miss Emerson gets back to her desk and passes along a little more gossip. "At the party last night, we all played party games. Some are a little rough but they're really gay and they really, really warm up a party."

The Faye Emerson show, I assume, is aimed primarily at women, but I know several men, including this one, who are helplessly fascinated by it for reasons which I'm sure never occurred either to C.B.S. or to Miss Emerson. The favorite program from the male point of view was one in which Denise Darcel appeared. Miss Darcel had quite a wrestling match with a strapless evening gown which kept trying to fall off but didn't quite.

Incidentally, the Faye Emerson show was originally to have
been the Diana Barrymore show. Well, I was on hand with pencil
and paper to record the first show. In place of it there appeared a
sign: "The program originally scheduled will not take place."
Television Guide explains that a piece of plaster came loose from the
ceiling and conked Miss Barrymore on the head. You're at liberty
to believe that, if you like.

--John Crosby in New York Herald
Tribune (January 23, 1950).

*   *   *

Somewhat peevishly, I take pen in hand today to set Miss
Faye Emerson straight on her neckline. Never, never did I think
any woman would consult me on where to wear her neckline. Never
has any woman even consulted me about where to wear her hem line.
I have, it's true, expressed some forcible opinions about both necklines and hem lines from time to time, but these opinions have never
been sought by women and have, in fact, been greeted by derisive
laughter from all the ladies within earshot.

The Faye Emerson controversy, which threatens to start a
civil war unless firmly handled, started innocently enough when I
reviewed Miss Emerson's television program, in which I used the
phrase--borrowed, as it happened, from someone else--"the plunging neckline Woollcott." Miss Emerson seized upon this phrase, and
that night on her program she told her rapt admirers that I dis-
approved low necklines. What, she asked, did the rest of the listeners think? In short, write.

Well, it was a nice stunt and brought Miss Emerson bushels
of mail, much of which she read over the air and 95 per cent of
which upheld the low neckline. Epithets of all nature were heaped
on my innocent skull. Even my alma mater was dragged through
the mire. "I never heard of any other Yale graduate," wrote one
Connecticut housewife, "even ones who majored in archeology, advo-
cating Mother Hubbard gowns."

I never did either, including this one. For your information,
Connecticut housewife, Yale men have been admiring pretty shoulders
since your great-great-grandfather's day. The fact is, I have been
maligned, misrepresented, traduced, defamed and slandered. Not
once in that column did I express or imply disapproval of Miss Emerson's revelatory costumes. I simply described them in the most
graceful prose I could muster at the moment. It is one of the func-
tions of criticism, Miss Emerson, to outline to the readers the general nature of the entertainment and the entertainers. To have
avoided outlining your own spectacular--uh--outlines would have been
a shameful neglect of my duties.

If there was any opinion at all expressed in that column, it

was one of helpless admiration. Several of the sentences positively
leered. I want to go on record right now--the rest of Yale University can speak for itself--as heartily in favor of all necklines--high,
low and upper middlebrow. In fact, Miss Emerson, I don't care if
you take the damned dress off.

I now retire hurriedly from the field of feminine fashions. If
any of the rest of you girls are having troubles with your peplums,
your sheath silhouettes, you'll have to consult someone else. I got
enough work of my own.

--John Crosby in New York Herald
Tribune (March 31, 1950).

*   *   *

There is a scurrilous rumor going around that there are really
seven Faye Emersons, that no one girl could meet so many people,
attend so many parties, be guest star on so many programs (while
still not neglecting her own) and, at the same time, finger stage and
screen offers.

Well, its a dirty lie. I happen to know there are only five
Faye Emersons. There is one actress Faye Emerson who handles
stage, screen and television dramatic work; another Faye Emerson,
the smartest of the five, who appears on quiz programs; still another
Faye who handles her own program and attends all the parties; there
is the weight-lifting Faye Emerson and there is one spare. The
spare is carried around in a velvet lined case, like Charlie McCarthy,
in case any of the others break down.

The spare is the most versatile of the crowd. There was a
bad period last winter, when all the four regular Faye Emersons
broke down. The spare Emerson was rushed in with only a hurried
briefing, and, gads, what a job she did! In that one heroic week
the spare Emerson attended twelve parties, was linked--as they
say--romantically with six different men in six different columns,
appeared on four different quiz programs (and got everything right),
lifted a 250-pound man over her head, took the lead in an hour-
long dramatic program and scored three times for C.C.N.Y. against
the University of Kentucky in the last three minutes of play at
Madison Square Garden. She's now back in her velvet case, breathing heavily.

The multiplicity of Miss Emerson is not the only case of its
kind, though, of course, it's the most conspicuous. Radio always
fell easy prey to multiplicity. (Take your dirty hands off that
word, editors. I like that word.) There was one dizzy period
two years ago, when, as the leading scholar of radio multiplicity,
I drew up a chart of guest appearances, the darndest thing you
ever saw. Bing would appear on Fred Allen's program; Fred would
appear on Jack Benny's program; Benny would appear on George

Burns's program; George would appear on Bing's program and then
Benny would. ... Well, you can't explain it. You have to diagram
it.

                              --John Crosby in New York Herald
                              Tribune (May 12, 1950).

• DAVE GARROWAY

     Dave Garroway, otherwise self-referred to as "the very low-
pressure guy," "old tiger," and various other odd--or as he would
probably say--incandescent labels, has made a fairly large splash on
television. But N.B.C. also offers an awful lot of Garroway on
radio, where you can sample the pure, undistilled Garroway.

     The pure Garroway, I'm informed, is the embodiment of the
bop movement. He is, as the bop crowd likes to describe it, a very
cool guy. Or to put it in pure bop: "The coolest." The noun is
unnecessary. The idea is to be as languid as possible about everything, and this is expressed by little shrugs, little liftings of eyebrows, and small flutterings of hands, by a general bonelessness
both in physiognomy and in point of view. One must never get
excited about anything. One must be terribly, terribly, terribly
casual about everything and relaxed almost to the point of stupor.

     This, if it's not too ambitious a word, is the philosophical
basis for all the Garroway shows, both radio and television, and it
must be admitted from the outset that this philosophy doesn't appeal
to just everyone. A great many people are decidedly cool to this
very cool guy. In Chicago, where Garroway first got his foot in
the door and from which he still broadcasts his network shows, Garroway attracted many devout admirers. There were others--quite an
impressive band too--who would like to wring his neck.

     For this reason, I have small doubts that Garroway will ever
win the popular acceptance of, say, Arthur Godfrey, which, it appears, is N.B.C.'s aim. He is a special taste, possibly a little fey
for wide esteem. There have been visible efforts to tone him down,
conceivably to avoid this charge. He once had an addiction for
words like incandescent, tenuous, gruesome, serene, gauzy, proto-
plasmic, esoteric, hassel, carbohydrated, resilient. He used to address his listeners as "my lissome," "old delicate," "my translucent"
and "my tawny." Of a singer he once remarked: "Listen how she
holds that note and then she forces her hands around its throat
and sort of shakes it."

     There is a good deal less of this now, though Garroway still
can't quite resist when some tenuous word wells up in his esoteric
throat. "You'll find nothing big, nothing upsetting here," he tells

his audience on his radio shows. The words, you'll note, are reasonably earthy; the philosophy is unchanged. Relax, kids. Nothing
is worth getting excited about.

They are very quiet musical shows, featuring an instrumental
quintet, a couple of singers--Connie Russell, who has one of those
sex-starved voices, and Jack Haskell, about whom I don't appear to
have anything at all in my notes--solos on various instruments and
Mr. Garroway, his cool self. He engages more and more in philosophy of the mildest sort, little snippets of news that strike him as
funny, and anecdotes about the cast.

Occasionally there are guests (Henry Morgan has been on a
couple of times) and there are a lot of little novelty numbers, not
all of which comes off. Restful is the word for it, I suppose. Incidentally, the origination of what might be described as the bop attitude stems way back to Bing Crosby, that very relaxed man, but
it has traveled so far from its starting point that neither Mr. Crosby
nor the bop addicts would recognize one another.

Just one other word about Mr. G., his philosophy and his
pretensions. His hobby is automobiles. He owns five--a Jaguar,
Model T, Lincoln Continental, Swallow and Rolls Royce. The Jaguar
is upholstered in natural alligator, the Lincoln in Harris tweed.
Mr. Garroway upholstered them himself.

--John Crosby in New York Herald
Tribune (January 6, 1950).

● ARTHUR GODFREY

There looms a financial struggle which threatens to eclipse
the titanic battle between Jay Gould and Cornelius Vanderbilt for control of the Erie Railroad. Looms, hell. It's already on us, and any
widows and orphans among you had better take to the hills. The
issue is orange juice. The contestants are those two great financial
typhoons--Bing Crosby and Arthur Godfrey. (A typhoon, junior,
is a tycoon who sings. Then there's the buffoon, a tycoon who makes
jokes. Like Bob Hope. What's a poltroon, you ask? Well, a poltroon
is an eight-gaited comedian who sings, dances, makes jokes, makes
faces, juggles, does high-wire acts, and makes a terrible amount of
money. There's only one living poltroon--Milton Berle. For heaven's
sake let's get on with this.)

The issue was joined last week when Arthur Godfrey, director
and stockholder of the Hi-V Corporation, maker of orange juice con-
centrate, took to the air for his--let's see now--third distinct and
separate television show. He teaches the ukulele and merchandises,
by a striking coincidence, orange juice. Way ahead of him in this

business is Bing Crosby, director and heavy stockholder in Minute Maid, who sings and merchandises his brand of orange juice every morning. At least in New York he's on in the morning. Out of town you may find the program, which is transcribed, almost any time of the day or night.

Years ago, back in the Paleozoic Age when reptiles and radio comedians roamed the earth, a sponsor could procure the services of an entertainer by paying him, if you'll excuse the expression, money. Then there was a period, the Second Ice Age, when money was a joke. You offered a man money to appear on a radio program and he doubled up with laughter. Today, money has progressed-- or, I suppose, degenerated is the word--even further. Money is no joke today. Money is an insult. To offer money to a comedian is like making derogatory remarks about his ancestry. Or even worse, about his ability.

The comedian wants stock in the enterprise. Or better yet, just turn the plant over to him and pay him dividends. Little by little the entertainers are going to wind up owning everything, like Rockefellers. The playboys of future generations won't be named Manville or Vanderbilt; they'll be Godfreys, Crosbys, Hopes and Jolsons. Inevitably, they'll start intermarrying like true aristocrats. You'll encounter names like Arthur Godfrey Crosby IV, of Sands Point, Deauville and Palm Beach. Arthur Godfrey Crosby IV will marry Hope Jolson, the most spectacular debutante of the year, daughter of Skelton von Bergen Jolson and great-great-granddaughter of Al Jolson, whose portrait hangs in the great hall of Aiken.

Well, let's stop wool-gathering.

The latest addition to Mr. Godfrey's empire is a fifteen-minute ukulele lesson. Godfrey has threatened to teach the nation how to play the ukulele for some time. He is now carrying out that threat. The ukulele--this is for the benefit of the younger members of the class--is a stringed instrument which passed into what I consider a well-deserved obscurity for a number of excellent reasons twenty years or so ago. Godfrey's attempt to revive it strikes me as something like ordering the tide to recede. But you can't tell. Godfrey is a remarkable man. There is a body of opinion harbored by Arthur's more worshipful admirers that if it had been Godfrey instead of canute, the tide would have receded.

Anyhow, the noted capitalist on this program strums his uke, explains basic finger movements, utters strong opinions about good ukes and bad ukes, which may cause a little consternation among ukulele manufacturers, and also demonstrates and drinks a little Hi-V orange juice. As a ukulele player, Arthur has twenty-one years of experience behind him and I suppose he is pretty good at it. I wouldn't know. I'm tone deaf to the charms of a ukulele.

Decades ago, popular myth held that a ukulele was potent courting equipment. My own experience never bore this out. The young blades in my vicinity considered a ukulele player no competition at all for the favors of young maidens. In fact, any one who couldn't elbow aside a ukulele player generally had some basic defect in his personality--like one eye in the middle of his forehead. However, we never ran up against Arthur Godfrey in these mating struggles.

--John Crosby in New York Herald
Tribune (April 10, 1950).

• THE GOLDBERGS (CBS, 1949-1951; NBC, 1952-1953; Dumont, 1954)

At the other tables in the Plaza's Oak Room, most of the patrons were taking their minds off the mugginess of the afternoon by sipping tall, cool and reasonably alcoholic beverages. So when the pleasant-faced woman in the black hat ordered hot tea, the waiter stared at her blankly. Then his look of puzzlement gave way to a smile of recognition as he said, "I'll get you the tea, Mrs. Goldberg, but please don't talk about it on the television. Nobody gets rich from tea-drinkers, except maybe Arthur Godfrey."

Gertrude Berg (for indeed it was she) laughed and resumed her conversation with the visiting magazine writer (who didn't order tea). "You see," she said. "Being recognized that easily is a thrill I'll never get over. It happens on the street, in a department store--all over. It's an experience common to people who perform on TV, but what I enjoy most is that they always break into a great, big smile when they spot me. No awe--just friendliness. And that makes me feel wonderful."

Equally as heartening to "Molly," of course, is the fact The Goldbergs have returned to television (WNBT, Fridays, 8 to 8:30 p.m.). They'd been off the channels for a whole year. Except for her guest appearances on the Milton Berle Show ("How I love working with that man!") Mrs. Berg has been virtually idle, a state that she finds quite intolerable. "I'm not happy unless I'm working," she says positively. Just what did she do with herself during the past 12 months? "Let's face it," she answers, "I cleaned closets."

The Goldbergs absence was not for want of a sponsor, but for lack of a suitable time slot. The drug sponsor whose sales increased by $5,000,000 during the 22 weeks of backing The Goldbergs early last year was understandably eager to pick up the show again for last fall, regardless of the night or hour. "But I wouldn't do it," Mrs. Berg explained, "because the only times available were those opposite Godfrey or Lucille Ball. It would have been foolish for me to jeopardize the entire future of The Goldbergs for the sake of a 39-week contract."

The 53-year-old Mrs. Berg, who speaks without a trace of her alter ego's Yiddish accent, has made a few changes in her Tremont Avenue contingent. Husband Jake is now being played by Robert H. Harris, a veteran stage and TV actor who's been seen on the program before as Jake's partner, "Mendel." The story has son "Sammy" serving in the Armed Forces, so that part won't have to be cast for a while. "And for the first time since the radio days," said Mrs. Berg, "we have a 'Mrs. Bloom.' Somehow, no name sounds as right as 'Mrs. Bloom,' right after a yoo-hoo. So she's back."

Back, too, are Eli Mintz, as "Uncle David" and Arlene Mc-Quade as "Rosalie." Arlene is prettier than ever, but her "advancing years" have posed something of a problem to Mrs. Berg. "In writing the scripts," she says, "I have to make sure that I don't have Rosalie doing anything childish. You see, she knows that her real-life boy friends are watching the show, so she balks at doing anything that would make her look or sound unsophisticated. And who can blame her?"

A major institution since 1929, The Goldbergs is a series whose writing and acting standards have always been the loftiest. Mrs. Berg is aided by the able Mike Morris on the plot-outlines, but writes the actual scripts herself, and there are few craftsmen in any branch of literature who have her faculty for dialogue. It is a genius that has paid off. There is nothing on Tremont Avenue, for example, that can match the Bergs' 17-room country home in Bedford Hills or their seven-room, Park Avenue duplex, lined with original works of such brush-wielders as Millet, Picasso, Rembrandt and Lautrec.

Some of the warmest Goldberg scripts have revolved around Molly's sporadic attempts to acquire "culture" overnight. The real-life Berg family is swarming with the stuff, none of it gained hurriedly. Both Gertrude, a Columbia University graduate, and her husband, Lewis, a consulting engineer, are ardent students of the arts. Son Cherney, 29, who produces the TV series, is a composer of serious music, and daughter Harriet, 26, is currently working toward her Ph.D. in 18th century literature. As Mrs. Berg puts it, "When you have about all the money you need, what else is there but culture?"

As a televiewer in her own right, Mrs. Berg is partial to Groucho Marx and the mystery shows. She steers clear of the situation comedies, for fear they may influence her own scripts. And she has never watched herself perform, either on the motion picture screen (the film, Molly was a highlight of the 1950 season) or on a kinescope of the TV show. "Like most people," she says, "I prefer

to think of myself as I was at 18. Seeing myself on the screen now
would only make me unhappy." Be that as it may, watching an artist
like Mrs. Berg perform isn't likely to make anyone else unhappy.
Both Tremont and Park Avenues can be proud of her.

> --Philip Minoff in Cue (July 11,
> 1953), page 13.

• HOWDY DOODY (NBC, 1947-1960)

There are two things you can do with Howdy Doody. You
can congratulate the people who are responsible for the program,
and you can censure them in hearts and spades.

Howdy Doody is quite harmless. For keeping it so, you can
congratulate the producers--that such is a back-handed compliment
is definitely intended. But, the impact of the innocuous characters
and situations on a small child are amazing. Almost every night I
am told of the ridiculous exploits of Banana Louie, Flub-a-Dub,
Clarabelle and a host of others.

While the son-and-heir's fondness for all of them seems quite
equally apportioned, I must own, not without a blush, that there
is one character I have reluctantly grown to care for. She is
Princess Summer-Fall-Winter-Spring, as cute a little Indian puppet
as you've ever seen. I suppose I like her so much because any
time Billy wants to get something out of his small sister he simply
reminds her that if she does what he wants she will be "just like
the princess." Since I am inclined to regard the lass as a princess
in fact, I'm inclined also to be fond of her prototype.

You may gather, though, that there is very little substance
in Howdy Doody. Think of the opportunities they are missing.
They have all the ingredients to capture the childish imagination
and interest. They now have that interest, but there it ends.
What good are they doing the children who follow the exploits of
this admixture of puppets and human beings through ridiculous
meanderings on the television screen?

They don't even take the obvious opportunity to stress
such national virtues as cleaning your teeth regularly, though a
well-known dental cream is a sponsor. They don't stress good
manners, obedience to "your mummy" and so on. Ah, well, chalk
up another program for the "lost chances" department of America's
fastest growing communications medium. Now, if I had the chance to
do a TV show for kids, I'd....

> --William H. Shriver, Jr. in
> Catholic World (March 1951),
> page 461.

• I MARRIED JOAN (NBC, 1952-1955)

Perhaps one of television's greatest contributions to art is
its creation of a type of program we shall call, for lack of a better
term, the Half-Hour Domestic-Comedy-Situation-Farce-Husband-and-
Wife Playlet-Plotlet. I have no doubt that in the years to come,
when the historians of television get down to the heartbreaking
task of classifying early television programs, the Half-Hour Domestic-
Comedy-Situation-Farce-Husband-and-Wife Playlet-Plotlet will be
known by another name. Meanwhile, for the purpose of getting along
with the thesis, we will abbreviate the term to HHDCSFHAWPP, or,
better, FHAWPP.

There are a number of Fhawpps on television these days,
and they have several things in common. They involve, as their
name suggests, a husband and wife who are ensnarled in some domestic situation, around which a thirty-minute playlet with a gimmick has been written. This analysis encompasses, of course, only
the bare framework of a Fhawpp. Examined more closely, these
programs reveal that both the husband and the wife, although living
in passably decorated homes with large living rooms, large bedrooms,
and all-electric kitchens, have mental ages that hover between eight
and twelve. For another thing, the husband and wife in a Fhawpp
have stepped, historically, from the comic strips, rather than from
the farce of either stage or screen. Thus, although television marks
a great advance in the technique of electronics, it has gone back, at
least in Fhawpps, to that earlier means of communication, the newspaper. Small episodes within the half-hour span of a Fhawpp come
and go with the rapidity of daily installments in the funnies; minor
climaxes are reached every five or six minutes, just as minor climaxes are reached in the comics in every third or fourth frame; and
by the close of a Fhawpp the audience has watched the equivalent
of a whole week of funnies. Television has improved upon the comics
somewhat by abandoning, for underlining climaxes or sub-climaxes,
the use of the words "Zowie!," "Whaam!," and "Kerplunk!" Instead,
in Fhawpp climaxes or sub-climaxes a character slaps a hand to his
mouth, pops his eyes, and shakes his head in utter bewilderment.
Variations consist of rubbing the chin, popping the eyes, and shaking
the head; pursing the lips, popping the eyes, and shaking the head.
Otherwise, there is less difference between a comic strip and a
Fhawpp than between your butter knives and your grandmother's.

Let us inspect in somewhat closer detail a specific Fhawpp,
I Married Joan (Wednesdays, 8-8:30 p.m., N.B.C.). The first
person singular of the title is Judge Bradley Stevens (judges are
setups for leading roles in Fhawpps; they lend an easily punctured
dignity to the proceedings, and they can tidy things up at will by
calling upon the forces of law and order), who is married to Joan
Stevens, a blonde of the type known as "dizzy." Since her husband
is the judge of what I take to be a criminal court in a small town, her

particular brand of dizziness is especially embarrassing to him, and
he is forever fearful that one of her emptyheaded notions will cause
him serious trouble. On I Married Joan the other night, we first
saw the Judge and his wife at breakfast. Mrs. Stevens, who was
reading the morning paper, announced that the Blond Bandit, a
local criminal, was still at large. "She's struck again," said Mrs.
Stevens. "What for?" asked the Judge. "Better pay?" Once the
tone of the Stevens household has been thus established, the Judge
sets out for work, carrying with him a suitcase he wants to have re-
paired. Mrs. Stevens, eying the suitcase, wonders whether he is
giving her the heave-ho, and, to show interest in his work, asks
his permission to visit his court that morning. The paragon of
justice grants his consent.

We next see the Judge questioning a man suspected of breaking into a safe. The man is on the witness stand, he looks like a
thug, his name is Rocky Slattery, and he answers no questions,
merely grunting, "I stand on de Fift' Amendment." The Judge's
wife is seated in the rear of the courtroom, alongside a blond young
lady who turns out to be Mrs. Slattery. Later, when she and
Mrs. Stevens go outside for a cup of coffee, she convinces the
Judge's wife that poor Rocky is innocent. Mrs. Stevens takes Mrs.
Slattery home for supper that evening. The entrance of the Judge
into his house, his astonishment at encountering the wife of a man
on trial in his court, his attempt to explain the ethics of the situation to the two ladies, and his harassed cry of "Well, let's eat!"--
here was Fhawppery at its best! A rapid-fire sequence of events
followed. Mrs. Stevens is certain that her husband is about to
convict Rocky on circumstantial evidence alone. To prove that circumstantial evidence is not enough, she pretends to be the celebrated
Blond Bandit. The Judge becomes aware of her plot and turns the
tables on her in a manner that I simply do not have the strength to
relate. At the close of the Fhawpp, the Judge and his wife are
about to go to sleep. Placidity and an air of quiet domesticity have
returned to the Stevens' house. Mrs. Stevens thinks that her little
adventure has made her husband ponder circumstantial evidence more
carefully than in the past. No, not at all, says the Judge. He
looks pretty arch. Mrs. Stevens might like to know, he goes on,
that Rocky confessed that morning, and that the Blond Bandit is
none other than Mrs. Slattery. Mrs. Stevens slaps a hand to her
mouth, pops her eyes, and shakes her head in utter bewilderment--
a perfect ending to a perfect Fhawpp.

--Philip Hamburger in The New
Yorker (January 24, 1953),
pages 69-70.

• THE KATE SMITH EVENING HOUR (NBC, 1951-1952)

The Kate Smith Evening Hour struck me at the outset as

being marked by a certain air of desperation. It occurs on Wednesday at 8 p.m., an hour which on N.B.C. last year was sacred to
comedians. However, N.B.C., I guess, just ran out of comics and
somehow the full-throated and extensive Miss Smith was thrust in
there to stem the flood of Arthur Godfrey, who appears at the same
hour on what is known as another network.

It's hard to tell what Miss Kate, one of the perennial glories
of daytime or female radio, is doing on evening television when the
men are home, presumably in search of relaxation. In fact this
show is pretty hard for me to explain in any terms. Miss Kate is
not a mistress of ceremonies, not even an Ed Sullivan or "What-on-
Earth-Am-I-Doing-Here" type emcee; she's not, apart from her singing, an entertainer; she doesn't--as she does on radio--burden the
air with profound reflections on the sanctity of matrimony (which
she has never experienced).

She is above all that. She is presented as a sort of American
institution, like Thanksgiving, something that doesn't require explanation. Ted Collins, her personal Svengali who has guided her des-
tiny--if that's not too sweeping a word--for several generations, ac-
cords her a reverence which I found damned irritating. The con-
founded show even opens with a shot of waves breaking on our rock-
encrusted shores, pans next to a shot of the American flag, con-
centrates briefly on the star-studded section of the flag and dwells
finally on a single star--symbolizing, as I gather it, Miss Smith,
America, motherhood, and the National Broadcasting Company.

"God bless everybody in no trump," I murmured as this ma-
jestic opening faded and Miss Smith herself hove into view to sing
"Vampin' Till You're Ready." It's a rather odd selection to follow
such a patriotic introduction--I half expected her to sing the Constitution in C sharp minor--and Miss Smith didn't improve matters
much by jiggling like a kootch dancer and snapping her fingers.
If Miss Kate wants to be an American institution, she ought to model
herself a little more closely on the behavior of other American insti-
tutions like, say, the stone lions at the steps of the New York Public Library.

The rest of the show is a mish-mash. Olsen and Johnson,
another American institution, came aboard to deliver that sketch
wherein they are in a hotel room, just trying to get a little sleep,
and everybody, including an N.B.C. guided tour, conspires to get
in the way. I first saw Olsen and Johnson do this bit in Milwaukee--
let's see now--about 1932 and I must admit they've rounded it, improved it and polished it a lot since then. It may be the most
popular sketch on television, having pretty well done the rounds
of all the shows. A classic, in short, which ought to be ready in
another year or so for the Library of Congress. This is a real
classic show.

Three guys and two dolls followed with a song number in which they bounded about without dropping a note, an impressive but exhausting mixture of athletics and vocalism. Miss Smith reappeared to sing "Longing." This led into a big dance number in which several thousand yards of crinoline were unfurled. From time to time, Mr. Collins, dinner-jacketed and acting a little like the curator of the American wing at the Metropolitan, showed up to talk about Miss Smith. There was a brief, muddy dramatic sketch, starring Sylvia Sydney and Sidney Blackmer, which proved that crime doesn't pay. It was acted in almost total darkness without scenery.

None of this was very bad but nothing was very good either. In any case, it didn't add up to anything that resembled a television show and I can't quite figure out what Miss Smith is doing there. They're trying, I speculated, to make a female Arthur Godfrey out of her. But is there any great need for a female Arthur Godfrey or, for that matter, a male Arthur Godfrey? I just don't understand the thought processes that led to the construction of this show and I'm afraid I never will.

--John Crosby in New York Herald
Tribune (October 14, 1951).

• LEAVE IT TO BEAVER (CBS, 1957-1958; ABC, 1958-1963)

I was all set to give a gold star for merit to Leave It to Beaver, the new CBS-TV "domestic comedy" program, but now it must go to the bottom of the class for poor conduct on a recent Friday night. I'm sorry to have to do this, because I could grow fond of pre-adolescent Theodore, nicknamed "The Beaver." the rather serious, freckle-faced youngster who is the star of the show; of Wally, his elder teen-age brother; and of their Mr. and Mrs. Average-American parents living in their typical Good Housekeeping home. The Beaver's weekly boyhood adventures are written, it is given out, by authors who are fathers themselves; the situations reflect, with tasteful humor, the entanglements that often arise in "family-oriented" homes where the parents are pals as well as disciplinarians. It was the Beaver at school which furnished the plot, however, the night he fell from grace.

He took a mass I.Q. test, along with all the pupils in his school. The family expected no exceptional results, as the Beaver's scholarship is mediocre. The surprise was great when the principal informed them that their son had earned the highest score in the school, which was also the second highest score ever achieved anywhere in the same test. The Beaver's parents were told that the school was not equipped to develop the gifts of a "genius," and the principal advised them to enroll him in a private school. They took him to be interviewed by the headmaster of a "progressive" school, which boasted no baseball diamond and where the emphasis was on cooperation rather than competition. Father, who had played football when he was at school, was let down by the interview, and the Beaver was uneasy. The boy's doubts about the prospective change were underscored by the shut-out treatment he now received from his public-school classmates who wanted to have nothing to do with a "genius."

The world was set right again by his shamefaced teacher who suddenly revealed that Theodore wasn't a genius at all. A new boy in the class had carried the test papers to the principal's office, and had seized the opportunity on the way to switch names on his paper and the Beaver's. The new boy hated being a genius, and he had chosen Theodore's paper, particularly, because everybody liked the Beaver. Father and mother were genuinely relieved; even the teacher confessed that she liked the Beaver "better this way." All the excitement about having a genius in the family had vanished before the winds of unpopularity. Well--so much the better for the Beaver. That progressive school wouldn't have been much fun: all it had was a swimming pool, gymnasium, and excellent laboratories. The headmaster was made to appear pretty much of an ass--with his accent on cooperation and his downbeat on competition.

Our deeper concern, however, is with that new boy who switched the test papers. Would his parents place him in the progressive school which he hated? Or would they permit him to remain Wally's classmate and be happy being liked--what matter if he never fulfilled his promise? The real dilemma was left untouched not merely, because Leave It to Beaver is just television entertainment, but because the choice which in true life presses upon us as a nation is too painful to face. Do we not desperately need geniuses for survival? How shall we make them eat calculus and like it--if their own desperate, inner compulsion is to be the captain of the football team and the most popular man in the class? President Eisenhower, his Cabinet, and Congress may lay heroic plans for producing the brainpower the nation requires, but citizen lip-service to the cause is not enough.

Neither will money manage the trick. Before we can mass-produce genius we must respect and honor genius. We are certainly not going in the right direction if we teach our children to suspect and dislike it or to assume that a high development of intellect is incompatible with "normalcy" or popularity.

--Robert Lewis Shayon in Saturday Review, Vol. 41, No. 5 (February 1, 1958), page 26.

• LIFE IS WORTH LIVING (Dumont, 1952-1955; ABC, 1956-1957)

Another strong, complex personality, Bishop Fulton J. Sheen, is visible each Tuesday evening from eight to eight-thirty over Du Mont. I know of no other program in which one man, speaking for thirty minutes, makes the time pass so quickly, and this is due not only to what Bishop Sheen has to say but to the strangely hypnotic and persuasive way he says it. His programs seem to me to be unfailingly interesting, thought-provoking, and, in the best sense, full of fun, even if at times the Bishop's jokes are somewhat strained. The other evening, he spoke with deep feeling and great competence of the work of Einstein and other physicists who have labored in the field of relativity, and refuted what he referred to as "the false charge" that atomic scientists are atheistic and godless. "Science," he said, "is not atheistic and godless. It is not concerned with God or moral values." He went on to tackle, with the help of a piece of chalk and a blackboard, the theory of relativity itself, and the result was a most rewarding half hour.

> --Philip Hamburger in The New
> Yorker (December 13, 1952),
> page 147.

• MR. PEEPERS (NBC, 1952-1955)

A comedian who instantly endears himself to the public because he offers a sympathetic extension of themselves, is Wally Cox as Mr. Peepers. Here is a characterization only slightly exaggerated. Mr. Peepers, for all practical purposes, could exist. Accepting the realism of the character, no one is ever too disturbed by some of the fanciful situations which overtake him.

In a comparatively short time Mr. Peepers has become a national figure. So much so that when he was dropped from the air, a storm of protest from vocal admirers brought him back with a new sponsor. If you have not yet watched this superbly subtle comedian, be warned that he is insidious, and will win you over as a confirmed fan and booster.

> --Fortnight (January 19, 1953),
> page 7.

• MY FRIEND IRMA (CBS, 1952-1954)

Time now for a look at some of television's humorous, or allegedly humorous shows. A typically Hollywood entry in this field

is the Marie Wilson starrer, <u>My Friend Irma</u>. Let us grant first off
that Miss Wilson has a body with several points of interest; having
conceded that, we have said almost everything in the least bit favor-
able about the program.

<u>Irma</u> is a rehash of the radio show of the same name, and
oddly enough both of these shows bear a striking resemblance to
the Broadway hit of yesteryear, <u>My Sister Eileen</u>. The resemblance
stops with the similarity of characters, however, because Ruth
McKenny's <u>Eileen</u> had wit, freshness, charm, and originality--all
qualities which are sorely missing in <u>Irma</u>.

It is a little difficult to place exactly wherein lies the blame
for the dull thud this show makes week after week. The actors are
competent, the writers average, direction and production good.
Why, then, this "blah" of a show? It would seem that something
basically is wrong; the original conception of what makes for humor
is off. Once launched on a false premise, everything must of necessity wind up on a slightly sour note. The writers try to twist
their talents to conform, the actors are forced to portray illogical
characters, and the director must do his best to make an unlikely
situation seem real.

In using exaggerated human characterizations as the springboard for humor, the originator of <u>Irma</u> is using sound comedy techniques. What he forgets is that the exaggeration must have a
realistic foundation. Just as caricature is based on real people, TV
humor must pick up actual human foibles and by enlarging and poking fun, achieve comedy.

A program such as <u>Irma</u>, which is built on phony situations,
phony people, and ridiculous antics, can never achieve the universal
identification which truly great comedy demands.

--<u>Fortnight</u> (January 19, 1953),
page 7.

• OMNIBUS (CBS, 1953-1956; ABC, 1956-1957)

Fortunately for the industry, and for the sanity of viewers,
an occasional television show turns out to be a completely well
rounded gem. Falling into that category is <u>Omnibus</u>, seen on the
CBS network at 1:30 on Sunday afternoons.

This is the show which received so much advance hoopla as
the first effort of the Radio-Television Division of the Ford Foundation. The rapturous preliminary ballyhoo was a little frightening to
people long accustomed to big build-ups for mediocre shows. In this
case however the preview praise was fully justified.

Omnibus runs a full hour and a half, and commands attention
through every moment. It is difficult to allocate this show to any
pat category; it is just what its name implies--an Omnibus of all
the worthwhile things which can be assembled for a particular week.
No attempt is made to fit the different items into the rigid broadcasters' limits of 15 or 30 minutes. If a particular segment needs
9 minutes or 17, or 43, that is the time it receives.

Alastair Cooke as the over-all coordinator of the show brings
a modest, refreshingly intelligent approach to the job of narrator or
host. The viewer is never exhorted or cajoled into feeling that
what he is seeing is the "greatest," or the "finest," or even the
"newest" thing to be found. Omnibus seemingly doesn't worry
about selling itself to the viewer. Whatever ballet, drama, scientific information, or discussion it presents is served up to the public
simply, for what it is worth. If the public likes it, fine; if not,
perhaps they will prefer something else in the weekly omnibus.

Actually of course the apparent effortlessness of the show is
deceptive. To arrive at the relaxed mood takes extremely clever
and capable hands in all departments. It is no easy task to assem-
ble all the various elements for a show which can present, all in
one afternoon, a complete ballet, a television premiere of Menotti's
The Telephone, a discussion of the development of plastics, a
dramatization of Lincoln's assassination, and a review of the life of
Leonardo da Vinci.

This is entertainment in its truest sense--not socko stuff,
but the kind of solid, meaty material which survives, and let us
hope will continue to survive.

Credits on this show are too numerous to list here, and
incidentally provide another clue to the quality of the entire effort.
At no time during the hour and a half are credits blasted out at the
viewer--there is no vieing for honors, only a simple straightforward
listing at the end of the show. Omnibus stands out as one of the
truly significant contributions to the new medium.

--Fortnight (December 8, 1952),
page 4.

• JACK PAAR

His mother and Billy Graham think he should have been a
minister. He himself thinks perhaps he should have tried to be a
missionary, like Albert Schweitzer. Some of television's unseen but
much-heard word merchants think he would have made a fine gag
writer. Walter Winchell plainly thinks he should have been put into
an ablative nose cone on a one-way rocket trip to the moon. Sponsors

of late movies think he should have stayed in daytime television,
and all across the land people who like to go to sleep early think
he should have stood in bed--and given them a chance to get to
bed too.

But about 5,000,000 fans--along with happy NBC executives,
satisfied advertisers and fellow entertainers whom his show helped
to success--think that Jack Paar should be precisely what he is: a
first-rate, refreshingly different TV performer who in a single year
has come out of nowhere and made a huge hit of a special kind of
entertainment. What Paar brings into American living rooms five
nights a week is both more and less than a comedy, variety or
chatter show--it is a special show business blend that Paartisans
consider uniquely satisfying.

He is one of a whole new class of TV-age entertainers--the
just talkers. But his appeal has little in common with Steve Allen's
brash sidewalk zaniness or Arthur Godfrey's somnolent saloon drone.
When Paar appears on screen, there is an odd, hesitant hitch to his
stride. For a split self-effacing second he is a late arrival, worried
that he has blundered into the wrong party. His shy smile--he has
developed one of the shiest smiles in the business--seems to ask a
question: "Is this applause for Me?" Then he remembers: he is
really the host. Almost diffidently he pulls up a chair. What Paar
calls his "cute little Presbyterian face" beams puckishly. With his
voice wavering between a whisper and a sigh, he begins to engage
his guests in quiet conversation.

He is surrounded by a band, singers, guest comedians, skits.
But what really gives the Paar show its shape is the L formed by a
scarred desk and a well-worn couch. Behind the desk, Jack is
barricaded; the couch supports a "panel" of regular or irregular con-
versationalists. Says Paar: "The show is nothing. Just me and
people talking. Historic naturalness. We don't act, we just defend
ourselves."

Most of the time, Paar is merely a good listener with a knack
of asking the right questions. He may be as fast on the ad-lib
draw as the next gag-toting desperado, but again and again he lets
himself be "topped." He is all the world's straight man. And yet,
Paar can hit. A caustic remark, a misconstrued question, a real or
fancied attack in or out of the studio can provoke stinging repartee.
When Winchell attacked him for a misstatement made by Elsa Maxwell
on the show, Paar counterpunched fiercely, guessed--on the air--
that Winchell's "high, hysterical voice" results from his "too-tight
underwear." Often, Paar punches with less provocation--massive
retaliation, as one of his former writers puts it--for no act of ag-
gression. When Perfectionist Paar berates stagehands ("the tippytoe
squad") for being slow, his writers for providing dull jokes, the
studio audience for not laughing, it is all done in fun--but there is
a serious, waspish edge in the laughter.

The same element of unpredictability--the suggestion that a mild explosive has been put into the prominently displayed tumblers of Sponsor Lipton's tea--derives from the widespread belief that Paar permits off-color humor. On the whole the charge is unjust. The show's most celebrated blue note was struck while Paar was on vacation and Stand-In Jonathan Winters allowed Anthropologist Ashley Montague to talk about how lack of breast feeding gives American males a bosom fixation. Jack says he would never have permitted it ("After breast feeding, there's just no place to go"). But Paar does occasionally tarry near the brink of the blue, and this brinksmanship is another reason why the Paar show provokes the implicit question: "What's going to happen next?"--and why the show is a hit.

The Big Gamble. When asked about Jack Paar, the late Fred Allen once said: "Oh, you mean the young man who had the meteoric disappearance." A year ago the description still fitted Paar, sometime minor movie actor and perennial radio-TV summer replacement. He had done well with a radio program and a daytime television show of his own, but never well enough to make it big. One TV executive dismissed him as strictly a "pipe and slipper type." What happened next is told by NBC's Board Chairman Robert Sarnoff: "We faced a critical decision. The America After Dark version of our Tonight show was a shambles. Sponsors were shunning the program. Some stations were defecting from the NBC late-night line-up in favor of old Hollywood movies. We were under heavy pressure to give up late-night live programing. After much soul searching we staked everything on an amiable young man named Jack Paar--and never has a network program gamble paid off more handsomely."

As it moved into its second year last week, the show had chalked up five industry awards and a higher rating than successful Steve Allen several years ago in the same time slot. At a time when live shows are fading fast from every channel, the Paar show is seen over a record 115 stations and has collected as many as 38 sponsors, ranging from Minipoo shampoo to Corega denture fastener. One measure of the show's import is the loyalty of most of the guests; they are paid only "scale" ($320 per appearance), but most of them love the show for its fun--and for the publicity.

Today it is already fashionable to forget how few people gave the show a chance to survive at all with a tough TV audience--night people already addicted to six-gun cowpokes or to the time-defying charms of late movies, with their youthful Gables and ageless Garbos. Could the All-American boy with the dimpled chin and the dinky toupee move the merchandise against such competition? At first NBC bigwigs were talking about a well-integrated variety show. Says Paar: "A television executive doesn't know what he wants to do, but he can put it on paper. I let them all talk and write memos and I secretly made plans."

The Characters. Paar's plans consisted mostly of organized planlessness. During the past year Jack has tantalized a tame lion with doses of catnip, tangled with a pickpocket named Dominique, who lifted his wallet, belt and wrist watch, sweated through a few falls with a professional wrestler named Killer Kowalski. He has worn funny hats, taken off his pants, climbed up the studio walls. But always, the high points were provided by the talkers--guided or goaded, driven or drawn out by Jack.

There was Dody Goodman, corn-fed elf and professional bird-brain, whose irrelevance and irreverence were fun until Paar got rid of her in an unseemly family squabble (Time, March 24). Elsa Maxwell appeared for weekly off-with-their-heads chats, chopped at so many well-known necks (including Winchell's, Presley's, Princess Grace's) that Jack was only half kidding when he rolled his eyes and groaned: "Call the lawyers." For a few frenetic nights, Zsa Zsa Gabor leaned over her cleavage and rattled her host into some now famous fluffs. "It will cut him!" she squealed, in the middle of his Norelco razor pitch. "It won't cut anything!" roared Jack, who could have happily cut off Zsa Zsa's blonde tresses when he realized what he had said.

Gradually a corporal's guard of regulars formed, including gifted Pianist José Melis, suave Announcer Hugh Downs and Singer Betty Johnson, who all served as Paar's foils. The regulars became as familiar as comic-strip characters. Leading characters at present: Genevieve, French singer with a haphazard haircut and accent to match, and an oldtime comedian named Cliff Arquette, with drooping pants and rustic repartee. Despite her sophisticated air, it is naively charming Genevieve who represents innocence on the show and Cliff, despite his cornball appearance, whose trigger-quick ad libs speak for sophistication. But the biggest character remains Jack Paar--and he represents neither innocence nor sophistication, but something in between.

Paar claims that he is just being himself on the show, and to a very large extent he is. Unlike an actor, he cannot take refuge behind a script or a false beard; he must convince the audience that he is exposing his true face. The result is that the traits of the "real" Paar are very like those of the TV Paar--the difference being that off screen they loom much bigger. Says he: "It is not true that my personality is split. It is filleted. On the air all I do is hold back. If I gave too much of myself on the show, it would be too much for the cable." If the on-screen Paar can be kind and sentimental, the off-screen Paar often weeps like a baby. If the public Paar can be waspish and oddly defensive, the private Paar often seems like a hunted and inordinately suspicious man.

As he sees it, the soft green leaf may well be a nettle in disguise, and danger lurks on all sides. It is hard to trust people --"If they slap me on the back, maybe the next time they slap me they'll have a knife." On the other hand, so few people are really grateful to him: "It's not that I need credit. But somewhere along the line the dog should be patted on the head." If some neighborhood toughs honk their horns outside his house to annoy him, he speaks of being "hounded by degenerates."

This feeling of being hunted may be explained by past failures, by the very real back-stabbing that goes on in show business, and by the pressure of Paar's schedule--for in his life, almost every night is opening night. Each show is preceded by a private warmup, ranging from gnawing anxiety to panic. During the hours of preparation--which must end in laughter or failure-- Paar is probably doing his hardest work. At noon on a recent, typical pre-show day, Jack was prowling his barn-red twelve-room house in suburban Bronxville, N.Y. His breakfast had been spoiled by an unfriendly newspaper comment on the previous night's show; now he was worried about the coming performance.

What to do? He calls Assistant Producer Monty Morgan at his Manhattan office. "It looks pretty nothing tonight," Jack complains. "The red flag is up. We're in trouble, we're really in trouble..."

2:05 p.m. Glumly Jack selects a Cuban cigar from his humidor. He is afraid to smoke cigars in public lest he look like a "wise guy." Pipes too have been forced into the privacy of his home since Marlboro cigarettes became one of the show's sponsors. Wandering aimlessly once more, like a man in search of work, Jack walks into the living room and picks up a newspaper. "What the hell can I say about the new women's hemlines?" he asks sadly. "I've already advised them to have their knees lowered."

2:50 p.m. He walks out to the swimming pool behind the house and seems surprised to discover that his nine-year-old daughter Randy is off swimming at the country club. "I never played with other kids. Most of the time Randy would rather sit and daydream like I do."

4:25 p.m. A call from an NBC attorney informs Jack that as a bonus for signing his new contract (which runs for two more years), he gets six weeks of vacation with pay. Now his salary comes to $2,750 a week, plus a percentage of the income from commercials, but he has no time for pleasure. "I don't know what in hell we're going to do tonight," he moans.

4:45 p.m. Still groaning about the "absolute lack of material" for the night's show, Jack suddenly cocks his head to the sound of a car horn and catcalls in front of his home. "The degenerates again," he says softly to a visitor. "See, Pal, I kid you not."

4:57 p.m. Talent Scout Tom O'Malley calls to announce that old Prizefighter-Clown Maxie Rosenbloom will be available for the night's show. "Tell Rosenbloom to be himself," Jack warns. "No prepared jokes." The warming is hardly necessary. Responsible for signing most of the guests on Paar's show, O'Malley is well aware of the rules of the game. Forbidden are "Lindy" comedians--the brash, Berle-type gagsters given to dialect jokes and continuous excitement. Says Paar: "I'm not interested in comedians named Joey or Jackie--no rock 'n' roll, no jazz."

5:10 p.m. After a brief dip in the pool ("I spend all my time keeping it clean and I'm seldom in it"), Jack settles down with a Jack Daniel's softened by water. "Do you know that right now, tonight, there is not one single written word, and now--WHAT TIME IS IT? We're in panic, NOW!"

5:27 p.m. Miriam Paar, Jack's pretty and patient wife, appears at poolside with a dinner tray--brook trout, corn on the cob, string beans, mixed green salad. Jack tops it off with a chocolate sundae garnished with whipped cream and peanuts.

7:10 p.m. Dressed in a blue suit, pink shirt and dark glasses, Jack is ready for the hired limousine that has come to take him to the show. He settles into the back seat with a groan, convinced that he is on a short ride toward disaster.

7:54 p.m. Jack hurries into the rear door of the Hudson Theater on West 44th Street and climbs upstairs to his dressing room. En route, he is cornered by Chris Carroll, an old Army buddy now serving as feature editor of the show (i.e., the procurer of oddball talent--pickpockets, performing chimpanzees, professional wrestlers). "You want Paul Anderson on the show?" Carroll asks hopefully. "Strongest man in the world. Hold you up over his head." Paar nods. Inside his dressing room he sits down and studies a mimeographed "status report" of talent bookings; peremptorily he scrawls "O.K.," "No" or "Investigate" after each listing.

8:01 p.m. Paar studies the scripts for the commercials, reads a part planned for a visiting comic, says "Whew!" and shoves the papers aside in disgust.

8:09 p.m. Writer Walt Kempley comes into the dressing room with the news that he has found a gun that shoots soft bullets. How about a duel with Genevieve to see who can draw the fastest? Often such gimmicks are the bright spots of a show (a mechanical fish-eating fish was brought back for numerous encores, as was a pair of "binoculars" that were actually half liquor flask). But tonight, Paar is not in the mood. "I need a show," he snaps.

8:16 p.m. Jack reads a skit called "Famous Last Words" and discards it as no good. Finally he begins to stitch together a few lines himself for his opening monologue, thinking aloud, jotting down the words in a stenographic notebook. "We have a wonderful evening planned just as soon as the show is over ... This show comes to you in compatible color; this means my shirt and socks match."

8:45 p.m. Onstage, Jack takes time to rehearse a skit, then
wanders around asking questions, checking on props, apparently
calm. Abruptly, he strides into his dressing room. On the dim,
dusty stage of the Hudson Theater, technicians keep rummaging about
the little world of cables, cameras, and dingy sets that will look sump-
tuous on the home screens. The band rehearses in shirtsleeves.

10:35 p.m. After a long, embarrassing interview with an English actress who was scheduled for a guest appearance, Jack comes
onstage again, explains with a sour face: "She made a movie with
Noel Coward, she did this, she did that. I said, 'Can you talk
about these things?' She said she wanted to be a cook, a creative
cook. That's not believable. A good-looking girl with a build
wants to be a cook? The audience would think she was lying, that
I was lying. It would destroy the naturalness of the show. I had
to let her go."

10:58 p.m. Genevieve shouts: "Zhonnee, I have no shoes,
dahling. I cannot go without red shoes. I left them in apartment."
A stage manager marches off to get the shoes, muttering.

11:01 p.m. Paar is frantic. "That wastebasket is filled with
routines by the writers. This is what I end up with--two sheets
from my own notebook."

11:14 p.m. Paar stands in the wings alone. The show theme
strikes up. Out front, Announcer Hugh Downs, who has been
warming up the audience, chuckles with the nightly enthusiasm:
"Now here's Jack." In that instant Jack Paar strides onstage, smiling shyly, snapping his fingers. He makes his little joke about hemlines and the men behind the TV cameras smile at him as if they
meant it. The show is on its way, following a complex timetable of
station breaks and commercials as the network gathers stations and
moves west across the night.

Tough Damn Job. From this moment on, Paar is assured,
professional, unfaltering. During each station break, after every
commercial, whenever he is off camera, he finds a moment to lean
over to chat with a guest, give instructions to an assistant director,
and check the time schedule. The peering cameras, the producing
teleprompters, the signaling technicians seem not to bother him; he
is at home. With Jack Douglas, head writer of his show, whom he
puts on as a guest from time to time, he ad libs quickly and surely.
With other guests, he is gentle, humble, anxious not to seem brighter
than anybody else.

By midnight it is plain that the show is a hit. A cameraman
smothers a laugh and says, "Jack's flying. He'll be home now."
Henny Youngman, a charter member of the Lindy comedians Jack so
often criticizes, has dropped in to watch--as many show business
pros do. Says Youngman: "This guy gives 200%; he wants to be

double good. He gives out a feeling of love, that's why they look
at this man. This is a tough damn job."

A few moments after 1 a.m. the lights go down, and Jack is
surrounded by exuberant writers. "Rosenbloom was great," says
one. "Douglas killed them," chimes in another. Jack says: "I
thought me was pretty good, too." He wipes off his make-up, grabs
his briefcase and pushes his way to his car--he never joins the rest
of the cast at the corner bar. At home in Bronxville, where Miriam
is waiting up, he has a cup of soup and a beer. At 3:15 a.m., after
reading two scripts that Writer Douglas has put together for future
shows, Paar turns out the light.

Balloon Breaker. To last through this kind of performance
five nights a week takes a talent spawned by radio, toughened by
Hollywood and burnished by the demands of an unforgiving clutch
of television cameras. No comedian in the U.S. can boast a more
abundant supply of the necessary skills than Jack Paar. He has
been practicing them almost all his life.

A sort of migrant Middle Westerner, thanks to his father's
job with the New York Central Railroad, which kept the family forever on the move, Jack Paar was born in Canton, Ohio on May 1,
1917. With time out for a stretch in Detroit, he did most of his
growing up in Jackson, Mich. But wherever he went, his childhood
memories are almost all somber ("I never had a childhood. I was
born an old man"). When he was five, an older brother was killed
by a car. All that comes back to Jack from his tenth year is the
death of his best friend. "I went to the funeral," he remembers
now, "and I didn't know what to do. My heart was breaking, and
all I could think of was to break balloons through the service. Then
I went home and bawled."

He stuttered badly as a boy, but cured himself by cramming
buttons in his mouth and reading aloud. At 14 he spent six months
in bed recovering from tuberculosis. He quit high school at 16. He
was already working as an office boy and part-time announcer at a
station in Jackson (WIBM) for $3 a week. Oldtimers still remember
his style. "This is Jack Buh-Buh-Buh-Boo Paar, your announcer,"
he would croon, or "This is your young and popular announcer, Bing
Paar." He kept a discarded microphone in the attic at home. It was
hooked up to nothing, but he sat before it by the hour, reading
aloud from plays, books, magazines. At 18 he left home and began
to bounce around the country on his own, handling microphones in
Indianapolis, Youngstown, Cleveland, Pittsburgh, Buffalo. He was
married by then, for the second time to the same girl, and for the
second time the marriage was breaking up. ("The first time we
were divorced it was my fault. The second time it was her fault.
When we felt that we were even, we quit.")

Caine Mutiny. In 1942, when Paar was 25, he was called up

into the Army and was put in the 28th Special Service Company as
member of an entertainment troupe. Jack's first weeks in service
were miserable. "I still talked like an announcer, and they didn't
understand me." Even in Special Services, the average draftee did
not dig his insistence on clean fingernails. Things were better
overseas. Crossing to Guadalcanal on an Army troop transport, he
took on a Caine-type commander who kept the soldiers on a near-
starvation diet. One day during an alert, Paar got into a lifeboat
and announced: "I've been asked to make an announcement that
there was a Japanese submarine in the vicinity, but unfortunately
the Navy gun crews have driven it off. I say unfortunately because
the Japanese submarine was trying to bring us food." Recalls Paar
sadly: "The men laughed until they cried. That was the greatest
joke of my life."

On the South Pacific's one-a-day, island-hopping vaudeville
circuit, Paar became the open enemy of all brass. Once, in New
Caledonia, a show was delayed and 5,000 men were kept waiting by
a Navy commodore, who finally arrived with a nurse on his arm.
"We were going to have six lovely girls do the dance of the virgins,"
announced Paar. "But they broke their contracts by being with the
commodore." The commodore threatened a courtmartial. "The Army
got me out of it," claims Paar, "by promising to send me to Okinawa."

Deus ex Machina. His wartime success got Jack a job in
Hollywood shortly after he came home. RKO and later 20th Century-
Fox put him under contract but rarely got around to putting him in
front of a camera (he did once play opposite an unheard-of starlet
named Marilyn Monroe). In 1947 he was hired as the summer replacement on NBC-Radio's Jack Benny Show. His fresh, natural
style was a success, and in the fall American Tobacco put the Jack
Paar Show on the air on ABC. It lasted until Christmas Eve. In
his radio days Paar squabbled with everyone, fired a whole set of
writers, feuded with a Daily Variety columnist named Jack Hellman
(Paar put a nameplate--"Hellman"--on a chimpanzee and paraded it
through Hollywood).

But on the ABC show, says Jack, "a fellow named Ernie
Walker ruined me. He sold the network a bill of goods that he had
a machine to analyze comedians." Walker's machine reported that
Jack got laughs all right but that he had no character, like Benny's
"cheapness," Gracie Allen's "dumbness." "There is nothing to tune
back to each week," reported Walker, and the Paar option was
dropped. Today, says Jack, he is just as glad that he did not
play along with the phony character bit: "I have no character except what I am--complicated, sentimental, lovable, honest, loyal,
decent, generous, likable and lonely."

Who Loves Him? In New York, where he moved five years
ago, Jack got a chance to go on talking on a shortlived CBS radio
show called Bank on the Stars. Then he moved into TV as a replacement for Arthur Godfrey, finally replaced Walter Cronkite on

the Morning Show, which he quit after eleven months ("Too much
pressure for me to help soften up sponsors"). After that, guest
appearances with Ed Sullivan kept him going until NBC signed him
up to take over the Tonight show.

Perhaps the only person who knows him well and does not
quite believe he has arrived is Jack Paar himself. Like any TV performer, Paar watches himself on a monitor set during the show, but
he also seems to be watching himself on an imaginary monitor when
he is not performing. Compulsive and candid talker that he is,
he looks for signs of having said the wrong thing or having been
misunderstood. He still broods "When will they start tearing me
down?" Or "I wonder how many among my group really love me?"
Says a former agent of his: "He has no armor. You can pierce
him with a piece of Kleenex."

A small kindness from anyone seems to be a large emotional
shock, and Paar still weeps often. When he went through the
motions of an on-screen reconciliation with Dody Goodman fortnight
ago, he broke into tears. When he was told that a Lindy comic had
liked his show, he was "Leaky Jack" once more, his eyes misting as
his own hostility melted.

It may be necessary for Paar to live at the top of his emotions, because to such a large extent in his work, feeling takes the
place of a specific talent. He is no actor, singer or dancer. He is
a gifted comedian, but not in the Lindy standup-and-knock-'em-
dead sense. His comedy is low pressure and has to be, if it is to
be tolerated on a nightly 1-3/4-hr. show. "Nine hours a week,"
says one awed performer of Paar's stint. "My God, that isn't over-
exposure, it's practically nudism." But Paar seems to have found
the formula for beating the dreaded "over-exposure" problem.

He has found a way of being unobtrusive in the somnolent,
night-time living room, of providing just enough surprises to keep
the audience from falling asleep but not so many shocks as to jolt
them really wide awake. He has developed a knack for picking
good guest performers, has made his show one of the prized show-
cases for new talent. The program can be dull and pointless but,
as Paar himself says, "there's nothing like it." He adds with a
wry smile, "I'm so lovable. I have a love affair with this whole
continent."

It may not be love, but it is certainly more than one of those
quick-cooling TV infatuations, one of those flirtations that wither in
weeks, leaving only an old pile of fan letters and musty ratings.
The fact is that Paar is less a comedian than a personality--and
personalities usually outlast comedians.

                                        --Time (August 18, 1958), pages
                                        53-56.

* ROBERT MONTGOMERY PRESENTS (NBC, 1950-1957)

    Robert Montgomery puts on one of the best TV shows. It
is well-rehearsed, well-acted, well-directed, well-produced. Only
drawback is that it still isn't television. It's still a combination of
films and theater and radio. Even so, it's pretty fine.
                                    --William H. Shriver, Jr. in
                                      Catholic World (December 1950),
                                      page 224.

* SEE IT NOW (CBS, 1952-1955)

    After his interrogation by Senator Joseph R. McCarthy a few
weeks ago, General Ralph Zwicker, the commandant of Camp Kilmer,
turned to his aides, according to the papers, and remarked, "Boys,
now you've had an education." I felt the same way the other night
after watching Edward R. Murrow's half-hour report on the Senator,
over his weekly See It Now program, sponsored by the Aluminum
Company of America (C.B.S., 10:30-11 p.m. on Tuesdays). Mr.
Murrow brought off an extraordinary feat of journalism by the simple
expedient of compiling a pictorial history of the Senator, complete
with sound track, that showed him as he has performed in a variety
of places and under a variety of circumstances during the past few
years. Mr. Murrow let the Senator do most, but not all, of the
work. We saw McCarthy speaking in Milwaukee, we saw him speaking
in Philadelphia, we watched him conduct an investigation of the Voice
of America, we heard a tape recording of a speech he delivered in
Charleston, West Virginia, and we watched some of his operations
during the 1952 Presidential campaign. We also got a pretty good
look at the fellow--the best that I, for one, have ever got. To begin with, he's a big man, with big hands and a large head. Most
of the time, he has a petulant, droop-jaw expression, as though, at
the very instant he was all set to challenge everybody in the place
to step outside, he was convinced that everybody in the place was
about to jump him. He has a soft, almost silky, droning voice,
which he tries somewhat too obviously to control. His laugh is
frightening. He uses his hands a great deal for emphasis. While
interrogating a witness, he gives the impression that all light, all
truth, and all honesty belong at the moment to him alone, but then
destroys the impression by appearing, curiously and unexpectedly,
to be uncertain of his next move.

    Mr. Murrow's intent was to pick the Senator up in a series
of contradictions. He quoted the Senator as having declared in Milwaukee seventeen months ago, "If this fight against Communism is
made a fight between America's two great political parties, the
American people know that one of those parties will be destroyed,

and the Republic cannot endure very long as a one-party system."
He then let us hear the remarks of the Senator in Charleston on
February 4th of this year: "The issue between the Republicans and
Democrats is clearly drawn. It has been deliberately drawn by those
who have been in charge of twenty years of treason. The hard fact
is that those who wear the label 'Democrat' wear it with the stain of
a historic betrayal." We saw the Senator in many moods--arrogant,
aroused, fierce, and humble. To depict this last mood, Murrow
threw a shot on the screen of a political dinner somewhere. An
elderly gentleman at the speaker's table who was introducing the
Senator became almost overwhelmed with emotion. He said he could
not express what was in his heart, and he reached across the table
and plucked some flowers from a floral arrangement, remarking:

> "Ah, 'tis but a dainty flower I bring you,
> Yes, 'tis but a violet, glistening with dew,
> But still in its heart there lie beauties
>   concealed.
> So in our heart our love for you lies un-
>   revealed."

McCarthy arose, gulping, and said, "You know, I used to
pride myself on the idea that I was a bit tough, especially over the
past eighteen or nineteen months, when we have been kicked around
and bull-whipped and damned. I didn't think that I could be touched
very deeply. But tonight, frankly, my cup and my heart are so full
I can't talk to you." And he turned away, almost in tears.

Throughout the program, Mr. Murrow quietly added comments
of his own. He made no attempt to hide his strong feelings of distaste and shock at the methods and language of the Senator. Murrow
is, of course, a master of pictorial presentation and rarely forgets
that television is designed for the eye as well as the ear. His most
effective use of pictorial technique, it seemed to me, came in his
discussion of the Senator's charge that "extreme Left Wing elements
of press and radio" were attacking his committee over the Zwicker
affair. Mr. Murrow had before him two stacks of newspapers, and,
pointing to one, he said, "Of the fifty large-circulation newspapers
in the country, these are the Left Wing papers that criticized."
Then, pointing to the other, he said, "These are the ones that supported him. The ratio is about three to one against the Senator.
Now let us look at some of these Left Wing papers that criticized the
Senator." Thereupon he read editorial excerpts from the Chicago
Tribune, the New York Times, the Washington Times-Herald, the
New York Herald Tribune, the Washington Star, the Milwaukee
Journal, the World-Telegram & Sun, and others.

Just before the conclusion of his program, Mr. Murrow fixed
the audience with an almost glassy stare and read, solemnly and deliberately, an editorial he had composed for the occasion. I thought
that he was especially impressive when he remarked, "This is no

time for men who oppose Senator McCarthy's methods to keep silent,
or for those who approve. We can deny our heritage and our history,
but we cannot escape responsibility for the result. There is no way
for a citizen of a republic to abdicate his responsibilities.... The
actions of the Junior Senator from Wisconsin have caused alarm and
dismay amongst our allies abroad and given considerable comfort to
our enemies, and whose fault is that? Not really his; he didn't
create this situation of fear, he merely exploited it, and rather successfully. Cassius was right: 'The fault, dear Brutus, is not in
our stars, but in ourselves....' Good night, and good luck."
                              --Philip Hamburger in The New
                              Yorker (March 20, 1954), pages
                              63-64.

                    *   *   *

This is an old team starting a new trade," remarked Edward
R. Murrow at the outset of See It Now, C.B.S.'s enormously impressive new television news show. He was seated in the control room
of Studio 41--a logical spot, he explained, to start out from--and
presently he called on Camera 1 to bring in the Atlantic Ocean.

The Atlantic Ocean, a small wet segment of it, swam into view
on one monitor screen. Then Murrow called on the crew in San
Francisco to show us the Pacific. The Pacific, overhung with San
Francisco's customary fog, was a less telegenic body of water, but
we did catch a glimpse of it. Then Murrow, more or less acting
as quarterback, called on his crews to show us first the San Francisco Bay Bridge, then the Brooklyn Bridge, the New York skyline,
then San Francisco's skyline--all on live television.

"We are impressed," said Murrow, "by a medium in which a
man sitting in his living room has been able for the first time to
look at two oceans at once."

I am, too. I am also impressed by the intelligence of the men
--chiefly Murrow and his producer, Fred W. Friendly--who dreamed
up this simple trick to bring home to the viewers the wonder of
this electronic miracle. See It Now, which has been in preparation
for six months, is the logical extension to the highly successful album of records, "I Can Hear It Now," and to its radio counterpart,
the Peabody award-winning Hear It Now. It is not--and is not intended to be--a complete review of the week's news; it is, instead,
an almost entirely new form of journalism, "told in the voices and
faces" of the people who made the news; a technique that offers a
deeper insight into the headlines and the people who make them--
who they are and what sort of people they are.

There was, for example, a film of Winston Churchill during
his London Guildhall speech, an aged, aged Churchill, the great
voice dimmed by time, the prose style--though a great improvement

on Clement Attlee's--subdued into just a whisper of its former thunder. A deeply revelatory picture it was. There were other pictures
--of Eden in Paris telling Vishinsky to stop laughing and read the
disarmament proposal, of Sen. Taft purring with a cat-like content-
ment while Sen. Dirksen told an assemblage what a great candidate
he was.

        Murrow--handsome, relaxed, urbane--sewed the pictures to-
gether with a running commentary which, I should say, neither
overplayed nor underplayed the significance of the events, and also
conducted interviews with some of the C.B.S. news staff members--
Eric Sevareid, in Washington; Howard K. Smith, in Paris. (Smith
remarked good-naturedly of the relations between Russia and the
West that "the mutual ill-will is entirely unimpaired.")

        Then Mr. Murrow shifted us to Korea for one of the most inti-
mate and instructive glimpses into that battleground that I have yet
seen. This bit was especially remarkable in its avoidance of all the
newsreel clichés. There wasn't a single shot of a soldier yanking
a lanyard on a 105-mm. cannon, no shots of bombers tearing great
holes in the Korean real estate. Instead, the cameras concentrated
on the soldiers of Fox Company of an infantry regiment, catching
them as they ate and slept and gambled and groused and joked,
catching the tedium of warfare, the waiting, the humor of an essentially unhumorous occupation, the humanity of an essentially in-
human profession.

        We followed Fox Company as they took position in the front
line on a mountaintop and left them there, anticipating trouble that
had not yet come. Evening had fallen; the rocket flares were out;
a few shells sounded their cricket calls in the distance; the Chinese
were astir; but nothing had happened yet. It was a dramatic close.
"We wanted," said Mr. Murrow, "to narrow the distance between
those of us sitting comfortably at home and those in the line." The
news of the week from Korea was the murder of 5,500 captive American soldiers. This was the other side, more dramatic in its sheer
uneventfulness.

        I think they have the feel of the thing already, but I expect
it'll get better as it goes along, that Mr. Murrow and Mr. Friendly
have the simplicity of mind and the sweep of imagination to understand what television can do best in the news field and what television cannot do and should not attempt.

                                        --John Crosby in New York Herald
                                        Tribune (November 23, 1951).

● PHIL SILVERS

        As we knocked on the open door of Phil Silvers' suite at the

Delmonico, we could see the comic seated at a desk, using a fountain pen on a sheet of colored stationery. He was alone. The place was silent--a testimonial to the engineering of the pen as well as to the good manners of Park Avenue traffic on the street 30 floors below.

At our knock, Silvers rose. Except for a jacket, he was fully dressed. His tie was carefully knotted at the throat, and his white shirt was what the ad-writers call "squeaky-clean" in the sunlight that streamed through the windows. He greeted us warmly, then asked us to excuse him for just another moment while he put a last line on the letter he was writing to a friend in California.

As we watched him, we suddenly thought that this was the first time, in several years of interviewing professional funny-men, that we'd ever come upon one in the midst of writing a letter. It was just a thought. But for that moment, it made Silvers a peculiarly serene figure among his contemporaries.

A minute or so later, we were talking about his new series for TV, a filmed situation comedy called You'll Never Get Rich. Several of the films are already in the can, and a preview we saw the other morning leads us to guess the series will make Silvers the biggest draw in video since Joseph Welch.

At this writing, alas, CBS has not yet been able to find a suitable time-slot for the venture, a difficulty which doesn't seem to bother Silvers nearly as much as it should--considering that he's to get half the profits from the series. "My mother," Silvers was saying, "My mother's the one who's worrying. I'm getting a nice salary for the series even now, but she says she won't believe I'm getting paid until she sees my picture on her TV screen."

You'll Never Get Rich is a comedy series about Army life, and if your instantaneous reaction to that news is "Oh, no!", that's exactly what Silvers said when veteran comedy-writer Nat Hiken suggested the TV idea last summer.

"All I could see," recounted Silvers, "was Abbott and Costello in a hoked-up Army drill routine. Not for me. The public had had enough of that. Then Hiken started talking, and the outlook didn't get any better. He's a lousy guy at telling a story. 'You're a sergeant--y'know--and you meet this fellow--y'know.' Every other second it was 'you know,' and I had to keep on telling him I didn't know. It was futile. But I liked the guy--because in the middle of all the discussion, he'd say, 'Let's take time out to watch the ball game.' My kind of guy."

It was only when Hiken wrote his ideas out on a typewriter that Silvers saw the possibilities inherent in the series. "And now I'm terribly confident about the whole thing," he said. "In fact, I'm willing to let my whole reputation rise or fall on that very first film."

Them's strong words--especially for an avowed worrier like
Phil--but he feels that the character of Sergeant Ernie Bilko is one
of those parts that comes along once in a lifetime. "Bilko's a big-
time operator from away back. Technically, he's in the Army, but
he's really in business for himself. He always has half a dozen
angles going for him, and half a dozen GI's--also opportunists--
anxious to be on his team. He's a crook at heart, but there's
something lovable about him, too. The brass puts up with him
largely because he's a guy who keeps things like the motor pool
running efficiently, but also because he's lovable."

Silvers has an abiding distaste for comedians who pontificate
about their style of humor, but he is aware that one of his own
strong points is his likability as a performer. "If that weren't so,
I could never play this Bilko role. Why, if another kind of comic
did some of the things I do in this series, they'd shoot him."

Bilko is not, of course, a complete, unalloyed rogue. He
always shows a proper degree of respect for the company chaplain,
for example, although it's true that the same sky-pilot is frequently
made the unwitting custodian of a strong-box containing GI wagers.

"In case you're wondering," assured Silvers, the only man we
know, incidentally, who smiles while holding a cigarette in his teeth,
"our series has the full approval of Washington. They feel it'll help
the recuiting program." We had a sneaky feeling that a guy named
Bilko had made one or two trips to the Pentagon in recent months.

There was no financial urgency for Silvers to embark on a
major-league TV venture this year. The Broadway, Hollywood and
theatre-touring versions of Top Banana (his most successful vehicle to date) have brought him peachy-keen returns. "But it's a
question of ego," he said. "Today a performer, if he has any vanity
at all, just HAS to be in TV. You want to be admired when you
walk down a street. You want to be recognized when you get
into a taxi. What does that as well as television?"

The persistence of his ego did not mean, Silvers pointed out,
that he hadn't matured in certain ways over the past few years.
"I've grown up a lot," he said. "I used to think that my career,
for example, was a goal in itself. I never thought of it as anything
else. No more. Now, I see it simply as a means of doing some of
the things I'd really like to do. See Europe, say. I mean see it
like a tourist."

Silvers, who's now a young-looking 43, sees himself as a guy
who acquired sense much too late in life. Even his five-year marriage to beauty Jo Carroll Dennison could have turned out different-
ly, he feels, if he'd had a little empathy--just a bit of understanding
for the emotional needs of those around him. "Why, on our honey-
moon, the poor kid found herself in New York at a table with me,

Toots Shor and Joe DiMaggio. In my own ignorance, I thought she'd
be impressed with that kind of socializing. She hated it. 'Phil,'
she'd say to me, 'why don't we just go for a nice walk in Central
Park together?' I'd look at her like she was crazy. 'Why on earth
would you want to do that?' I'd tell her. 'I'm just a bald guy with
glasses. Why would you want to walk with me in Central Park?'
I just didn't understand."

     Something else Phil learned rather tardily was that he didn't
always have to be "on" to win the acceptance of people. "Laughter
isn't my passport any more," he says. "I used to be the guy they
invited to all the Hollywood parties for yaks. Everyone at the parties would roar at my jokes--everyone but Jo. She didn't have to.
She didn't love me because I was a funny man. She loved me for
me."

     Silvers long ago decided that he doesn't have the psychologi-
cal make-up ever to be an ecstatically happy person, but he thinks
he's learning how to come to terms with himself. Above all, he is
becoming aware that he's a much more conventional person than he'd
ever allowed himself to believe. "I was never one of those comedians," he says, "who needed a big entourage following me around
every time, but I used to think it was shameful to be seen eating
alone. It's taken me a long time to be able to walk into a place by
myself and ask for a hamburger."

     We thought back an hour or so to the picture of Silvers calm-
ly writing a letter in the silence of his hotel suite, and it was only
now that we sensed it was not always thus. "A guy grows up,"
Silvers was saying. "You take that 'Glad to see ya' line. I never
use it any more. After a while, a tag phrase like that becomes a
monster. Know why I used to come up with 'Glad to see ya?' Because I couldn't think of anything else to say, that's why. But
sooner or later, you've got to grow up. Even Bilko's got to learn
that eventually. But I hope he lets the series run a few years
first."

                              --Philip Minoff in Cue (January
                                 22, 1955), pages 20 and 46.

• THE $64,000 QUESTION (CBS, 1955-1958)

     The Greeks had a word for The $64,000 Question: a tragedy.
Sophocles's audience, the whole population, came early, prepared to
spend the day in the bleachers (Francis Ferguson tells us in the
brilliant work The Idea of a Theatre); "the actors were not professionals in our sense, but citizens selected for a religious office,
and Sophocles himself had trained them and the chorus." The bold,
imaginative Louis G. Cowan, who created the Revlon international

episode (Tuesday nights, CBS-TV), would blush, I am sure, to be
joined to such august company as the author of Oedipus Rex, and
yet the analogue is accurate. Gino Prato, Gloria Lockerman, Captain McCutchen, et al., are citizens, not actors in the professional
sense. But "religious office"?

The point is: there on the Revlon stage, as on the platform
in Sophocles's time, a modern scapegoat is to be offered who will
purify us of our baser lusts for certified checks, harmonize our
obscurities and frustrations, and render our unpublicized, individual
lots palatable till "the next plateau." Gino Prato a scapegoat? But
$32,000, four pressagents, a $10,000 a year job, reunion with Papa
on a mountain in Statale, Italy, after thirty-three years? Alas,
scapegoat, indeed.

One has merely to follow Gino Prato's itinerary, from standing
ovation at La Scala, in Milan, to sidewalk cafe in Rome with Madame
Ambassador Claire Luce and ex-outfielder Joe DiMaggio, to appreciate the parallel. From the time of Oedipus's exile from Thebes (according to the play's sequel, Oedipus at Colonos) he became a sort
of sacred relic, like the bones of a saint; perilous, but "good medicine" for the community that possessed him. Antigone, his daughter,
went with him on his blind wanderings. Of Gino recently the Associated Press reported that he "climbed a mule trail on foot to reach
his birthplace in the north Italian mountains. Church bells rang and
nearly every resident gathered in the town square to welcome him."
Riding beside him on a mule was--his daughter.

But what of the scapegoat theory? Struggle, dismemberment,
death, and renewal--this was the passion, the pathos of the perennial
winter-spring conflict which underlay the Greek theatre. Now, consider the Revlon isolation booth, into which the tragic heroes of
The $64,000 Question must enter when they approach the ultimate
mystery of pumpernickel bread or antidisestablishmentarianism. Regard the agonizing loneliness of the spotlighted figure in the sound-
proofed booth. He is face to face with the very meaning of his life,
with the most desperate crisis of his aspiration. And the community,
the audience, the 50,000,000 who pity and fear, who echo the un-
utterable prayer of a Mammon-culture--observe (courtesy of the
clever, naked, searching camera's eye) how they are dismembered by
the trial, the suspense, the unendurable torment of the hero who is
expiating publicly their private, unacknowledged sin of greed.

Aristotle, who set forth on the basis of the Greek plays
spread out before him some still-viable insights into the art and
value of the tragic drama, would have appreciated the cunning of
The $64,000 Question. Even as the television public appreciates and
commends and enjoys its success. Aristotle was no old, moralizing
fogey like Plato. Aristotle opined that the end of poetry (or literature or TV) was--simply and unashamedly--"delight."

Nevertheless, this program, passing a phenomenon as it may be, has struck so big a note precisely because it is an unconscious communal ritual. We, the people, imitate here no rites of fertility. The womb of The $64,000 Question glitters with the appearance of life. Still, it is sterile. Oedipus was an essentially noble human being, innocent, affectionate, of uncalculating benevolence and public spirit. At Colonos he died, redeemed from the consequences of his error (patricide and incest) and at peace. Mr. Prato, kindly man, is but the instrument, in these paragraphs, of a literary device. We wish him the fulness of his innocent good fortune--and all the other conquerors of the golden plateaus. But their roles in the Revlon rites suggest sobering afterthoughts. Let us hope that another and perhaps greater Sophocles will arise to purge the Thebes of our national conscience of the sinister corruption that lives behind the window where no sound comes save the riddle of the Manufacturers Trust Company.

--Robert Lewis Shayon in Saturday
Review, Vol. 38, No. 39 (September 24, 1955), page 26.

• SMALL WORLD (CBS, 1958-1960)

In Small World Edward R. Murrow has, not for the first time, combined good planning, technical skill, and sound intelligence to create what broadcasting perpetually needs: the sense of something new happening, the atmosphere of experiment. The decisive moment came early in the series when Dr. Willard Libby, who seems to make a habit of being maladroit on Murrow's programs, wondered whether Bertrand Russell's remarks on the suppression of birth-control information would remain in the edited version of the program. There was something of cold steel in Murrow's, "You'll see. They'll be there."

The complaint that Small World is only a radio talk-program with cameras to film the speakers is not only beside the point--it actually indicates the program's great virtue, that the talk is as simple as radio talks used to be. The combinations, which seem at first calculated only to bring incommensurables together, work out well. There was a point in putting Rickover between Rebecca West and Mark Van Doren because they talked about education, and, although Lauren Bacall obviously could have outwitted men of ten times their stature, Malcolm Muggeridge and Eric Johnston were, in the theatrical sense, "adequate." On the first program bad editing left Aldous Huxley out of the program too long at one stretch and the atmosphere was a little on the strained jocose side, but there are basic conflicts between Nehru and ex-Governor Dewey and, before the half hour was over, these had emerged and Dewey had not been overcome by the cooler intellect he challenged.

The remarkable thing is that not only the ideas, but the character-in-action of each of the participants comes out so clearly. They are separated by the seven seas, but they are intent on one another, they listen with passion. I shall not soon forget the startled look that crossed Rebecca West's face when she heard Admiral Rickover say that Matthew Arnold had revolutionized the English school system nor the deep, malicious satisfaction with which Lauren Bacall watched Mr. Muggeridge digging the pit (woman's place is in the home) into which she neatly tumbled him. Not to mention Rickover's unbending determination to prevent anyone from liking him--in which, unfortunately, he was hugely successful.

Small World doesn't attempt to take the place of See It Now and runs the danger of becoming chummy, of coming apart into separated threads of conversation. The basic success of Murrow and Fred Friendly is to have captured the right tone, the atmosphere in which good conversation can take place. It is in this, and not in its world-spanning techniques, that it is superior to two other talk programs of the season.

--Gilbert Seldes in Saturday Review, Vol. 41, No. 50 (December 13, 1958), page 27.

- TO TELL THE TRUTH (CBS, 1956-1968; syndication, 1969 to present)

Another increasingly lucrative profession--in what Walter Lippmann calls our purposeless society--is time wasting. The great merchant princes of time wasting are Goodson and Todman, who have expended time wasting into a commercial empire. One of the flowers of this great empire is To Tell the Truth, which is the very model of a quiz show.

That is: empty-headed. It requires nothing of the observer but the temporary excercise of his eyeballs. It's cheap. That means it can sell cigarettes and other products at a marvelously small cost per thousand. And it occupies a splendid half hour of prime evening time on an important network, thus successfully preventing that half hour from being put to any important use, which is the highest aspiration of the time-wasting profession.

Ah, when you think of thirty million pairs of eyeballs fixed on To Tell the Truth successfully getting through another half hour of eternity without a flicker of thought or a motion or the use of a muscle, you realize the superb achievement of the Messrs. Goodson and Todman in the fine twentieth-century profession of wasting other people's time and charging them money for it. Quiz shows, in the opinion of some philosophers, have supplanted the chewing of gum as the great nirvana of the masses.

Now then, To Tell the Truth has a somewhat ironic gimmick: the chief ingredient is lying. That is, three people are gathered together, two of them to tell lies about who and what they are to a panel that tries to guess which of the three is telling the truth. Years ago, before Congress took a dim view of the matter, who had schlockmeisters who gathered loot for the giveaway shows. Now we have liemeisters who gather liars for To Tell the Truth. I don't know what posterity is going to say about this--that a grown man could earn his living looking for liars. Just as Diogenes went through the streets looking for an honest man with a lantern, the Truth people go out looking for liars, but whereas Diogenes couldn't find any honest men, they find lots of liars. There's a commentary on our civilization in there somewhere, but I haven't time to look for it.

> --John Crosby in With Love and Loathing (McGraw-Hill Book Company, 1963), pages 199-200.

- TOAST OF THE TOWN (CBS, 1948-1955)

I think it's time to catch up with the fellow who remarked, a great many years ago, that vaudeville is dead: Somebody must have said it first, and for all I know he may still be around, living out his life in some dreary cold-water flat--poring over old Keith-Albee programs and smiling sadly as he recalls his weekly seat on the aisle at the Palace, where he watched the comedians and the tumblers and the odd, tall female singers with ostrich feathers in their hats. Someone had better catch up with this fellow and hustle him off to a television set. He'll be surprised to discover that vaudeville is far from dead. It may not be the tranquil, disarming vaudeville he re-members, and it may not be especially healthy or display any notable charm, but it's vaudeville, all right.

These thoughts bring me to Mr. Ed Sullivan and his mon-strously lavish, all-network, all-glamour variety show, Toast of the Town (Sundays, 8-9 p.m., C.B.S.). I've been watching Toast of the Town for more Sunday nights that I care to remember, and it occurs to me that its weekly budget must equal that of many of the larger municipalities in this country, and surpass, by several thou-sand fish, the semiannual budget of most of what we refer to as the backward nations. Sullivan and his weekly guests spend money with an almost thoughtless and arrogant abandon. Let any performer, anywhere, come to the attention of an agent, or receive acclaim from some segment of the population, and he or she will inevitably turn

up on Toast of the Town. A dog in Racine can recite the opening
lines of "Il Penseroso"? He will be grabbed up for the Ed Sullivan
show. A man in New Orleans can faultlessly render "La Marseillaise"
on a kazoo stuck in his ear? He'll turn up right after the dog act.
A musical opens on Broadway, and a glittering new singing star is
"discovered"? She'll soon be on C.B.S. on a Sunday evening. Week
after week, the celebrities parade before the cameras, introduced with
a strange pride by Mr. Ed Sullivan. This Mr. Sullivan is a study.
He's always impeccably dressed, wearing neat and what I take to be
light-weight suits, with padded shoulders. His pocket handkerchiefs,
which are prominently, but not too prominently, on view, are folded
in the square, or box, manner. His dark hair is greased to a fine,
but not too fine, gloss. His smile is a mixed smile, betraying a good
deal of sorrow, and even suffering, as though he not only partici-
pated in every act but was aware of the struggle the performers
had to go through to reach perfection. He seems to be saying that
his only wish is that they, and he, and you, could do better. He
is obviously a theatre buff--a performer at heart--and after all these
years he still stands in awe of the notion that human beings, not
to mention dogs, seals, and horses, can display so damned much
ability in public. While he is instinctively enthusiastic and optimis-
tic about live performers, he can be just as enthusiastic and optimis-
tic, if not more so, about the Lincoln and Mercury cars advertised
on his program. He can really whip himself up over a new Lincoln
or Mercury! His voice assumes a special lustre of tone, and he is
almost beside himself with quiet, deep-running, abiding pride in the
performance of the automobiles he's selling. If I were Mr. Lincoln
or Mr. Mercury--or even Mr. Ford--I would certainly hold onto
this fellow, for his faith is the faith that can sell a million cars.

As for the programs themselves, they are vaudeville, or at
least a species of vaudeville, with an overlay of a rustic amateur
night. The other evening, the program got under way with a brief
appearance by a young lady from Manly, Iowa, and her steer,
Shorty, which had just won the big prize at the International Live
Stock Exposition in Chicago. Shorty weighed eleven hundred
pounds, was fifteen months old, and was completely uninterested in
the proceedings around him. The girl was a member of a 4-H Club,
and she was proud of the steer. Her family was on hand, and so
were some people who seemed to own a restaurant in Chicago.
"They have all been flown in from Chicago by United Air Lines,"
said Mr. Sullivan, tossing us that bewilderingly appreciative smile.
Mr. Sullivan spoke briefly of his own small farm in Connecticut
("with the Ford tractor"), congratulated all hands, except the
steer, and made a passing reference to the possibility of the steer's
turning up someday at the restaurant in Chicago. I felt that this
last touch was unnecessary. The Ames Brothers--four of them,
and all singers--were next on the agenda, and they went through a
variety of routines. Some of them popped their eyes, some of them
sang while others pretended to sing, and, all in all, they were
rhythmic and extremely proficient, if you enjoy hearing four brothers

sing. Mr. Kirk Douglas appeared. Mr. Sullivan said that Mr. Douglas was in town on a holiday and was making his appearance pretty
much out of friendship for Mr. Sullivan. At the sound of the compliment, Mr. Douglas's muscles rippled gently, and he was gone. We
next saw shots from the forthcoming movie There's No Business Like
Show Business. (This is a favorite stunt of Mr. Sullivan's--shots
from new pictures and forthcoming pictures.) Afterward, Jackie
Miles, a comedian, turned up in a routine having to do with an incident in a movie house. He was holding a seat for someone in a
crowded theatre. Then came Eartha Kitt, first as some sort of
Parisian waif, all bundled up in a greatcoat and howling "Hey,
Jacques!," and later as herself--strident, choky, and wonderful.
There were many more acts, including the remarkable Miss Carol
Haney, who danced. At the close, of course, there were tumblers.

> --Philip Hamburger in The New
> Yorker (December 18, 1954),
> pages 81-82.

• TODAY (NBC, 1952 to present)

My alarm went off, by prearrangement, at two minutes to
seven one chill, windy morning last week, and, rising swiftly in the
dark and noting with satisfaction that my wife was still asleep, I
grabbed a bathrobe and afghan and padded to the television room.
There was not a sound in the house. A rapid survey revealed that
the two small boys who board with us were still in the land of Nod,
their faces bathed in expressions of such supernal innocence as to
mask completely their diabolical plans for the day. At the stroke of
seven, I sat down before the tiny screen as a program entitled
Today, broadcast over N.B.C. five mornings each week from seven
to nine, hove into view. "You are watching the World Communication
Center," a voice announced, adding that the master of ceremonies of
Today, Mr. Dave Garroway ("the Master Communicator," the voice
called him), would handle matters for the next two hours. Mr. Garroway, a likable young man with a bow tie and an incredibly wide-
awake look, was seated behind an immense horseshoe desk. In back
of him was a battery of clocks, revealing the time in Honolulu, Cal-
cutta, Moscow, Chicago, Tokyo, and many other points where names
make news. All around him was a tangled skein of cables, wires,
rattling machines, and people. The people were tapping away at
typewriters, fiddling with the rattling machines, stepping over the
cables, or just sitting at desks, perhaps too stunned to move.

"This is today," said Mr. Garroway, somewhat ominously,
"the day you're going to live." I got up and turned on the radiator
as Mr. Garroway, carrying a pointer, moved over to a huge blackboard, on which a number of news photographs had been posted.
Mr. Garroway announced that he would give us a capsule summary

of the day's news in two minutes, and for the next two minutes he gave a capsule summary of the day's news. "I will put you in touch with the world," said Mr. Garroway. "This is today, the day you're going to live." From somewhere to Mr. Garroway's left, a phonograph began playing "I Want a Regular Man," a tape bearing the message "MOSSADEGH GETS DEATH THREAT" ribboned its way across the tiny screen just below Mr. Garroway, and a voice cut in to say that the temperature was thirty degrees, the humidity sixty-eight per cent, and the prospects clear and colder, with wind.

Mr. Garroway picked up a telephone and got in touch with a man in the Weather Bureau in Washington. The Master Communicator was now standing before another large blackboard, on which was an outline of the continental United States. He had discarded the pointer in favor of a piece of chalk. The voice at the Weather Bureau, clearly audible both to Mr. Garroway and to me, told us that a great deal of cold air had come down from Canada over the weekend. "There's warm air up through Texas," the voice said. "Watch out for storms in the plains area tomorrow." Mr. Garroway nodded vigorously, chalked in several arrows and sweeping semicircles on the map, thanked the man in the Weather Bureau, and sat down again at the horseshoe desk. I gave the radiator two or three good kicks, and went out to the kitchen to put on the coffee.

When I got back to Today, the tiny screen was filled with still another blackboard. This one listed the weather in selected cities thorughout the nation. It was snowing in Cleveland, drizzling in Kansas City, clear in Los Angeles, foggy in Miami, clear in Philadelphia, windy in Syracuse, and extremely cold in my television room. A man called James Fleming, standing amidst the cables and holding a sheaf of press messages, read out some of the important news of the day. "Thank you, James," said Mr. Garroway. He announced that he was about to call Frankfurt, Germany. He picked up a telephone. "Frankfurt, are you there?" he said. "Speak to me, Ernest." Evidently, Ernest answered the phone, for although I could hear no sound from Germany, Mr. Garroway went on to say, "All right, Ernest. Do you think the Germans this time will make good soldiers?" Ernest, I gathered, delivered himself of a ready opinion, but still I could hear nothing. "I can hear you, Ernest," said Mr. Garroway, "but I don't think our audience can. Check transmission from the field, Ernest. I can hear you, Ernest. Stand by, Ernest. I can hear you, but N.B.C. doesn't seem to have you on the program circuit." Mr. Garroway sheepishly put down his phone and told us that we would now watch some newsreels. We saw Cardinal Spellman returning from Europe, Captain Carlsen visiting the Hall of Fame, and a man trying to sink a putt. The older boarder, clutching a Teddy bear, stamped into the television room. "Put on your slippers," I told him. "Teddy doesn't wear slippers. Why should I?" he said. I escorted him to his room and, employing reason and force, put his slippers on him. Teddy, the boarder, and I returned to the television room. "The temperature is thirty degrees,

the humidity is sixty-eight per cent," a voice was saying. It predicted fair and colder.

A man appeared on the screen, seated at a piano and singing
a song. "They told Marconi wireless was a phony," he sang, while
behind him, on a small puppet stage, a puppet puppy appeared.
The dog, whose name was Buttons, was carrying an umbrella. "It's
snowy, windy, and cloudy!" he shrieked. "The temperature is
thirty degrees, the humidity sixty-eight per cent." "If you're
cheerful until ten in the morning, the rest of the day will take care
of itself," said that man at the piano. My wife entered the television
room. "Good God," she said, looking at the screen. "Quiet, I'm
working," I said. "Get back on relief," she said, removing herself.
"Goodbye now," said the puppy. "I want breakfast," said the older
boarder, removing himself. "Here's today's weather," said Mr.
Garroway. "Temperature thirty degrees in New York. Colder
tonight, and windy." The weather blackboard was again exhibited.
It was fifty-six degrees and cloudy in Jacksonville, twenty-three
degrees and snowing in Erie, and thirty-one degrees and clear in
Baltimore. Then a man who was making a valiant effort to stay
awake talked to me from Chicago. He was of the opinion that Taft
was pretty strong out there, thanks to the support of Colonel Mc-
Cormick and his friends. Mr. Fleming reread the highlights of the
day's news, Mr. Garroway interviewed a taxi-driver who had made
his début the night before as a baritone, someone announced that
the temperature was thirty degrees and the humidity sixty-eight per
cent, the younger boarder awoke with a bloodcurdling cry, the phone
rang, the older boarder would not eat his cereal, my wife announced
that she had no intention of serving breakfast in shifts, and I turned
Today off and began to live.

> --Philip Hamburger in The New
> Yorker (February 2, 1952),
> pages 61-62.

• TRUTH OR CONSEQUENCES (CBS, 1950-1951; NBC, 1954-1958)

If you've never heard Ralph Edwards' Truth or Consequences,
which seems inconceivable, you must at least have heard some nasty
rumors about the granddaddy of giveaway shows, all of them true.
The latest and nastiest rumor of all is that Truth or Consequences
has taken to television. I'm afraid the latest rumor is true, too. I
got witnesses.

In girding his loins for this latest assault on my sensibilities,
Mr. Edwards declared: "From the time the show first went on the
air over ten years ago, we knew we had a Number One television
show, but we also knew that it could not be simulcast. On the air
for ten years we have aimed our stunts at a listening audience and

thrown out stunt after stunt because it was too visual. These
stunts were filed against the day of television."

Altogether, that's an extraordinary statement designed to
show what an astute student of show business Mr. Edwards is, and
the fact that there isn't a great deal of truth in the statement could
only be caviled at by people who go around caviling at everything.
Me, for instance. Mr. Edwards' device for aiming a stunt at a listening, as opposed to a visual, audience consisted generally of
dunking some innocent into a tank of water (splash), throwing a
pie in his face (squish), or making him kiss a cow under the illusion that it is a pretty girl (moo). As any fool can readily see,
these are primarily auditory stunts, not conducive to a visual or
television audience.

Well, I was right there, pencil in hand, to see how well Mr.
Edwards had converted himself to visibility. On his first TV show
a blindfolded man was persuaded to kiss a cow under the illusion that
it was a pretty girl. No, no pies in the face yet. But then this is
only the first show.

The main stunt of the evening consisted of dressing a lot of
outlandish contestants in outlandish costumes and perpetrating them
on an audience full of dance lovers in another auditorium as a serious
dance group. This must have been one of the stunts that Edwards
had lying around in his files waiting for television. Probably waiting
since 1942, when Edwards pulled a similar stunt on a bunch of music
lovers at Town Hall in New York, introducing a housewife from New
Jersey who had never touched a violin as the "distinguished European concert violinist, Yifnuff."

She scraped away at the violin while the Town Hall audience
stared incredulously. Essentially, the same thing happened on the
TV show. A collection of paunchy middle-aged men and women, who
looked as if they had been swept out of a convention in Los Angeles,
were dressed in ballet skirts, doublet and hose, and feathers and
they inflicted what Mr. Edwards referred to as "The Dance of the
Delirious Deer" on an audience of astonished dance lovers who were
at first astonished and then embarrassed. Of course, a ballet is a
little more visual than a violin, but otherwise it was the same eight-
year-old stunt.

I'm afraid I can't agree that Truth or Consequences is a
natural for television. The radio version, which is still on the air,
was the ultimate in silliness, but at least it was decently veiled. Its
television counterpart is a monstrosity of vulgarity. It reminded me
strongly of Bedlam, the first English lunatic asylum, whose inmates
provided amusement to throngs of spectators.

The shrieks of laughter from the studio audience were enough
to drive the children from the room gibbering with fright. New York

children, of course, are well inured to bloodshed in all its most
devilish forms. They're not yet accustomed to lunacy. The quality
of this laughter--if that's the word for it--is quite different from
that at even the dizziest comedy show. You'll find traces in it of
embarrassment, of sadism and of drooling idiocy. It's a frightening
noise, and to be sure you can see it as well as hear it, the cameras
are frequently turned on the audience while they are in labor.

The visible Mr. Edwards is a pop-eyed gentleman with a
wolfish grin who acts and even looks a little like a maniacal Bob
Hope. The participants are indescribable except to someone with the
gifts and the space of Charles Dickens. Their appearances are not
helped much by the fact that this horrible operation is on kinescope, which is murky enough to malign them and not quite dark
enough to obscure them entirely.

--John Crosby in New York Herald
Tribune (September 12, 1950).

- WHO'S THERE (CBS, 1952)

It would not be surprising to learn that radio listening has
taken a considerable spurt doing the summer months. The summer
doldrums have hit the television channels far more acutely than they
ever affected radio. One reason seems to be that television has made
no attempt to develop new formats for summer listening. The one
standard answer for a new TV show is still the panel program.

Even worse, "panel program" has come to mean almost invariably one form or other of the old Twenty Questions game. There
is now an absolute glut of such shows as What's My Line?, Knock,
Knock, Masquerade Party, I've Got a Secret, and on and on into
the night, ad nauseum.

Let it be said in fairness that What's My Line? started the
current cycle and is still by far the best of the lot. Moderator
John Daly has the easy manner and deft sureness to keep the program going as he wants it to go. There is some intelligent good
humor coming from the panel, and even occasionally some sophisticated barbs not ordinarily found on television.

Someone at CBS, following the strange line of tortured reason-
ing which substitutes for thinking in television programming circles,
came through with the notion that since Arlene Francis was a par-
ticipant on the successful What's My Line?, she could successfully
moderate a panel show of her own.

T'aint so. Miss Francis is a decorative bit of fluff as a panel
member, but when it comes to handling a show on her own she misses

badly. To begin with, Who's There, which is the handle for her version of the same old show idea, lacks any spark of real original-ity.

Gimmick is that panel hears a knock, Miss Francis say sprite-ly, "Who's There?," and guest personality appears to studio audience, while the moderator overcome with the mirth of knowledge unknown to the panel, rocks gleefully in her chair. Next the panel is shown three or four objects which have some vague connection with the personality whose identity they must guess. You can fill in the rest yourself.

Perhaps it's only natural that television should follow the same pattern as motion pictures. Climbing on the bandwagon and start-ing a cycle of imitations as soon as a picture is a hit has long been standard practice of the film-makers. It's a dreary process for the audience, and one reason for poor movie attendance. Do television programmers have to learn the hard way, too?

--Fortnight (August 18, 1952),
page 8.

• ED WYNN

Halfway through his premiere telecast from the West Coast the other evening, Ed Wynn boasted, "I know as much about tele-vision as anyone--I've been in it for fifteen minutes now." Well, if the rest of the show were as strong as that gag, we'd have been compelled to agree with him. But the truth is that Mr. Wynn, a revered veteran of stage, screen and radio, has many things to learn about a medium which is a strange combination of the other three.

After introducing himself as "Keenan Wynn's father," the comedian proceeded to hold the stage virtually by himself for the next fifteen minutes or so, a considerable fraction of the half-hour show, and what he had to say and do did not warrant that sort of monopoly. He wasted too much time between jokes, and when gags are not very funny in the first place, the wisest course to pursue is to make them follow each other in rapid succession. Don't give the audience time to mourn.

Mr. Wynn, like the late Joe Cook, is at his best when working with screwball props, so it wasn't surprising that two of his most comical bits on the premiere were in this line. In the first, he dem-onstrated a church collection box that released a banner marked, "Tilt," whenever a button was tossed into it. The other prop was a cash register with a bottomless drawer. As a jewelry store clerk, Wynn rang up a sale, thrust the bill into the drawer with one hand

and removed it from below with the other.   These two pieces of
business were priceless, but two swallows don't make a meal, and
the rest of the pickings were very slim, indeed.

The weekly show (WCBS-TV--Thursdays, 9 to 9:30) is being
staged "live" on the Coast and brought East by kinescope (television
recording).   Technically, it is one of the best kinescoping jobs we've
seen, but it still does not have the clarity and definition of a live
telecast.   It seems to us that the other "big names" who've been
waiting to see Wynn's kinescopes before attempting TV programs of
their own from Hollywood, are going to wait just a little longer.   It
could be that the "Perfect Fool" has rushed in where more cautious
souls have feared to tread, but he is so well loved by so many millions that his special charm may surmount all the standard obstacles.
                                        --Philip Minoff in Cue (October
                                        22, 1949), page 20.

• YOUR SHOW OF SHOWS (NBC, 1950-1954)

A few years back, Sid Caesar appeared in a local stage revue
and, among other antics, impersonated a chewing-gum vending machine in a subway station.   As the vending machine, Mr. Caesar,
alone on the stage, choked, spat, spluttered, disgorged imaginary
pieces of gum, got out of order, pretended to be kicked severely by
irate purchasers, and so on.   As I recall this dreadful act, Mr.
Caesar felt sorry for the vending machine; indeed, he was shattered
by the plight of every vending machine on earth.   Vending machines,
he implied, were far more miserable than Okies or children with
rickets, and their suffering hurt him deeply.   I thought at the time
that his performance was perhaps the least funny thing I had ever
seen anywhere, and I wrote him off as a misplaced comic with a
heart of Cream of Wheat.   Now, I have been watching Mr. Caesar
on television lately and, although I still shudder when I think of
that vending machine, I have concluded that he is not only a genuinely funny man but one of the two or three funniest men on television.   He has been appearing each Saturday night over N.B.C.,
in an excellent revue called Your Show of Shows, and he has almost
consistently accomplished what he has undertaken to do.   He is a
master of pantomime and the possessor of an astounding collection of
dialects, and he can shift from dialect to dialect with remarkable
ease.   One moment he is a true-blue Latin, the next moment a distinguished citizen of Minsk.   If a patina of Minsk overlays even his
Mediterranean interpretations, who knows but that therein may lie
one of the secrets of his humor?   Among my happiest coaxial memories is Caesar, in a recent monologue, impersonating a Russian
movie director.   Having just arrived in this country, the director
was attempting to explain--to ship-news reporters, I gathered--the
significance of his latest film, an epic of coal mining in Russia.

With desperation, he tried to impress upon them the deep, primordial
beauties of his creation. Because of language difficulties, he was
forced to resort to deep, primordial grunts and groans and a few
scattered guttural English phrases. The miners in his film, it seemed,
were real, earthy fellows, uninhibited by union rules or safety de-
vices. When they wanted coal, they pulled at it until it came loose.
"Shovels, nah! Picks, nah! Phooey!" shrieked Caesar, his face
alight with the agonies of primitive labor. In addition to being a
shrewd commentary on conditions in the Workers' Paradise, the monologue was a classic of high good humor.

Caesar has been co-starred on Your Show of Shows with Imogene Coca, who is, I'd say, not one of the two or three funniest
comediennes on television but far and away the funniest. There is
a fetching quality to Miss Coca's work that is hard to define. A
large part of her success derives, I suspect, from her comprehension of the medium in which she works. Every move she makes,
whether she is an ugly duckling in a dance hall or a fashion model
trailing hideous pelts, is aimed at an audience seated at home in a
relatively small room. She avoids completely the broad gestures and
loud tones required of comics on the legitimate stage, who must
think not only of the people in the first rows but of those in the
back. This may seem an elementary point--in fact, it is an elementary point--but few television performers are on to it. The celebrated Mr. Berle, for example, throws away a good many of his
"jokes" by screaming them at his studio audience rather than direct-
ing them toward his victims at home in the living room. Perhaps
Miss Coca's extensive experience as a night-club entertainer taught
her to confine her personality to a small area. In any event, she
has solved the problem of transmitting that personality from the point
of origin to the television screen. More important than her technique,
of course, are her gaiety, her intelligence, and her humor. She is
one of those rare persons who are funny per se; she has the comic
spirit, all right, and that's enough for me.

                                    --Philip Hamburger in The New
                                    Yorker (May 27, 1950), page 80.

                         *   *   *

The big music and comedy extravaganzas are all beginning to
seem a little limp, only half way through the season. The best
publicized of them all, Your Show of Shows, seems to be showing
the strain more than most. This is the show, you will recall,
which features Sid Caesar, Imogene Coca, and a huge company of
dancers, singers, guest stars, opera divas and whatnot.

Many of the component parts are excellent, but the show suffers from the effort of trying to make everything, within its hour
and a half, a colossal production. Good musical revues, as Broadway producers found out long ago, must have their big production
numbers. But other less pretentious moments are needed to give
both audience and performers a breathing spell.

The constant hammering of elaborate production on number after number is as wearing on the viewer as it must be to the production staff. One feels like murmuring to the staff, "Relax boys--don't work so hard." That admonition would apply particularly to the star of the show, Sid Caesar. The comic works so hard, punches so much, is so obviously exhausted at the end of a number, that it takes away much of the fun of watching.

And this same show of shows deplorably wastes guest talent. Every week a top name in entertainment is "host" for the show. The duties usually consist only of introducing each number, although occasionally the guest is used in a dramatic sketch. But all too seldom.

The show has suffered recently with the illness of Imogene Coca--the co-star. The series of fill-ins have all appeared to be no more than that--temporary substitutes, not making a real effort. Perhaps the often rumored internal bickering between the stars is affecting the spontaneity of the show. Whatever the cause, this high priced effort is growing weaker and weaker.

                              --Fortnight (January 19, 1953),
                              page 7.

• INDEX OF CRITICS •

CECELIA AGER
  Radio: Jessica Dragonette

RICHARD SHERIDAN AMES
  Radio: The Screen Guild Theatre

DALE ARMSTRONG
  Radio: Gene Autry's Melody Ranch; Ted Husing; Pot o' Gold;
    Sherlock Holmes; Walter Winchell

BEN BODEC
  Radio: The Chesterfield Show; The Jello Program

FRANCIS CHASE, JR.
  Radio: Father Charles E. Coughlin

WILLIAM A. COLEMAN
  Television: TV in 'fifty-three (1953); The American Road;
    John Daly

JOHN CROSBY
  Radio: The Bickersons; Lassie; mr. ace and JANE; Bill Stern
  Television: Fred Allen; Amahl and the Night Visitors; Milton
    Berle; Faye Emerson; Dave Garroway; Arthur Godfrey; The
    Kate Smith Evening Hour; See It Now; To Tell the Truth;
    Truth or Consequences

ORRIN E. DUNLAP, JR.
  Television: What's Happened to Television? (1940)

CYRUS FISHER
  Radio: Norman Brokenshire; The Easy Aces; Fred Allen's Bath
    Club Revue; Ipana Troubadours; Little Jack Little; One Man's
    Family; The Sal Hepatica Revue; The Story of Myrt and Marge;
    The Town Crier; Vic and Sade; Tony Wons

JERRY FRANKEN
  Radio: The Rudy Vallee Show
  Television: RCA-NBC Inaugural Program; NBC Second Regular
    Program

195

HERB GOLDEN
  Radio: The Lone Ranger

B. H. HAGGIN
  Radio: Arturo Toscanini and the N.B.C. Symphony Orchestra

PHILIP HAMBURGER
  Television: The American Week; Milton Berle; Bob and Ray;
    Jimmy Durante; I Married Joan; Life Is Worth Living; See It
    Now; Toast of the Town; Today; Your Show of Shows

DON HEROLD
  Radio: The Amos 'n' Andy Show; Boarke Carter; Father Charles
    E. Coughlin; W. C. Fields; Major Bowes' Original Amateur
    Hour; The March of Time; Deems Taylor; Alexander Woollcott;
    Your Hit Parade

WOLFE KAUFMAN
  Radio: Les Miserables

ROBERT/BOB LANDRY
  Radio: Critics and Criticism in Radio (1938); Hamlet; The Pep-
    sodent Show; The Sal Hepatica Revue; Kate Smith

HOWARD LONG
  Radio: Johnny Got His Gun

MARY McSKIMMING
  Radio: Abe Burrows; Candid Microphone; Leave It to the Girls;
    Noah Webster Says; What Makes You Tick?

MAX MILLER
  Radio: Al Pearce

PHILIP MINOFF
  Television: Red Buttons; Sid Caesar; The Goldbergs; Phil Sil-
    vers; Ed Wynn

CURTIS MITCHELL
  Radio: Walter Damrosch

JOE SCHOENFELD
  Radio: Al Jolson

GILBERT SELDES
  Radio: The Amos 'n' Andy Show; The Cuckoo Hour; Leopold
    Stokowski
  Television: Hollywood's Greatest Enigma--Television (1938);
    Small World

ROBERT LEWIS SHAYON
  Television: Leave It to Beaver; The $64,000 Question

WILLIAM H. SHRIVER, JR.
    Television: Howdy Doody; Robert Montgomery Presents

AGNES SMITH
    Radio: Walter Damrosch; Nils T. Granlund; "The Happiness
        Boys"; Graham McNamee; Moran and Mack
    Television: Television (In Case You're Interested) (1928)

A. M. SULLIVAN
    Radio: Radio and the Poet (1934); Radio and Vaudeville Culture
        (1935)

DOROTHY THOMPSON
    Radio: The War of the Worlds